MW01093416

knitting light

20 ~Mostly~ Seamless Tops, Tees, & More
for Warm Weather Wear

Marie Greene

Founder of Olive Knits™ and author of *Seamless
Knit Sweaters in 2 Weeks* and *The Joy of Yarn*

PAGE STREET
PUBLISHING CO.

For my Knit Campers, who've been asking
(pleading?) for this book for years.
This is for you, my friends.

PAGE STREET
PUBLISHING CO.

Copyright © 2024 Marie Greene

First published in 2024 by
Page Street Publishing Co.
27 Congress Street, Suite 1511
Salem, MA 01970
www.pagestreetpublishing.com

All rights reserved. No part of this book may be reproduced or used, in any form or by any means,
electronic or mechanical, without prior permission in writing from the publisher.

Distributed by Macmillan, sales in Canada by The Canadian Manda Group.

28   27   26   25   24   1   2   3   4   5

ISBN-13: 978-1-64567-857-1
ISBN-10: 1-64567-857-1

Library of Congress Control Number: 2023936579

Cover and book design by Molly Kate Young for Page Street Publishing Co.

Photography by Annie Loaiza
Illustrations by Carlee Wright
Technical editing by Bristol Ivy

Printed and bound in the United States

Page Street Publishing protects our planet by donating to nonprofits like The Trustees,
which focuses on local land conservation.

contents

introduction

My first experience with plant-based fiber came in the form of good, old-fashioned kitchen cotton. It was inexpensive, came in one weight ("too thick"), wasn't particularly soft, and was most certainly not intended for anything other than dishcloths. Once, in a state of desperation, I used kitchen cotton to knit myself a summer tank top. It was the heaviest thing I've ever made—far heavier than any of my wool sweaters. I wore it exactly zero times, and it ended up in the donation bin.

One can only knit so many dishcloths.

As a self-proclaimed sweater knitter (and one prone to wool snobbery), I've found that it always made more sense for me to knit with wool and wool blends. I rarely go a single day without knitting, regardless of the temperature outside, but *wearing* what I knit year-round is another story. Though wool can be moisture-wicking and breathable, it's never been my first choice for a hot summer day. Luckily for me (and you), the world of wearable plant-based yarns has bloomed into a wide array of tantalizing textures and blends. Now we can wear what we knit all year long.

The transition from working with wool to plant-based fiber, though, is not as simple as swapping a skein of wool for a skein of cotton; it's decidedly more nuanced. It's more like the difference between traditional baking and gluten-free baking: It doesn't matter how much experience you have because the old rules just don't apply. You must relearn everything you thought you knew, even if you're an experienced knitter.

This book is my love letter to year-round knitting and, more importantly, to the joy of wearing what you make year-round, too. Why should fall and winter have all the fun? The resources in this book reflect what I've learned in my own plant-based knitting adventures, along with twenty all-new patterns for lightweight tops that will help you round out your handmade wardrobe twelve months a year.

If you've shied away from plant yarns like cotton and linen because you don't love the way they feel, keep reading. Many of the patterns in this book include blends with plant AND protein fibers, offering you the option to enjoy the best qualities of both, while retaining the lightness necessary for warm weather wear.

Whether you're knitting for a warm climate, for your own personal summer, or just to round out your handmade wardrobe for all seasons, you'll find both timeless and contemporary styles in inclusive sizing on the pages of this book. Plus, I'll share the very best tips, tricks, and techniques to support you along the way.

Let's knit light!

Marie Greene

getting started

The patterns in this book feature a healthy blend of plant fibers; some are balanced with protein fibers like wool, alpaca, or silk, while others feature exclusively plant fiber, in varying combinations. This range of fiber blends creates an approachable gateway to working with plant-forward yarns. In a nutshell: There's something for everyone, whether you enjoy knitting with cotton or not.

But the shift from wool to plant fiber is not as straightforward as one might assume. The balance of fiber, the ply, the weight, the yardage, and the method of production each play a vital role in the way the yarn will behave in your project. For best results, pay special attention to the recommended yarn in the pattern and take note of any additional tips to help guide your efforts. What might seem like a small difference on paper can make a noticeable difference on your needles.

Whatever one might know about knitting with wool must take a seat—at least temporarily—to make space for the very different set of rules for knitting with plant fiber. To help you navigate the unique characteristics of these fibers, you'll find tips and tricks throughout this book, with a special section on how to care for your plant-based garments over time (see Blocking & Care [page 196] for more).

Most importantly, if this is new territory, I hope you'll give yourself a break as you dive in. For all its virtues, plant fiber is NOT wool. I know you know this, but it's important to really KNOW IT—deep down—so that you can adjust your expectations for what plant fiber can and cannot do. True success comes from learning how to work with each fiber's unique personality, embracing the differences, and adjusting your technique, when necessary, to get the results you want.

adding plant-based yarn to your fiber diet

knitting with cotton

A modern wardrobe wouldn't be complete without cotton; it's a staple for most of our clothing. But when it comes to knitting garments, it can be a hard sell.

The kitchen cotton of my youth can't hold a candle to the options we have at our fingertips today; but even so, they come with a bit of a learning curve. Cotton is less elastic than wool, less forgiving, and more likely to stretch out of shape over time. So much depends on the quality of the fiber, the manufacturing method, and the way you use it. Where cotton really shines, though, is when it's combined with other fibers. When you marry cotton fiber with nylon, linen, silk, or even wool, the result is a lighter, heat-wicking, moisture-wicking garment that celebrates the best of both worlds.

Cotton is strong (stronger than wool) and gets stronger when it's wet. Try breaking a wet strand of worsted weight cotton with your bare hands, and you'll see what I mean. It can absorb around twenty times its weight in water and can quickly evaporate to help cool you down, making cotton the perfect choice for summertime wear. Keep in mind, though, that handknit cotton garments must dry completely before putting them away; this fiber can be prone to mildew if it doesn't get a chance to dry.

Cotton won't bounce back the way wool does (we call this the "fiber memory"), and this is why it's not appropriate for just any pattern. It's important to consider the style, shape, and desired fabric to ensure that cotton is the right choice for the project. If your cotton ribbing is stretched out, it will stay stretched out. Depending on the project, that might not be an issue, but sometimes cotton will need a little help from other kinds of fiber to retain its shape.

Because of the inherent heaviness and lack of elasticity, cotton can both stretch with wear and shrink when it's washed and dried. Patterns in this book that were designed for cotton (or cotton blends) have taken the characteristics of cotton into account for best results and wearability.

Something to keep in mind: Since we're creating lightweight, breezy fabrics in this book, we shouldn't run into the pitfalls that might otherwise concern you about working with this fiber. I was very intentional with my use of cotton in these patterns, ensuring that the recommended yarn both supports and enhances the design details.

knitting with linen

Linen is one of my favorites, not so much for the way it feels as I'm knitting it (linen can be somewhat unpleasant to work with), but for its myriad benefits as a wearable fiber. Linen is a bast fiber, meaning it comes from the internal tissues of the flax plant. It's one of the most sustainable fibers in the world, but your experience working with it will vary depending on the quality of the fiber and how it's produced. Linen yarn is relatively stiff, especially in the beginning, but it softens with time and wear.

Linen is the strongest natural fiber—coming in at about 30 percent stronger than cotton—but it is far less heavy and dries faster than cotton, too. Linen garments can be worn for decades, making them one of the best investments for your time and effort. As a hand knitter, I love knowing that I'm investing my energy and resources in something I can wear for a lifetime, not just the next few seasons.

Many fiber blends incorporate linen for the added breathability, moisture-wicking properties, and strength, so if working with 100% linen isn't your cup of tea, look for blends that contain other fibers (like cotton, silk, or wool) to find a winning combination that is softer on the hands but retains some of linen's remarkable qualities. I'm convinced that the more you work with linen, the easier it will be to appreciate the way it performs in handknit garments.

If you haven't worked with linen, you may be surprised by the way the fiber behaves when you put your swatch or your finished project into blocking water. While wool gets softer in water, linen seizes up and gets stronger when it's wet. Don't be alarmed; it will soften again (in fact, more so) once it dries.

Some knitters prefer to pre-soak their linen with a softening fiber wash, then dry it gently in a laundry bag while still in the skein, all before they cast on for their project. If you've been around me for a while, you know I can't be bothered with such fuss. I'd rather get busy knitting and let my hands adjust along the way (and they do).

But here's a trick: Linen is much easier to work with if you relax your hands as you go, allowing yourself to knit with less tension in your hands than you might normally use. I often need to go down one or two needle sizes from what I would use with a wool yarn of the same weight to achieve the gauge I need. As you work through the patterns in this book, keep in mind that the

knitting with bamboo, rayon, & more

According to the legend Clara Parkes, **bamboo**—and other cellulosic fibers—were invented in an effort to create silk-like fiber without the silkworm.* Innovation is fascinating, isn't it? Bamboo yarn, which originates from the cellulose fiber of the bamboo stalk, is soft, bouncy, and absorbent—three things we admire for summer yarns. If cotton and linen feel unpleasant to your hands, you'll be delighted by the softness of bamboo. Plus, its fiber reveals excellent stitch definition when used in textured patterns.

It's important to note, however, that the bamboo manufacturing process can be less environmentally friendly than that of other plant-derived fibers. While, on the one hand, bamboo grows quickly and is a sustainable fiber, many of the processing methods involve heavy chemicals, so consider yarns labeled "bamboo" rather than "bamboo rayon" for less heavily processed options, and do your homework when researching new yarns.

Speaking of rayon, fiber labeled "**rayon**" can be made from a variety of natural sources (like corn, bamboo, milk, seaweed, or even trees!), but—as you can imagine—these ingredients require more chemical intervention to become yarn. Through the miracle of modern processing, the

suggested needle size is merely a starting point; each knitter is different, and you may find that your particular knitting style or needles require that you go up or down in needle size to achieve the correct gauge. You might also find that your usual needles are too slippery for linen (or other plant fibers), so if you run into trouble achieving gauge or can't seem to keep the stitches on your needles, it's worth considering whether a different kind of needle (like wood or bamboo) might give you better results. I'm too stubborn to make the switch (and have managed to get the results I want in spite of myself), but many knitters report that changing to needles with a little more "drag" has helped tremendously.

*Clara Parkes, The Knitter's Book of Yarn (2007), 38.

resulting rayon fibers are soft with a delightful sheen, making it an appealing choice for dressier but still wearable knits. Keep in mind that rayon *can* grow heavy (especially if the pattern involves cables or other heavy textures), and you may run the risk of your garment stretching out of shape. Knitting with 100% rayon can also be quite slippery on the needles, so look for fiber blends that benefit from some of the best qualities of rayon without sacrificing control while you knit. As with linen, it can help to use wood or bamboo needles to help you maintain control.

While we're here, let's talk briefly about **silk**. While silk is technically a protein fiber created by silkworms (not plants), it has similar characteristics to plant fiber in terms of how it behaves on the needles, and silk can be found in many plant-forward blends. Silk can come from domesticated silkworms (resulting in mulberry silk) or wild silkworms (resulting in tussah silk). This luxuriously soft fiber is quite strong and inelastic, meaning that it has very little (if any) "give." On the needles, it reminds me of plant fiber in that it doesn't have a spring to it and retains very little fiber memory, or the ability to bounce back to its original shape when stretched (although it does have slightly more memory than most plant fiber). Because of silk's inherent strength, you'll find a small percentage of silk in many sock yarns, but for the purposes of sweater knitting, silk adds drape and sheen, too. Because silk production is still so labor intensive, you may notice that it comes with a slightly higher price point than that of other common fibers, but even just a bit can make your project shine.

tips for knitting with plant yarn

Knitting with plant fiber is an opportunity to expand the boundaries of your handmade wardrobe—and your skills as a seasoned garment knitter. The lessons and opportunities of this range of fiber will extend the possibilities of knitting your own wardrobe and make it easier to knit (and wear) your creations year-round. If you try your hand at one kind of plant fiber and don't love it, don't give up on it entirely. There are many different methods used to produce plant-based yarn, and you may find that switching to a different brand or blend makes it easier to find the right fit.

Knitting with plant fiber is an adventure—one that I think is well worth the effort. So before you cast on for your next project, keep these three things in mind:

- **Adjust your needles.** Early in your plant-fiber knitting journey, you'll discover that you may need to vary your **needle type** and **needle size** from what you typically use. The suggested needle sizes in this book are the ones I used to achieve gauge, but you may find that you need to use a smaller or larger needle to get the same results; this is perfectly normal. If you find that the yarn is too slippery, try needles with a bit more drag (like bamboo, wood, or Karbonz).

- **Relax your hands.** Whatever flow you've established with wool, you'll need a different one for working with plant fiber. Because plant fiber can be significantly stiffer than wool (and other animal fibers), you'll see more space within *and* between your stitches than what you're used to. Your instinct might be to tighten your grip on the needles to eliminate those spaces, *but resist!* To create a light, breezy fabric (at the appropriate gauge), let your stitches have the space they demand. Forcing them into a tighter fabric will lead you on a frustrating journey—and it won't get you the results you want.

- **SWATCH!** If you've managed to skip swatching without dire consequences in the past, you won't have the same luck here. Sorry, my friend. You absolutely must knit a gauge swatch if you want success with plant fiber. This critical part of the process will give you the opportunity to get used to the feel of plant fiber on your needles, to learn how your own knitting style and needles affect your work, and to make sure you're using the right needle size and type—not to mention the right yarn—for the project. Even if you use the same yarn I used for the design and the very same needles, there's no guarantee your results will be the same. They're a starting point, but it's doubtful that your style and tension will be the same as mine in every situation, and that's okay. That's part of the fun of being a knitter! There's absolutely no such thing as "always getting gauge," so take the extra few minutes to knit your swatch and make sure you're on the right track before you cast on.

planning for a great fit

the levers of fit

The secret to a properly fitting sweater comes down to a few very important factors that I like to call "levers." These are the elements of fit that work together, like little levers in a machine, to influence your results. They are:

1. Yarn Choice
2. Swatching
3. Knowing Your Size
4. Understanding Ease

No amount of experience can make up for those four levers; not even if you've been knitting for fifty years or have made more than a dozen sweaters. I've been knitting for nearly four decades at the time of writing this book. I've knit and designed hundreds of sweaters in my lifetime, and I *still* start every project by making a careful yarn choice, swatching, confirming my size, and making sure the ease is where I want it. Every pattern is different, every yarn has its own personality, and every knitter varies. Planning your project with these levers in mind will save you time, money, and potential headaches.

yarn choice

First things first, when choosing yarn for your project, the recommended yarn is more than a mere suggestion; it's your guide for success. You may find yourself at the mercy of your budget or unable to get your hands on the exact yarn listed in the pattern, but you can still use the recommended yarn as a guide to find a comparable replacement. To do so, start with the fiber content. Variations in the blend of fibers (and the method of production) can result in very different kinds of yarn, and these differences can impact your results far more than you might expect. Often when knitters struggle with getting the correct gauge for the pattern, the culprit is the yarn. Look for blends with a similar combination of fibers and production method, or those that will behave in a similar way.

Next, check the weight and yardage. Even seemingly small variations in the yardage and weight ratio can have surprising effects on your gauge. You may find yourself able to achieve stitch gauge, but not row gauge, or perhaps you've achieved gauge without issue, but your fabric is significantly heavier or looser than it should be for the project. The more similar your yarn is to the recommended yarn in the pattern (both for fiber content and yardage/weight), the better your results will be.

Remember, too, that yarn choice should include considerations about stitch definition, drape, and heaviness (or lightness) for the project. Not to be dramatic, but the yarn you choose can make or break your project. For real.

swatching

If there's one thing I've learned in my journey of plant-forward knitting, it's that plant fibers have their own personalities. It's important to get to know them before you cast on for your project. You may be convinced that you "always get gauge" with a certain yarn weight and needle size, but I can assure you that whatever predictable gauge you might think you get with superwash merino is no match for the gauge you'll get in 100% linen. Always, always, always, always, ALWAYS swatch. *Always.*

When it comes to gauge, it helps to understand what it is we're trying to accomplish.

Gauge refers to the number of stitches, NOT the size of the swatch.

Measuring a swatch means measuring your stitches, not measuring edge to edge. For this reason, I always recommend knitting a larger swatch than the number of stitches you're supposed to count. That way you'll have enough room to measure whole stitches, away from the edges.

For example, if the pattern calls for a gauge of 20 stitches in 4 inches (10 cm), cast on 30 stitches and work in the recommended pattern until your swatch is about 5 inches (12.5 cm) long. This will give you a few extra stitches on each side, and a little more room on the top and bottom. Edge stitches are weirdos, and they will skew your results. If you really want to know your gauge, you'll need to measure whole stitches, and stay clear of the edges. The larger the swatch, the more accurate the information it will give you.

But knitting your swatch is just the beginning. You will also need to wet block your swatch and let it dry completely before you measure it. (You'll wet block your swatch in much the same way that you'll wet block the garment, so take a look at the blocking instructions for each pattern as a rough guide.) Most of the finished measurements in this book are based on wet blocking—especially any measurements related to circumference. The only time a pre-blocked measurement is provided is when you're knitting to a certain length (such as working the lower body until you reach a specific measurement). If it's something you'll need to measure on your needles while you're still working it, a pre-blocked measurement is provided. Blocking will almost always dramatically change your gauge, which is why it's so important to block your swatch first before you measure.

Stitch Gauge

Stitch gauge is measured side to side, and it's this measurement that will tell you if your stitches are the right size (widthwise) to achieve the appropriate fit in your finished sweater. If your stitches are smaller than they should be, your sweater will be smaller, and if your stitches are bigger than they should be, your sweater will be bigger. But we often underestimate just what a difference these seemingly slight variations can make. Too often I hear knitters say that their gauge was "close" but that their sweater doesn't fit the way they expected it to. "Close" isn't close when it comes to gauge.

Row Gauge

Row gauge is measured top to bottom, and it's this measurement that will affect how much yarn you'll use in your project, the overall drape of the fabric you're creating, and—depending on the pattern construction—may affect the way the garment fits in the shoulders, arms, or even the lower body. In patterns that are knit top-down, in the round, row gauge is especially important; it will determine the depth from the shoulder to the underarm. In bottom-up sweaters, row gauge isn't quite as critical, but it might still affect your yarn usage and the drape and feel of your fabric. In some cases, if your row gauge is significantly different, this can sometimes be a clue that your yarn choice may not be ideal for the project.

How to Adjust Your Gauge

When you first knit your swatch, begin with the recommended needle size. And while this may seem obvious, it's important to use the same yarn and the same needles you plan to use for your project. If you've done both of these things, and you've wet blocked your swatch and let it dry, the next step is to measure.

If you have the correct gauge on the first try, hooray! It's time to cast on! Consider it a gift from the fiber fairies and maybe buy a lottery ticket while you're out today. All jokes aside, few of us get perfect gauge the first try, every time. It has nothing to do with your skill or experience; it's just part of the knitting process.

If your gauge isn't what it should be, you'll need to make a few adjustments and swatch again. I know that knitting *one* swatch is bad enough, but sometimes you'll need to knit two. Maybe even three! (Gasp!) Tedious though it may seem, it's just a little more knitting; and it'll be worth the time and frustration it will save you in the end. I promise.

When it comes to adjusting your needle sizes for the next swatch, though, it can be a little puzzling; I get questions about it all the time. Let's demystify what that stitch measurement is telling you and which direction you'll need to go to get closer to your goal next time.

Let's pretend that your gauge swatch is a happy little neighborhood block in the suburbs. Imagine that on one side of the street there are five houses of equal size and with equal yards. On the other side of the street there are six houses of equal size and with equal yards.

Which side of the street has the larger homes? The size of the block is the same, but one side has managed to fit more homes into the same amount of space. The homes on the five-house side are larger than the homes on the six-house side.

If your gauge is supposed to be 20 stitches, but instead it's 22, many knitters see that larger number (22) and think their gauge is too big. Or vice versa, if your gauge should be 20 stitches but instead it's 19 stitches, that smaller number might trick you into thinking your gauge is smaller. But that's not how gauge works.

Going back to our example of the houses in the neighborhood, the six houses on one side of the street are smaller than the five houses on the other side. Sure, six is a larger number, but it doesn't mean the homes are larger. It means they're squeezing MORE houses into the same amount of space. The size of the space doesn't change; it's what you can fit INTO that space that matters.

Since gauge is a measurement of the number of stitches you can fit into a defined space, if you've fit more stitches into that space, it means your stitches are smaller. They don't take up as much room as they should. Smaller stitches need a larger needle to help them grow.

But let's say you have 19 stitches when you're aiming for 20. Even though 19 is a smaller number, having fewer stitches means they're actually bigger. Bigger stitches need a smaller needle to bring them down in size.

Here's an easy shortcut to help you remember:

If your number of stitches in 4 inches (10 cm) is a **smaller** number than the pattern gauge, go down to a **smaller needle** size and swatch again.

If your number of stitches in 4 inches (10 cm) is a **larger** number than the pattern gauge, go up to a **larger needle** size and swatch again.

Why the Gauge Matters

While it might seem that the difference of a few stitches shouldn't matter much in the scheme of things, those differences will multiply around the body of your sweater. Here's an example of what a "slight" gauge difference can do to the finished size of your project:

Let's say your sweater has 264 stitches around the bust for your size and the pattern gauge is 24 stitches in 4 inches (10 cm). You're expecting a finished measurement of 44 inches (110 cm).

Here's how that math works:

24 stitches in 4 inches (10 cm) = 6 stitches in 1 inch (or 2.4 stitches in 1 cm)

- 264 stitches divided by 6 sts per inch = **44 inches**
- 264 stitches divided by 2.4 sts per cm = **110 cm**

What happens if your gauge doesn't match the pattern gauge?

Example 1

22 stitches in 4 inches (10 cm) = 5.5 stitches in 1 inch (or 2.2 stitches in 1 cm)

(As we talked about in the last section, 22 is a smaller number than 24, but it means our stitches are bigger than they should be.)

- 264 stitches divided by 5.5 sts per inch = **48 inches**
- 264 stitches divided by 2.2 sts per cm = **120 cm**

In this example, our stitches are just a little bit bigger (22 vs. 24) but look at what a difference it makes in the finished measurements: 4 inches (10 cm) larger!

Example 2

26 stitches in 4 inches (10 cm) = 6.5 sts in 1 inch (or 2.6 stitches in 1 cm)

- 264 stitches divided by 6.5 sts per inch = **40.6 inches**
- 264 stitches divided by 2.6 sts per cm = **101.5 cm**

In this example, we have 26 stitches in 4 inches (10 cm) instead of 24, which means our stitches are too small. The stitch count remains the same, but now our sweater is nearly 3.5 inches (8.5 cm) smaller than it should be.

Even small discrepancies add up. Gauge matters.

choosing the perfect size

The next important lever of sweater fit is knowing your size, and before you roll your eyes and tell me you already know your own size, bear with me here. Not only do bodies change over time, but it's important to make sure that you're using the same metrics that knitting patterns use.

First, your bra size isn't your bust size (and if this is the first you've heard about that, don't worry—you're not alone). If you've been using your bra size to determine your sweater size, let's switch gears and use a more reliable method to help you achieve a much better fit. I'll explain which measurement you **should** use as we progress through this section.

Second, your size will change over time. I teach sweater fit classes to knitters around the world, and every time I do, my students are surprised when they take their measurements. Every. Single. Time. As knitters, we're likely to spend more time and energy thinking about the sizes we're making for others, but base our own sweater projects on the last time we measured, even if it's been decades. If it helps at all, I'm no saint in this department. I've been a sweater designer and educator for more than a decade, and I kept knitting myself the same size sweaters for years! (I'll blame the "cobbler's shoe" situation here, but really, there's no excuse.) Like so many others, I thought my gauge must be getting tighter with age. It was only when I stood in front of my students, demonstrating how to measure your bust, that I looked down and saw the writing on the wall—or, rather, *the tape measure.* My size had

changed. If it's been more than 6 months since the last time you measured, it's a good idea to do it again. Measure now, and your next sweater will be all the better for it.

Third, it's important to understand the difference between "sizes" and "finished measurements." The patterns in this book will list both sizes and finished measurements; *these are two different numbers, used for two different purposes.* Understanding these differences will help you knit beautiful sweaters that fit you perfectly—every time.

Imagine that you're shopping for sweaters at your favorite department store. When looking for your size on the shelf, you aren't holding a tape measure and taking measurements off the garment, are you? Of course not! You're checking the labels. You're looking for the familiar S, M, L, etc. to give you a starting point. You'll probably still want to try it on to check the fit, but the "size" is where you begin.

The finished measurements are the actual measurements of the garment. In knitting patterns, the finished measurements tell you what you can expect when you've finished knitting your top—assuming you've knit according to gauge and have wet blocked your garment for the perfect finish. Finished measurements will help you understand how the sweater will FIT.

When thinking about size and finished measurements, think of the SIZE as related to YOU, and the FINISHED MEASUREMENTS as related to the GARMENT.

Size = Your Body
Finished Measurements = The Garment

In many cases, the sizes will correspond to something familiar, like 2X, 3X, 4X, or 48, 52, 56. In either case, these correspond to body sizes or body measurements. When a pattern size doesn't clearly explain how it relates to your size (such as if the pattern gives sizing in a 1, 2, 3 format), check out the Fit Advice section for that pattern to understand how to choose the right size for the fit you need.

In most cases, you're not looking for finished measurements that match your own measurements exactly; that would result in a top that fits like a glove, which is generally not the right fit for a light and breezy summer style. Refer to the size information, Fit Advice, and recommended ease to choose the right size for your project.

"Ease" is the difference between your actual measurements and the finished measurements of the sweater, and in many cases, you'll be choosing the size that gives you a little extra room to move. For example, if your bust measurement is 36 inches (90 cm), and the Fit Advice says that the recommended fit has 2 inches (5 cm) of positive ease, then you would choose the size with a finished measurement closer to 38 inches (95 cm) to give you that extra 2 inches (5 cm) of room for a comfortable fit. These numbers don't have to be exact, but they will help you get close to the best size.

taking your measurements

Step One: Measure Your Full Bust Circumference

A full bust measurement will give you a good starting point for choosing your size. To get this measurement, remove any outer clothing (like shirts or jackets), but do measure over a good-fitting bra if you plan to wear one under your knit top. For best results, check that the tape measure isn't drooping or crooked in the back and that you're not holding it too tightly.

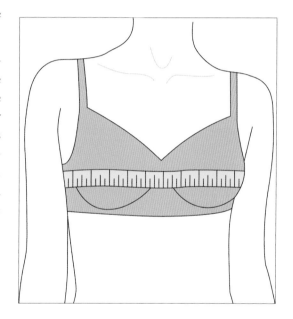

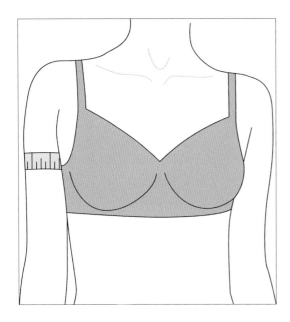

Step Two: Measure Your Upper Arm

Choosing the size that matches the fit for your bust will *usually* result in a decent fit in the arms, as well—but not always. It's important to know your own upper arm measurement so you can compare it to the finished measurements in the pattern; in some cases—especially if you're between sizes—your arm circumference might make it easier to choose which size is best for you.

Worth mentioning: The amount of ease in your sleeve can be significantly less than the ease in the body; in fact, a sleeve with a slightly closer fit is usually quite flattering. While the amount of positive ease in the bust and body of the sweater might be several inches/centimeters (or more) based on the intended fit of the design, the sleeve of this same pattern might fit with little to no ease at all—and that's okay. It depends on the design, of course; some patterns are meant for a looser fit around the arms, like Poppy (page 159), but more traditional sweater shapes, like Violet (page 75) or Marigold (page 181), can fit with positive ease in the body and minimal (or even zero)

ease in the sleeves. Zero ease means the finished measurement for that portion of the sweater is exactly the same as your own measurement. For example, if your upper arm circumference is 12 inches (30 cm) and the finished measurement for the upper sleeve is 12 inches (30 cm), that's zero ease.

It's fine if your sleeve does fit with a little extra room, but if it doesn't, that's okay too. If you're between sizes and can't decide, check out the finished measurements of the sleeve or armhole portion of the sweater to see which one is closer to your own measurements, and use that as a guide.

Here's a quick example of choosing between sizes:

Option 1: Let's say size 2 will give you 2 inches (5 cm) of positive ease in the bust, but only .5 inches (12.5 cm) of positive ease in the sleeve.

Option 2: Let's say size 3 would give you 5 inches (12.5 cm) of positive ease in the bust and 3 inches (7.5 cm) of positive ease in the sleeves.

First, check the Fit Advice section in the pattern to see how much ease is recommended in the bust. Let's say in this case, the amount of recommended ease is 2–3 inches (5–7.5 cm). Some knitters size up for fear that the sleeve will be too tight, but you may not want so much extra room in your sweater. It's up to you, of course, and depends on how you like to wear your tops. If it were me, I would choose the smaller size in that scenario because it offers the appropriate ease in the bust, and a closer sleeve fit works fine for me, but there's not a right answer here—it's just good to know your options and how to make a wise choice for the fit you want. Just remember that for most traditional pattern styles the amount of ease in your sleeves does not need to be the same as the amount of ease in the body.

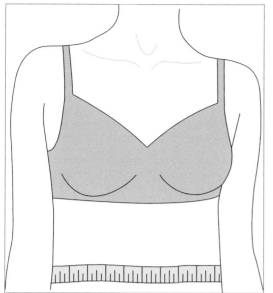 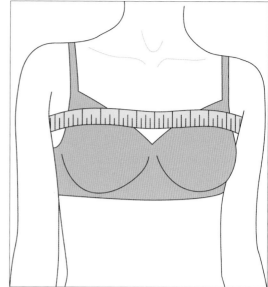

Step Three: Measure Your Belly

Bellies are important, too. If your midsection needs a little more room than your bust, look for patterns with a loose fit in the lower body, like Magnolia (page 63) or Chamomile (page 57), as a starting point, or size up on a pattern with a standard fit. If you're savvy with pattern math, you can also go up a needle size in the lower body or add a few stitches after the sleeve divide to give you some extra room.

Step Four: Measure Your Upper Bust

Upper bust measurements don't work for everyone, but they're useful if you're small in all places EXCEPT in the bust. If you've knit a few sweaters and find that knitting for your full bust measurement results in a sloppy, oversized top, your upper bust measurement might help you get the fit you're looking for. For those who fit this body style, you would use your upper bust measurement as your bust measurement when looking at the pattern sizes. This will result in a closer fit in the shoulders and arms, while gently hugging your bust.

One piece of advice, though: If you're new to sweater knitting and aren't familiar yet with the fit that works best for you, always start by using your full bust measurement to determine your size. Knit a few sweaters and learn from them; you'll need that information to know how to adapt your results for a better fit. Some knitters have been advised to *always* use their upper bust measurement, and I don't recommend this for everyone; the result can be frustratingly snug if that's not the right fit for your body. I try to avoid "always/never" statements when it comes to knitting (except when it comes to swatching and blocking), because what works for one pattern or one person rarely works in every situation for every knitter. I've seen far too many wonderful knitters follow this advice of always using their upper bust measurement and end up disappointed with a sweater that doesn't fit.

A Summary of Fit

Pay attention to the Fit Advice section for each pattern. It will give you valuable guidance for creating a sweater that fits the way it should. For less traditional shapes, the amount of ease can be an important aspect of the fit, so don't shy away from the recommended size just because the ease seems wildly out of bounds; in most cases, it's an important part of the fit and style. My first sample of Jasmine (page 175) started with about half of the amount of ease you'll see in the pattern now, but I didn't love the fit. I doubled down on my idea and went with a whopping 15 inches (37.5 cm) of ease and absolutely loved it. I wouldn't have imagined that's the fit I'd like, but in the right piece, it really does work. Be careful about sizing down for those unique ones; while the body may be oversized, the neckline, shoulders and sleeves likely already have a closer fit. Poppy (page 159) and Bluebell (page 93) are good examples of this. For these styles, sizing down can backfire.

There's nothing more wonderful than knitting a beautiful new top *that fits*. When you understand the levers of fit—how and where to measure, the relationship between size and finished measurements, pattern ease, and intended fit—you can knit with confidence, knowing that your project will fit the way it's meant to. Don't be disheartened if it takes a few sweaters to get the hang of it; we don't always know how much ease we like or which pattern styles feel best on our bodies until we knit them. Every sweater is an education, and you can use the experience from each one to refine your fit for next time.

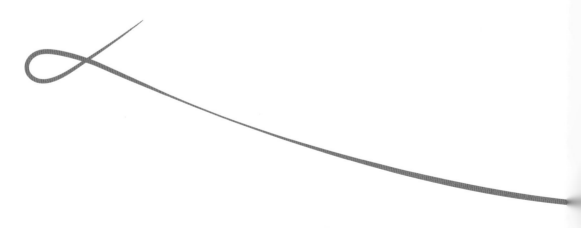

the patterns

I've been knitting since I was a little girl, but I didn't start knitting sweaters until my early twenties, and the first few weren't anything to write home about. I had a lot to learn about yarn, gauge, and fit; and it took time to discover that seamless (or mostly seamless) patterns were really all I wanted to make. But seamless patterns were much harder to find back then, and the ones I could find left a lot to be desired. So, I learned to design the sweaters I wanted to make—in the way I wanted to make them—and the rest is history. Seamless knitting has come a long way. And what you'll find on the pages of this book are mostly seamless designs in a range of styles and sizes. While seamless knitting is what I'm mostly known for, I wanted the flexibility of adding a few bottom-up designs. Every pattern in this book is knit in one piece, and they're seamless whenever possible, but some styles may require a small amount of seaming on the shoulders or underarms. The addition of bottom-up construction gave me a wider range of design possibilities; I exercised this freedom to the fullest degree possible, resulting in pieces that work beautifully for every size, style, age, and fit.

More importantly, I've taken the opportunity to feature plant-forward yarns in lightweight blends to make it easier to wear what you knit all year, from one season to the next. I hope you'll find many new favorites while you're here.

lace details

Lacework is one of the easiest (and most attractive) ways to lighten up your knitting. Openwork details create natural airflow and allow for movement and ease in the drape of the fabric, making them an easy choice for spring and summer knitting. While lace patterns may look complex, you'll find that most are easily memorized after the first few repeats, creating a steady but entertaining rhythm on the needles. I always look forward to the lace sections of a pattern; they're a fun diversion from straight knitting, and I love to watch the way the intricate details are revealed as I knit.

The patterns in this section are mostly classic shapes, with lace features that range from the showstopping centerpiece of Aster (page 29) to the easy, allover texture of Thistle (page 83). These details shine in plant-forward blends that, in many cases, include a bit of silk or rayon for added sheen. Wet blocking will make an amazing difference, as it will expand and enhance the lacework and make it easier to smooth and coax the edges into place.

aster lace panel tee

The pale blue cotton in this floral tee reminds me of summer, when just the barest wisp of a cloud swoops across the sky like a brush stroke. The delicate lace panel is the real showstopper in this one; it's absolutely stunning and looks complex, but it's not at all difficult to work (I promise). The detail creates a flattering vertical visual down the center of your tee, with classic details throughout. Knit in lightweight cotton, this airy design is wearable on a warm day, and the fabric is light enough to layer for cooler evenings. Dress it down with a denim jacket or dress it up with a silk shawl; Aster is a versatile piece you can wear year-round.

Skill Level
Intermediate

Construction
This breezy floral tee is knit top-down in the round (in one seamless piece) with round yoke construction and short rows. The increases are spaced evenly around the yoke (on either side of the center panel) as you work down toward the underarms. The top and sleeves are worked all in one down to the underarm, then the sleeves are separated onto waste yarn while you complete the rest of the body. The lace panel continues down the center of the body on a background of stockinette stitch, and the half sleeves are worked last. (You could easily make your sleeves shorter or longer, if you like—it's one of the perks of knitting a top-down, seamless style.) This classic design is finished with simple ribbed edges. Bonus: There's very little finishing since the neckline is worked right into the pattern when you cast on (there are no stitches to pick up).

Sizes
S (M, L, XL, 2X, 3X, 4X, 5X, 6X)

Fit Advice
Designed to be worn with 2–3 in (5–7.5 cm) positive ease.

Finished Measurements

A) Bust Circumference: 34.5 (37.5, 41.5, 45.5, 49.5, 54.5, 56.5, 58.5, 63) in / 86.75 (93.25, 104.25, 114.25, 124.25, 136.75, 141.75, 146.75, 158) cm – blocked

B) Yoke Depth: 7.75 (8.5, 8.75, 10.25, 10.75, 11.25, 11.5, 12, 12.25) in / 20 (22, 22.5, 25, 26.5, 28.75, 29.5, 30.75, 31.25) cm – blocked

C) Lower Body Length: 13 (14, 14, 15, 15, 16, 16, 16, 16) in / 33 (35.5, 35.5, 38, 38, 40.75, 40.75, 40.75, 40.75) cm – prior to blocking

D) Sleeve Circumference: 11.25 (13.25, 14.25, 15.75, 17.25, 18.25, 19.25, 20.25, 20.75) in / 28.25 (33.25, 35.75, 39.5, 43.25, 45.75, 48.25, 50.75, 51.75) cm – blocked

E) Cuff Circumference: 9.25 (11.25, 12.75, 13.25, 14.75, 15.25, 16.75, 17.25, 18) in / 23.25 (28.25, 31.75, 33.25, 36.75, 38.25, 41.75, 43.25, 45) cm – blocked

F) Sleeve Length from Underarm: 9.5–10 in (23.75–25 cm) from underarm – prior to blocking

G) Neck Circumference: 19.25 (19.25, 20, 20, 20.75, 22, 22, 22, 22.75) in / 48.25 (48.25, 50, 50, 51.75, 55, 55, 55, 56.75) cm – blocked

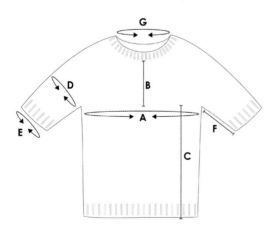

Abbreviations	
[ ]	brackets indicate a repeat
bet	between
BO	bind off
BOR	beginning of row/round
CO	cast on
dec	decrease/decreases/decreased
inc	increase/increases/increased
k	knit
k2tog	knit two stitches together (dec 1)
M1L	make one stitch, left leaning (inc 1)
p	purl
p2tog	purl two stitches together (dec 1)
PM	place marker
rep	repeat
rnd/s	round/rounds
RS	right side
sm	slip marker
ssk	slip one st knitwise, slip the next st knitwise, then return the two sts back to the left needle and knit the two together through the back loop (dec 1)
st/s	stitch/stitches
UM	unique marker
WS	wrong side
x	denotes sizes not represented in this line of instruction
yo	yarn over (inc 1)

Materials

Yarn	Fingering Weight | Rowan Summerlite 4 Ply | 100% Cotton | 191 yards (175 meters) in 1.76 oz (50 grams) | 1029 (1111, 1199, 1295, 1399, 1511, 1632, 1763, 1904) yards / 941 (1016, 1096, 1184, 1279, 1381, 1492, 1612, 1740) meters | **Color:** Cloud **Note:** Variations in yarn choice or row/round gauge may impact yarn consumption. If in doubt, round up to the nearest skein.
Needles	**Body:** US 3 (3.25 mm)* 16–40 in (40–100 cm) circular needle **Neckline and Lower Ribbing:** US 2 (2.75 mm) 16 in (40 cm) circular needle **Sleeves:** US 3 (3.25 mm) 12 in (30 cm) circular needle or DPNs **Sleeve Cuffs:** US 2 (2.75 mm) 12 in (30 cm) circular needle or DPNs *Or size needed to achieve gauge. Adjust other needle sizes accordingly.*
Notions	Stitch markers (including locking markers and a unique marker) Waste yarn or spare needles, for holding stitches Blocking pins and mats Darning needle to weave ends **A note about markers:** Unique markers will be placed to denote special details (like lace panels).
Gauge	24 sts and 32 rows/rounds in 4 in (10 cm) in stockinette stitch with largest needle, blocked

aster lace panel tee pattern

With US Size 2 (2.75 mm) 16-inch (40-cm) circular needle—*or size needed to achieve gauge*—CO 116 (116, 120, 120, 124, 132, 132, 132, 136) sts using cable cast-on method. Do not join in the rnd yet. (*Note: The cable cast-on begins your work immediately on the RS.*)

Set-Up Row (RS): [K2, p2] rep bet brackets to end. PM and join to work in the rnd, being careful not to twist your sts.

Ribbing Rnd: [K2, p2] rep bet brackets to end. Rep this rnd until neckline ribbing measures 1.25 in (3.25 cm), or slightly longer, if desired.

Next Rnd: With US Size 3 (3.25 mm) circular needle—*or size needed to achieve gauge*—k one rnd to begin the upper yoke.

Next Rnd: K58 (58, 60, 60, 62, 66, 66, 66, 68) sts, place a side marker, k58 (58, 60, 60, 62, 66, 66, 66, 68) sts to end. Stop.

Turn your work to the WS to begin 8 short rows using the Japanese short row method. You will need two locking markers for this technique.

Short Rows

Tip: If you prefer a different short row method, simply work 8 short rows in your preferred method, using these details as a guide for the turning point. Be sure to keep your BOR and side markers in place as you create the short rows.

Short Row 1 (WS): Slip first st to right needle (purlwise) without working it and place a locking marker on your working yarn (holding the marker to the WS of your work). P to the side marker. Stop and turn to the RS.

Short Row 2 (RS): Slip first st to right needle (purlwise) without working it and place a locking marker on your working yarn (holding the marker to the WS of your work). K to the gap that is marked with locking marker. Using the marker to pull, draw up the marked yarn from the WS of your work and place it on the left needle as if a new st (adjusting the BOR marker, as needed, to work the short row, and then replacing it to its original location), then knit it together (k2tog) with the next st on the left needle (closing the gap) and remove locking marker. K1, stop, and turn to WS.

Short Row 3 (WS): Slip first st to right needle (purlwise) without working it and place a locking marker on the working yarn (holding the marker to the WS of your work). P to gap that is marked with locking marker. Slip the next st to the right needle purlwise without working it (adjusting the side marker, as needed, to work the short row, and then replacing it to its original location). Using the locking marker to pull, draw up the marked yarn from the WS of your work and place it on the left needle as if a new st. Place the st that you previously slipped back to the left needle and purl it together (p2tog) with the "new" st (closing the gap) and remove locking marker. P1, stop, and turn to RS.

Short Row 4 (RS): Slip the first st to right needle (purlwise) without working it, place a locking marker on the working yarn (held at the WS of your work). K to gap that is marked with locking marker. Using the marker to pull, draw up the marked yarn from the WS of your work and place it on the left needle as if a new st, then knit it together (k2tog) with the next st on the left needle (closing the gap) and remove locking marker. K1, stop, and turn to WS.

Short Rows 5–8: Rep Short Rows 3 and 4 twice more. Do not turn work to WS after final repeat of Short Row 4.

Continue on RS, and work in pattern to end of rnd until you are one st before the final gap. Slip this st to your right needle purlwise without working it, then, using the marker to pull, draw up the marked yarn from the WS of your work and place it on the left needle as if a new st. Place the st that you previously slipped back to the left needle and knit it together (k2tog) with the "new" st (closing the gap) and remove the locking marker. Knit to end of rnd. Your short rows have been completed and your gaps should be closed.

Knit one rnd.

Pattern Begins

Note: Please refer to the Aster Lace Chart or Chart Written Directions on page 37 as you proceed.

Next Rnd: K11 (11, 12, 12, 13, 15, 15, 15, 16), place UM, work Aster Lace Chart (beginning with Rnd 1 of chart or written instructions, worked over 36 sts), PM, k to end.

To simplify the inc process for the duration of the yoke, we shall pretend the UM is the beginning of the round. We will return to the original BOR when it's time to separate the sleeves from the yoke, so keep the original marker in its place and just pass it when you reach it. As you finish this rnd, go ahead and k the remaining sts until you are at the UM to begin the next rnd. Make note that you will never be working inc in the section with the lace chart.

Work 2 rnds even in established pattern.

Inc #1 – Next Rnd: Work Aster Lace Chart (next rnd), sm, [k4, M1L] rep bet brackets to last 4 sts, k3, M1L, k1 – 20 (20, 21, 21, 22, 24, 24, 24, 25) sts inc.

Work 4 rnds even in established pattern.

Inc #2 – Next Rnd: Work Aster Lace Chart (next rnd), sm, [k5, M1L] rep bet brackets to last 5 sts, k4, M1L, k1 – 20 (20, 21, 21, 22, 24, 24, 24, 25) sts inc.

Work 4 rnds even in established pattern.

Inc #3 – Next Rnd: Work Aster Lace Chart (next rnd), sm, [k6, M1L] rep bet brackets to last 6 sts, k5, M1L, k1 – 20 (20, 21, 21, 22, 24, 24, 24, 25) sts inc.

Stitch Count Check-In
176 (176, 183, 183, 190, 204, 204, 204, 211)

> **Note:** Transition to longer circular needle when necessary for stitches to move comfortably.

Work 4 rnds even in established pattern.

Inc #4 – Next Rnd: Work Aster Lace Chart (next rnd), sm, [k7, M1L] rep bet brackets to last 7 sts, k6, M1L, k1 – 20 (20, 21, 21, 22, 24, 24, 24, 25) sts inc.

Work 4 rnds even in established pattern.

Inc #5 – Next Rnd: Work Aster Lace Chart (next rnd), sm, [k8, M1L] rep bet brackets to last 8 sts, k7, M1L, k1 – 20 (20, 21, 21, 22, 24, 24, 24, 25) sts inc.

Work 4 rnds even in established pattern.

Inc #6 – Next Rnd: Work Aster Lace Chart (next rnd), sm, [k9, M1L] rep bet brackets to last 9 sts, k8, M1L, k1 – 20 (20, 21, 21, 22, 24, 24, 24, 25) sts inc.

Stitch Count Check-In
236 (236, 246, 246, 256, 276, 276, 276, 286)

Work 4 rnds even in established pattern.

Inc #7 – Next Rnd: Work Aster Lace Chart (next rnd), sm, [k10, M1L] rep bet brackets to last 10 sts, k9, M1L, k1 – 20 (20, 21, 21, 22, 24, 24, 24, 25) sts inc.

Work 4 rnds even in established pattern.

Inc #8 – Next Rnd: Work Aster Lace Chart (next rnd), sm, [k11, M1L] rep bet brackets to last 11 sts, k10, M1L, k1 – 20 (20, 21, 21, 22, 24, 24, 24, 25) sts inc.

Work 4 rnds even in established pattern.

Inc #9 – Next Rnd: Work Aster Lace Chart (next rnd), sm, [k12, M1L] rep bet brackets to last 12 sts, k11, M1L, k1 – 20 (20, 21, 21, 22, 24, 24, 24, 25) sts inc.

Stitch Count Check-In
296 (296, 309, 309, 322, 348, 348, 348, 361)

Work 4 rnds even in established pattern.

Inc #10 – Next Rnd: Work Aster Lace Chart (next rnd), sm, [k13, M1L] rep bet brackets to last 13 sts, k12, M1L, k1 – 20 (20, 21, 21, 22, 24, 24, 24, 25) sts inc.

Work 4 rnds even in established pattern.

Inc #11 – Next Rnd: Work Aster Lace Chart (next rnd), sm, [k14, M1L] rep bet brackets to last 14 sts, k13, M1L, k1 – 20 (20, 21, 21, 22, 24, 24, 24, 25) sts inc.

Work 4 rnds even in established pattern.

Stitch Count Check-In
336 (336, 351, 351, 366, 396, 396, 396, 411)

> **Note:** As you proceed you will see an "x" as a placeholder for sizes that are no longer represented on that rnd.

Size S ONLY – Move ahead to "All Sizes Continue" before **Divide for Sleeves** on page 35.

All Other Sizes Continue

Inc #12 – Next Rnd: Work Aster Lace Chart (next rnd), sm, [k15, M1L] rep bet brackets to last 15 sts, k14, M1L, k1 – x (20, 21, 21, 22, 24, 24, 24, 25) sts inc.

Work 4 rnds even in established pattern.

Inc #13 – Next Rnd: Work Aster Lace Chart (next rnd), sm, [k16, M1L] rep bet brackets to last 16 sts, k15, M1L, k1 – x (20, 21, 21, 22, 24, 24, 24, 25) sts inc.

Stitch Count Check-In
x (376, 393, 393, 410, 444, 444, 444, 461)

Size M ONLY – Move ahead to "All Sizes Continue" before **Divide for Sleeves** on page 35.

All Other Sizes Continue

Work 4 rnds even in established pattern.

Inc #14 – Next Rnd: Work Aster Lace Chart (next rnd), sm, [k17, M1L] rep bet brackets to last 17 sts, k16, M1L, k1 – x (x, 21, 21, 22, 24, 24, 24, 25) sts inc.

Stitch Count Check-In
x (x, 414, 414, 432, 468, 468, 468, 486)

Size L ONLY – Move ahead to "All Sizes Continue" before **Divide for Sleeves** on page 35.

All Other Sizes Continue

Work 4 rnds even in established pattern.

Inc #15 – Next Rnd: Work Aster Lace Chart (next rnd), sm, [k18, M1L] rep bet brackets to last 18 sts, k17, M1L, k1 – x (x, x, 21, 22, 24, 24, 24, 25) sts inc.

Work 4 rnds even in established pattern.

Inc #16 – Next Rnd: Work Aster Lace Chart (next rnd), sm, [k19, M1L] rep bet brackets to last 19 sts, k18, M1L, k1 – x (x, x, 21, 22, 24, 24, 24, 25) sts inc.

Stitch Count Check-In
x (x, x, 456, 476, 516, 516, 516, 536)

Size XL ONLY – Move ahead to "All Sizes Continue" before **Divide for Sleeves** on page 35.

All Other Sizes Continue

Work 4 rnds even in established pattern.

Inc #17 – Next Rnd: Work Aster Lace Chart (next rnd), sm, [k20, M1L] rep bet brackets to last 20 sts, k19, M1L, k1 – x (x, x, x, 22, 24, 24, 24, 25) sts inc.

Stitch Count Check-In

x (x, x, x, 498, 540, 540, 540, 561)

Sizes 2X and 3X ONLY – Move ahead to "All Sizes Continue" before **Divide for Sleeves** on page 36.

All Other Sizes Continue

Work 4 rnds even in established pattern.

Inc #18 – Next Rnd: Work Aster Lace Chart (next rnd), sm, [k21, M1L] rep bet brackets to last 21 sts, k20, M1L, k1 – x (x, x, x, x, 24, 24, 25) sts inc.

Stitch Count Check-In

x (x, x, x, x, 564, 564, 586)

Size 4X ONLY – Move ahead to "All Sizes Continue" before **Divide for Sleeves** on page 36.

All Other Sizes Continue

Work 4 rnds even in established pattern.

Inc #19 – Next Rnd: Work Aster Lace Chart (next rnd), sm, [k22, M1L] rep bet brackets to last 22 sts, k21, M1L, k1 – x (x, x, x, x, x, 24, 25) sts inc.

Stitch Count Check-In

x (x, x, x, x, x, x, 588, 611)

All Sizes Continue

Work 3 (3, 1, 1, 1, 5, 2, 1, 3) rnd(s) even in established pattern.

To ensure that your panel is centered on the front of your body, reposition your markers, if needed, as follows:

Position your markers so that you have your BOR marker, then 66 (76, 86, 96, 107, 117, 123, 129, 135) sts, then your center lace panel (over 36 sts), then 66 (76, 86, 96, 107, 117, 123, 129, 135) sts, then side marker (which you can remove now), then 168 (188, 206, 228, 248, 270, 282, 294, 305) sts.

Divide for Sleeves

Before separating the sleeves from the body, you should have the following number of sts: 336 (376, 414, 456, 498, 540, 564, 588, 611).

Next Rnd: K33 (39, 42, 47, 51, 54, 57, 60, 60) PM (*Note: This marker is to save your spot for the edge of your right sleeve, which you will come back to as you finish this round.*), k33 (37, 44, 49, 56, 63, 66, 69, 75), sm, work Aster Lace Chart (next rnd), sm, k33 (37, 44, 49, 56, 63, 66, 69, 75) sts—this is the front of the body, place next 66 (78, 84, 93, 102, 108, 114, 120, 120) sts onto waste yarn (loosely, so you can try it on later)—this is the left sleeve. CO 2 (2, 2, 2, 2, 2, 2, 2, 4) sts under arm using e-loop (backward loop) method worked tightly and join to back sts. K102 (110, 122, 136, 146, 162, 168, 174, 185) sts—this is the back, place next 66 (78, 84, 93, 102, 108, 114, 120, 120) sts onto waste yarn (loosely)—this is the right sleeve, CO 2 (2, 2, 2, 2, 2, 2, 2, 4) sts under arm using e-loop (backward loop) method worked tightly—end of rnd. Place your new BOR marker at the center of these newly cast-on sts—this will be the start of each rnd going forward.

Your sleeves have now been separated from the yoke of your sweater. You will now transition to the Lower Body.

Stitch Count Check-In

208 (224, 250, 274, 298, 328, 340, 352, 379) sts in lower body

Lower Body

Next Rnds: K to center panel, sm, work Aster Lace Chart (next rnd), k to end.

Continue working the lower body in the rnd as established, repeating the lace chart rnds in order, until your lower body measures approximately 11 (12, 12, 13, 13, 14, 14, 14, 14) in / 28 (30.5, 30.5, 33, 33, 35.5, 35.5, 35.5, 35.5) cm from under-arm, **ending after a Rnd 16, 20, or 24.** (*Note: Your top will grow another 1–2 in [2.5–5 cm] in the lower body with blocking; if you'd like a little less length, stop sooner before you transition to ribbing.*)

Sizes S, M, 3X, 4X, and 5X ONLY – Next Rnd: Transition to US Size 2 (2.75 mm) circular needle—*or one size smaller than used to obtain gauge on the body*—and k one rnd.

Sizes L, XL, 2X, and 6X ONLY – Next Rnd: Transition to US Size 2 (2.75 mm) circular needle—*or one size smaller than used to obtain gauge on the body*—and k one rnd, increasing x (x, 2, 2, 2, x, x, x, 1) st(s) evenly using M1L inc, ending with a multiple of 4 sts for ribbing—x (x, 248, 272, 296, x, x, x, 378) sts.

Ribbing

Next Rnd: [K2, p2] rep bet brackets to end.

Rep this rnd until ribbed edge measures approximately 2 in (5 cm) in length. BO in pattern with medium tension (not too tight, not too loose—if the lower edge feels restrictive, BO more loosely).

Sleeves

Beginning with either sleeve, and with US Size 3 (3.5 mm) needle—*or size needed to achieve gauge*—transfer the sleeve sts from waste yarn to your needles, and pick up the sts cast-on under arm—68 (80, 86, 95, 104, 110, 116, 122, 124) sts. When all sts are on your needle, PM at center of underarm and join to knit in the rnd.

Knit one rnd.

Dec Rnd: K2, k2tog, k to last 4 sts, ssk, k2—2 sts dec.

Continue working sleeve in the rnd, decreasing every 1.25 (1.25, 1.25, 1, .75, .75, .75, .75, .75) in / 3.25 (3.25, 3.25, 2.5, 2, 2, 2, 2, 2) cm until you reach 58 (70, 76, 83, 88, 94, 100, 106, 108) sts and sleeve measures approximately 6 in (15.25 cm).

Sizes S, M, 3X, and 5X ONLY – Next Rnd: Transitioning to US 2 (3.25 mm) needle—*or one size smaller than needed to achieve gauge*—work one more Dec Rnd: 56 (68, x, x, x, 92, x, 104, x) sts.

Sizes L, 2X, 4X, and 6X ONLY – Next Rnd: Transition to US Size 2 (3.25 mm) needle—*or one size smaller than needed to achieve gauge*—and k one rnd.

Size XL ONLY – Next Rnd: Transitioning to US 2 (3.25 mm) needle—*or one size smaller than needed to achieve gauge*—k2, k2tog, k to last 4 sts, (ssk) twice—x (x, x, 80, x, x, x, x, x) sts.

All Sizes Continue

Ribbing
Next Rnd: [K2, p2] rep bet brackets to end.

Rep this rnd until ribbed edge measures 1.5–2 in (3.75–5 cm). BO in pattern with medium tension (not too tight, not too loose). If the cuff edge is restrictive, BO again more loosely.

Rep for second sleeve.

Finishing
Weave in ends on the WS and wet block for best results. Soak in lukewarm water with a splash of fiber wash for 20 minutes to gently cleanse and relax the fiber. Press out excess water, lay flat, and pin carefully in place along the front panel and neckline to ensure they dry flat and even. Because of the fiber content of the recommended yarn, minimal pinning would be advised; the other portions of your tee can be smoothed flat and dried without pinning. Turn as needed for even drying.

Chart Written Directions
Rnd 1: P1, k3, k2tog, k4, yo, p2, [k2, yo, ssk] 3 times, p2, yo, k4, ssk, k3, p1.

Rnd 2: P1, k2, k2tog, k4, yo, k1, p2, [ssk, yo, k2] 3 times, p2, k1, yo, k4, ssk, k2, p1.

Rnd 3: P1, k1, k2tog, k4, yo, k2, p2, [k2, yo, ssk] 3 times, p2, k2, yo, k4, ssk, k1, p1.

Rnd 4: P1, k2tog, k4, yo, k3, p2, [ssk, yo, k2] 3 times, p2, k3, yo, k4, ssk, p1.

Rnds 5–12: Rep Rnds 1–4.

Rnd 13: P1, yo, ssk, k2, yo, ssk, p2, yo, k4, ssk, k6, k2tog, k4, yo, p2, k2, yo, ssk, k2, p1.

Rnd 14: P1, k2, ssk, yo, k2, p2, k1, yo, k4, ssk, k4, k2tog, k4, yo, k1, p2, ssk, yo, k2, ssk, yo, p1.

Rnd 15: P1, yo, ssk, k2, yo, ssk, p2, k2, yo, k4, ssk, k2, k2tog, k4, yo, k2, p2, k2, yo, ssk, k2, p1.

Rnd 16: P1, k2, ssk, yo, k2, p2, k3, yo, k4, ssk, k2tog, k4, yo, k3, p2, ssk, yo, k2, ssk, yo, p1.

Rnds 17–24: Rep Rnds 13–16.

Rep Rnds 1–24 to create the lace panel.

aster lace tee panel chart

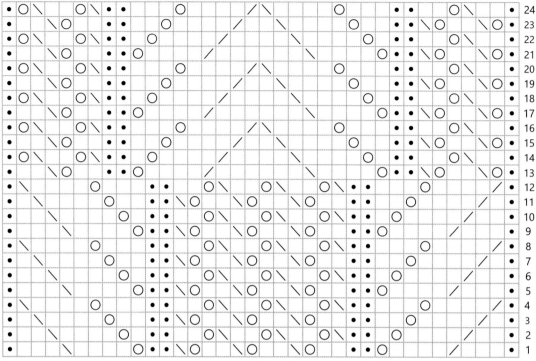

Key	
☐	knit
•	purl
/	k2tog
O	yo
\	ssk

freesia summer top

Lightweight elegance is the name of the game with this gorgeous summer-friendly top that's inspired by one of the world's most popular cut flowers. This is one of the first designs I wrote for this book, and I was stunned by how beautifully the yarn brought the details to life. I used a blend of cupro (a rayon created with cotton waste) and mulberry silk, resulting in stitch definition and sheen like almost nothing else. This featherweight top is the perfect option for a day of wine tasting or a lunch date with a friend. Pair it with cotton capris or a linen skirt and you'll be ready for a day out. Better yet, bring a light jacket to go with it—this delicate top is so lightweight, it's perfect for layering.

Skill Level
Intermediate

Construction
This light-as-air top is knit from the bottom up in the round with allover lace details and single-rib edges up the sides. The upper bodice transitions to stockinette stitch and is worked flat, but it maintains the side ribbed details up to the shoulders. This pattern is very nearly seamless, except for the simple seams on the shoulders. It's finished with a single rib at the neckline and arms.

Sizes
S (M, L, XL/2X, 3X, 4/5X, 6X)

Fit Advice
Designed to be worn with 2–3 in (5–7.5 cm) positive ease.

Finished Measurements
A) Bust Circumference: 34.25 (38.25, 44, 48, 52, 58.25, 62.25) in / 85.5 (95.5, 110, 120, 130, 145.5, 155.5) cm – blocked

B) Armhole Depth: 6 (6.5, 7, 7.5, 8, 8.5, 9) in / 15.25 (16.5, 17.75, 19, 20.25, 21.5, 22.75) cm – prior to blocking (should grow slightly with blocking)

C) Underarm to Hem: 13 (13, 13, 14, 14, 15, 15) in / 33 (33, 33, 35.5, 35.5, 38, 38) cm – prior to blocking

D) Neckline Width (with Ribbing): 10.25 (10.5, 10.5, 11, 11, 11.25, 11.75) in / 30.5 (31.5, 31.25, 32.25, 32.75, 33, 34.25) cm – blocked

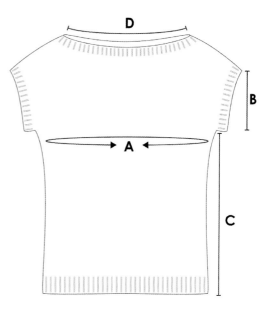

Abbreviations	
[ ]	brackets indicate a repeat
bet	between
BO	bind off
BOR	beginning of round
CO	cast-on
dec	decrease/decreases/decreased
inc	increase/increases/increased
k	knit
k2tog	knit two stitches together (dec 1)
M1L	make one stitch, left leaning (inc 1)
mX	marker "X" denotes which marker (mA, mB, mC, etc...)
p	purl
p2tog	purl two stitches together (dec 1)
PM	place marker
pmX	place marker "X" denotes which marker (pmA, pmB, pmC, etc...)
rep	repeat
rnd/s	round/rounds
RS	right side
sm	slip marker
smX	slip marker "X" denotes which marker (smA, smB, smC, etc...)
ssk	slip one st knitwise, slip the next st knitwise, then return the two sts back to the left needle and knit the two together through the back loop (dec 1)
st/s	stitch/stitches
WS	wrong side
yo	yarn over (inc 1)

Materials	
Yarn	Fingering Weight	Knit Picks Samia	80% Cupro, 20% Mulberry Silk	188 yards (172 meters) in 1.76 oz (50 grams)	875 (944, 1019, 1101, 1189, 1284, 1387) yards / 800 (863, 931, 1006, 1087, 1174, 1268) meters	**Color:** Abalone Shell **Note:** Variations in yarn choice or row/round gauge may impact yarn consumption. If in doubt, round up to the nearest skein.
Needles	**Body:** US Size 3 (3.25 mm)* 24–40-in (60–100-cm) circular needle **Lower Ribbing:** US Size 2 (2.75 mm) 24–40 in (60–100 cm) circular needle **Neckline:** US Size 2 (2.75 mm) 16-in (40-cm) circular needle **Sleeve Ribbing:** US Size 2 (2.75 mm) 12-in (30-cm) circular needle or DPNs *Or size needed to achieve gauge. Adjust other needle sizes accordingly.*
Notions	Stitch markers (including locking markers) Waste yarn or spare needles, for holding stitches Blocking pins and mats Darning needle to weave ends and seam shoulders
Gauge	26 sts and 34 rows/rounds in 4 in (10 cm) in stockinette with largest needle, blocked. The fabric of your swatch should be light and airy.

freesia summer top pattern

With US Size 2 (2.75 mm) 24–40-in (60–100-cm) circular needle—*or one size smaller than used to achieve gauge*—CO 224 (250, 288, 312, 338, 380, 406) sts using cable cast-on method. Do not join in the rnd yet. (*Note: The cable cast-on begins your work immediately on the RS.*)

Set-Up Row (RS): [K1, p1] rep bet brackets to end. PM and join to work in the rnd, being careful not to twist your sts.

Ribbing Rnd: [K1, p1] rep bet brackets to end. Rep this rnd until work measures 2 in (5 cm) from cast-on edge.

Next Rnd: Transition to US Size 3 (3.25 mm) needle—*or size needed to achieve gauge*—as you work this rnd. Work in rib as established over next 28 (20, 18, 30, 22, 22, 14) sts, pmA, work Freesia Lace Chart (beginning with Rnd 1 of chart or written instructions, worked over 21 sts) and rep chart a total of 4 (5, 6, 6, 7, 8, 9) times, pmB, work in rib as established over next 28 (20, 18, 30, 22, 22, 14) sts, pmC, work Freesia Lace Chart (beginning with Rnd 1 of chart or written instructions, worked over 21 sts) 4 (5, 6, 6, 7, 8, 9) times to end.

Next Rnd: Work in established ribbing to mA, smA, work Freesia Lace Chart (next rnd) to mB, smB, work in established ribbing to mC, smC, work Freesia Lace Chart (next rnd) to end.

Continue working the lower body in the rnd as established, repeating the lace chart rnds in order until your lower body measures approximately 13 (13, 13, 14, 14, 15, 15) in / 33 (33, 33, 35.5, 35.5, 38, 38) cm from cast-on edge, ending after Rnd 6.

Upper Bodice

Going forward, you will separate the front and back bodice sections and work back and forth on each section, flat, beginning with the front. You will return to work the back afterward.

Tip: As you begin working flat, be sure to keep your edges tidy. To do this, work the first st tighter than usual, then insert the tip of your needle into the second st, and pull the working yarn tight again to draw the first st a little tighter. Then proceed with the remainder of the row with normal tension. Do this at the start of every row (RS and WS) for nicer edges that will be easier to finish later.

Reposition your markers to begin working the upper bodice flat as follows:

Next Rnd: Work 14 (10, 9, 15, 11, 11, 7) sts in established rib, PM (*Note: This marker is to save your spot for your new BOR.*), work in established ribbing to mA, smA, knit to mB, smB, work 14 (10, 9, 15, 11, 11, 7) sts in established rib, stop.

Slide remaining 112 (125, 144, 156, 169, 190, 203) sts onto a long separate needle or waste yarn. (*Note: This includes the ribbing sts you just worked.*) You will work back and forth (flat) on the front section (only) for now.

Front

Next Row (WS): P1, work in established ribbing to mB, smB, p to mA, smA, work in established ribbing to last st, p1.

Next Row (RS): K1, work in established ribbing to mA, smA, k to mB, smB, work in established ribbing to last st, k1.

Rep these two rows until your flat section measures approximately 6 (6.5, 7, 7.5, 8, 8.5, 9) in / 15.25 (16.5, 17.75, 19, 20.25, 21.5, 22.75) cm from where you began working flat, ending after a WS row (ready to work a RS).

Front Shoulder and Neckline Shaping
Next Row (RS): BO 6 (8, 8, 10, 11, 13, 14) sts knitwise, then work in established pattern for 21 (25, 36, 40, 44, 52, 57) sts—this is the left front shoulder. BO next 58 (59, 56, 56, 59, 60, 61) sts knitwise for center front neckline. Work 27 (33, 44, 50, 55, 65, 71) sts in established pattern to end—this is the right front shoulder.

Place the 21 (25, 36, 40, 44, 52, 57) sts of left front shoulder onto a holder or waste yarn; you will return to work them later. You will now work only on the right front shoulder and neckline dec as you proceed in this section.

Right Front Shoulder
Next Row (WS): BO 6 (8, 8, 10, 11, 13, 14) sts purlwise, work in established pattern to end.

Next Row (RS): K1, ssk, work in established pattern to end—1 st dec.

Next Row (WS): BO 6 (8, 8, 10, 11, 13, 14) sts purlwise, p to end.

Rep these two rows once more (for a total of 2).

Next Row (RS): K1, ssk, k to end—1 st dec.

Next Row (WS): BO remaining sts purlwise.

Left Front Shoulder
Return left front shoulder sts to your needles and rejoin working yarn, ready to work a WS row.

Next Row (WS): P1, p2tog, work in established pattern to end—1 st dec.

Next Row (RS): BO 6 (8, 8, 10, 11, 13, 14) sts knitwise, k to end.

Rep these two rows once more (for a total of 2).

Next Row (WS): P1, p2tog, p to end—1 st dec.

Next Row (RS): K1, k2tog, BO remaining sts knitwise (including the first two).

Back
Return back sts to needles and join working yarn, ready to work a RS row of 112 (125, 144, 156, 169, 190, 203) sts.

Next Row (RS): K1, work in established ribbing to mC, smC, k to mD, smD, work in established ribbing to last st, k1.

Next Row (WS): P1, work in established ribbing to mD, smD, p to mC, smC, work in established ribbing to last st, p1.

Rep these two rows until your flat section measures approximately 6 (6.5, 7, 7.5, 8, 8.5, 9) in / 15.25 (16.5, 17.75, 19, 20.25, 21.5, 22.75) cm and is the same length as the front section from where you began working flat. End after a WS row (ready to work a RS).

Back Shoulder Shaping
Next Row (RS): BO 6 (8, 8, 10, 11, 13, 14) sts knitwise, work in established pattern to end.

Next Row (WS): BO 6 (8, 8, 10, 11, 13, 14) sts purlwise, work in established pattern to end.

Rep these 2 rows once more (for a total of 2)—88 (93, 112, 116, 125, 138, 147) sts.

Next Row (RS): BO 6 (8, 8, 10, 11, 13, 14) sts, then k8 (8, 19, 19, 21, 25, 28) sts—this is the right back shoulder. BO next 60 (61, 58, 58, 61, 62, 63) sts knitwise for center back neckline. K14 (16, 27, 29, 32, 38, 42) sts to end—this is the left back shoulder.

Place 8 (8, 19, 19, 21, 25, 28) sts for right back shoulder onto a separate needle or holder—you will return to work these sts later. You will now work only on the left back shoulder and neckline dec as you proceed in this section.

Left Back Shoulder

Next Row (WS): BO 6 (8, 8, 10, 11, 13, 14) sts purlwise, p to end.

Next Row (RS): K1, k2tog, k to end—1 st dec.

Next Row (WS): BO remaining sts purlwise.

Right Back Shoulder

Return the right back shoulder sts to your needle and rejoin working yarn, ready to work a WS row.

Next Row (WS): P1, p2tog, p to end—1 st dec.

Next Row (RS): BO 6 (8, 8, 10, 11, 13, 14) sts knitwise, k to end.

Next Row (WS): BO remaining sts purlwise.

Shoulder Finishing

Seam the shoulder sts together on each side to the neckline, ensuring that the front, back and shoulder bind-off sections line up perfectly. See seaming and grafting tutorials on my website here: oliveknits.com/grafting.

Neckline

With US Size 2 (2.75 mm) 16 in (40 cm) circular needle—or *needle one size smaller than needed to achieve gauge*—pick up and k approximately every available st around the neckline, ending with a multiple of 2. PM, and join to work in the rnd.

Ribbing

Next Rnd: [K1, p1] rep bet brackets to end.

Rep this rnd until ribbed edge measures approximately 1.25 in (3.25 cm). BO in pattern with medium tension.

Tip: You can adjust the size and feel of your neckline by doing one of the following: For a looser neckline, pick up every available st and ensure that your bind off is not too tight. If your neckline is too open (or your ribbing flares out), try picking up slightly fewer sts—such as 5 of every 6 available sts—and/or binding off a little more tightly. Necklines like this one are very easy to adjust with just a few simple changes to your technique.

Armhole Ribbing

Beginning with either armhole, and with US 2 (2.75 mm) 12 in (30 cm) circular needle or DPNs—*or one size smaller than needed to achieve gauge*—pick up and k approximately 5 of every 6 available sts around the first armhole opening, starting at the underarm and ending with a multiple of 2. Jot down the number of sts you've picked-up so you can match the same number on the other armhole. Starting at the center of the underarm, PM and join to work in the rnd.

Ribbing

Next Rnd: [K1, p1] rep bet brackets to end.

Rep this rnd until ribbed edge measures approximately 1 in (2.5 cm).

BO in pattern with medium tension.

> **Tip:** If your sleeve ribbing flares out, it means you've either picked up slightly too many sts or have worked your ribbing too loosely. If this happens, try again with slightly fewer sts and/or go down another needle size to work your ribbing more tightly. Your bind off can also make a difference, so adjust your tension as needed for best results.

Rep for second armhole.

Finishing

Weave in ends on the WS. Wet block for best results, soaking in lukewarm water with a splash of fiber wash for 20 minutes to gently cleanse and relax the fiber. Press out excess water and lay flat, smoothing into place on your mats. Draw out the sides and edges so they are even. Pin around the sleeve edges and neckline to encourage the ribbed edges to lay flat, and—if necessary—pin carefully down the sides to open the lace and encourage the body to dry into shape. Due to the nature of the recommended fiber, minimal pinning is advised.

Chart Written Directions

Rnd 1: [K1, yo, k3, ssk, k10, k2tog, k3, yo, PM] rep bet brackets to end (on subsequent repeats of this round, you will slip the markers that you already placed).

Rnd 2: [K2, yo, k3, ssk, k8, k2tog, k3, yo, k1, sm] rep bet brackets to end.

Rnd 3: [K3, yo, k3, ssk, k6, k2tog, k3, yo, k2, sm] rep bet brackets to end.

Rnd 4: [K4, yo, k3, ssk, k4, k2tog, k3, yo, k3, sm] rep bet brackets to end.

Rnd 5: [K5, yo, k3, ssk, k2, k2tog, k3, yo, k4, sm] rep bet brackets to end.

Rnd 6: [K6, yo, k3, ssk, k2tog, k3, yo, k5, sm] rep bet brackets to end.

Repeat pattern rounds 1–6 to establish lace design.

freesia summer top chart

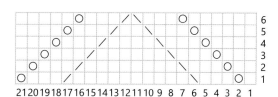

21 20 19 18 17 16 15 14 13 12 11 10 9 8 7 6 5 4 3 2 1

	Key		
☐	knit	\	ssk
O	yo	/	k2tog

verbena side detail tee

Transitions are one of my favorite parts of sweater knitting—moving from one section of the pattern to the next, from one stitch to another. Transitions help us mark time and progress as we work through a project and give us something to look forward to when the less interesting bits drag on, *as they do*. Verbena flowers have noticeable transitions between the leaves and the flowers. In some varieties, the flowers sit together in a colorful puffball on top of a lollipop stem with dark green foliage. You really notice them even though the flowers themselves are quite small. Verbena is a timeless tee, featuring fabric that is as soft and light as a butterfly's wing and delicate details that mark the transitions to the lower body. Lace panels adorn the sides like strings of blossoms, adding a touch of charm without overpowering the simplicity of the design. Want to spice up your look? The blank canvas down the front of the tee leaves room for a statement necklace.

Skill Level
Advanced Beginner

Construction
This ultra-lightweight, three-quarter sleeve tee is knit top-down in the round (in one seamless piece). The yoke is knit with raglan construction, which begins by working flat to shape the rounded neckline (without the need for short rows) and is then joined to work in the round. The yoke increases are worked at even intervals (on either side of the raglan "seams," which are not really seamed at all, but are rather a result of partnered increases). For all but the smallest size, these increases accelerate in pace near the sleeve divide to allow for a raglan shape. This tee has a flattering and comfortable fit, regardless of the size you make. The lace panels are worked from the underarm to the bottom ribbing.

Sizes
S (M, L, XL, 2X, 3X, 4X, 5X, 6X)

Fit Advice
Designed to be worn with 2–3 in (5–7.5 cm) positive ease.

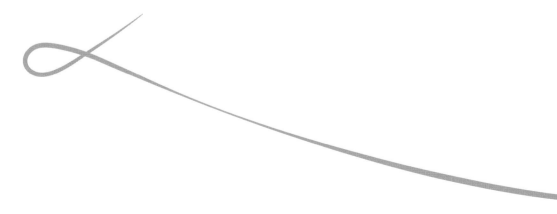

Finished Measurements

A) Bust Circumference: 36 (40, 44, 46.75, 49.25, 52.75, 54.75, 59.25, 63.25) in / 90 (100, 110, 116.75, 123.25, 131.75, 136.75, 148.25, 158.25) cm – blocked

B) Yoke Depth: 8.75 (9.25, 10, 10.75, 11, 12, 12.25, 12.75, 13.5) in / 21.75 (23.25, 25, 27, 27.5, 29.75, 33.5, 32, 34) cm – blocked

C) Underarm to Hem: 13 (14, 14, 15, 15, 16, 16, 16, 16) in / 33 (35.5, 35.5, 38, 38, 40.75, 40.75, 40.75, 40.75) cm – prior to blocking

D) Sleeve Circumference: 12.25 (13.25, 14.25, 15.75, 16.25, 17.75, 18, 18.75, 19.75) in / 30.75 (33.25, 35.75, 39.25, 40.75, 44.25, 45, 46.75, 49.25) cm – blocked

E) Cuff Circumference: 8.75 (9.25, 11.25, 12.75, 13.25, 14.75, 14.75, 15.25, 16.75) in / 21.75 (23.25, 28.25, 31.75, 33.25, 36.75, 36.75, 38.25, 41.75) cm – blocked

F) Sleeve Length: 14.25 (14.25, 14.25, 14.25, 14.25, 14.25, 14.75, 14.75, 14.75) in / 36.25 (36.25, 36.25, 36.25, 36.25, 36.25, 37.5, 37.5, 37.5) cm – prior to blocking

G) Neck Circumference: 18.25 (19, 19.75, 22.25, 23, 23.75, 23.75, 23.75, 23.75) in / 45.75 (47.5, 49.25, 55.75, 57.5, 59.25, 59.25, 59.25, 59.25) cm - blocked

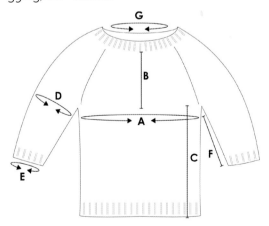

Abbreviations	
[ ]	brackets indicate a repeat
bet	between
BO	bind off
BOR	beginning of row/round
CO	cast on
dec	decrease/decreases/decreased
ea	each
inc	increase/increases/increased
k	knit
k2tog	knit two stitches together (dec 1)
M1L	make one stitch, left leaning (inc 1)
M1R	make one stitch, right leaning (inc 1)
mX	marker "X" denotes which marker (mA, mB, mC, etc...)
p	purl
PM	place marker
pmX	place marker "X" denotes which marker (pmA, pmB, pmC, etc...)
rep	repeat
rnd/s	round/rounds
RS	right side
smX	slip marker "X" denotes which marker (smA, smB, smC, etc...)
ssk	slip one st knitwise, slip the next st knitwise, then return the two sts back to the left needle and knit the two together through the back loop (dec 1)
st/s	stitch/stitches
WS	wrong side
x	denotes sizes not represented in this line of instruction
yo	yarn over (inc 1)

	Materials

Yarn	Light Fingering Weight/Heavy Lace	Knit Picks Voliere	40% Linen, 30% Mulberry Silk, 30% Baby Alpaca	274 yards (251 meters) in 1.76 oz (50 grams)	1210 (1307, 1411, 1524, 1646, 1778, 1920, 2074, 2240) yards / 1106 (1195, 1290, 1393, 1505, 1625, 1755, 1896, 2048) meters	**Color:** Galah **Note:** Variations in yarn choice or row/round gauge may impact yarn consumption. If in doubt, round up to the nearest skein.
Needles	**Body:** US Size 3 (3.25 mm)* 16–40-in (40–100-cm) circular needle **Neckline and Lower Ribbing:** US Size 2 (2.75 mm) 16-in (40-cm) circular needle **Sleeves:** US Size 3 (3.25 mm) 12-in (30-cm) circular needle or DPNs **Sleeve Cuffs:** US Size 2 (2.75 mm) 12-in (30-cm) circular needle or DPNs *Or size needed to achieve gauge. Adjust other needle sizes accordingly.*
Notions	Stitch markers (including locking markers and several unique markers) Waste yarn or spare needles, for holding stitches Blocking pins and mats Darning needle to weave ends **A note about markers:** Markers are labeled to make them easier to differentiate. Markers A, B, C, and D will mark the raglan "seams" or increase sections that separate the front, sleeves, and back. Unique markers will be placed later to denote special details (like lace panels).
Gauge	24 sts and 32 rows/rounds in 4 in (10 cm) in stockinette st with largest needle, blocked

verbena side detail tee pattern

With US Size 3 (3.25 mm) 16-in (40-cm) circular needle—or *size needed to achieve gauge*—CO 62 (66, 70, 84, 86, 90, 90, 88, 86) sts using cable cast-on method. Do not join in the rnd yet. (*Note: The cable cast-on begins your work immediately on the RS.*)

A few things to note: First, don't worry that some larger sizes begin with a smaller cast-on number; this is intentional and considers other aspects of size and shaping that will become apparent later. Second, you will work the pattern flat for a few rows to create the shaped neckline (This is a technique I "unvented" many years ago—as Elizabeth Zimmerman would say—in order to create a beautifully shaped neckline without short rows.); the pattern will indicate when to join in the rnd to continue your work. You will shape the neckline with new sts cast on at the start of each row until the shaping is complete. You will then join your sts to work in the rnd and will reposition your working yarn as indicated when the time comes.

Set-Up Row (RS): K2, pmA, k8 (10, 12, 18, 18, 20, 20, 18, 16), pmB, k42 (42, 42, 44, 46, 46, 46, 48, 50), pmC, k8 (10, 12, 18, 18, 20, 20, 18, 16), pmD, k2.

Set-Up Row (WS): P to end, slipping markers as you go.

Row 1 (RS): CO 2 sts using cable cast-on method worked knitwise (tightly)*, k to 1 st before mA, **M1R**, k1, smA, k1, **M1L**, k to 1 st before mB, **M1R**, k1, smB, k1, **M1L**, k to 1 st before mC, **M1R**, k1, smC, k1, **M1L**, k to 1 st before mD, **M1R**, k1, smD, k1, **M1L**, k to end—8 sts inc + 2 sts CO.

Row 2 (WS): CO 2 sts using cable cast-on method worked purlwise (tightly)*, p to end, slipping markers as you go—2 sts CO.

*Note: Going forward, all sts cast on at the start of a row will be worked using the cable cast-on method, either knitwise or purlwise, depending on the row. Keep your cast-on sts nice and tight to ensure a tidy neckline (it will make for nicer finishing, as well). Always work the new sts in pattern after casting them on.

Row 3 (RS): CO 4 sts, k to 1 st before mA, **M1R**, k1, smA, k1, **M1L**, k to 1 st before mB, **M1R**, k1, smB, k1, **M1L**, k to 1 st before mC, **M1R**, k1, smC, k1, **M1L**, k to 1 st before mD, **M1R**, k1, smD, k1, **M1L**, k to end—8 sts inc + 4 sts CO.

Row 4 (WS): CO 4 sts, p to end, slipping markers as you go—4 sts CO.

Stitch Count Check-In

Fronts (ea): 10 (10, 10, 10, 10, 10, 10, 10, 10)

Sleeves (ea): 12 (14, 16, 22, 22, 24, 24, 22, 20)

Back: 46 (46, 46, 48, 50, 50, 50, 52, 54)

Row 5 (RS): CO 4 sts, k to 1 st before mA, **M1R**, k1, smA, k1, **M1L**, k to 1 st before mB, **M1R**, k1, smB, k1, **M1L**, k to 1 st before mC, **M1R**, k1, smC, k1, **M1L**, k to 1 st before mD, **M1R**, k1, smD, k1, **M1L**, k to end—8 sts inc + 4 sts CO.

Row 6 (WS): CO 4 sts, p to end, slipping markers as you go—4 sts CO.

Row 7 (RS): CO 4 (4, 4, 4, 4, 4, 4, 6, 6) sts, k to 1 st before mA, **M1R**, k1, smA, k1, **M1L**, k to 1 st before mB, **M1R**, k1, smB, k1, **M1L**, k to 1 st before mC, **M1R**, k1, smC, k1, **M1L**, k to 1 st before mD, **M1R**, k1, smD, k1, **M1L**, k to end—8 sts inc + 4 (4, 4, 4, 4, 4, 4, 6, 6) sts CO.

Row 8 (WS): CO 4 (4, 4, 4, 4, 4, 4, 6, 6) sts, p to end, slipping markers as you go—4 (4, 4, 4, 4, 4, 4, 6, 6) sts CO.

Row 9 (RS): CO 10 (10, 10, 12, 14, 14, 14, 12, 14) sts, k to 1 st before mA, **M1R**, k1, smA, k1, **M1L**, k to 1 st before mB, **M1R**, k1, smB, k1, **M1L**, k to 1 st before mC, **M1R**, k1, smC, k1, **M1L**, k to 1 st before mD, **M1R**, k1, smD, k1, **M1L**, k to end—8 sts inc + 10 (10, 10, 12, 14, 14, 14, 12, 14) sts CO.

Neckline Join

The neckline shaping is complete. Cut the working yarn, leaving a tail. Bring your needles together to form a circle and find mD. This will be your new BOR. Slide the sts after mD to the left needle so they are ready to be worked and join the working yarn at mD to begin your new rnd. Be sure to check that your sts are all positioned correctly and are not twisted. (This is one of the few things that's impossible to fix later, so it's worth checking.) You will initially have a small gap where you've joined at the front neckline; don't worry! You'll weave it closed when you finish the neckline later.

Next Rnd (no inc): Starting at your new BOR (at mD), k to end of rnd, slipping markers as you go.

Stitch Count Check-In

Front: 52 (52, 52, 54, 56, 56, 56, 58, 60)

Sleeves (ea): 18 (20, 22, 28, 28, 30, 30, 28, 26)

Back: 52 (52, 52, 54, 56, 56, 56, 58, 60)

Next Rnd (inc): K1, **M1L**, k to 1 st before mA, **M1R**, k1, smA, k1, **M1L**, k to 1 st before mB, **M1R**, k1, smB, k1, **M1L**, k to 1 st before mC, **M1R**, k1, smC, k1, **M1L**, k to 1 st before mD, **M1R**, k1—8 sts inc.

Next Rnd (no inc): K to end, slipping markers as you go.

Rep these two rnds until you reach the following number of sts and have just completed a "no inc" rnd:

Stitch Count Check-In

Front: 106 (102, 102, 106, 108, 112, 114, 120, 128)

Sleeves (ea): 72 (70, 72, 80, 80, 86, 88, 90, 94)

Back: 106 (102, 102, 106, 108, 112, 114, 120, 128)

Size S ONLY – Move ahead to **Divide for Sleeves** on page 52.

> **Note:** As you proceed you will see an "x" as a placeholder for sizes that are no longer represented on that rnd.

All Other Sizes Continue

Next Rnd (extra inc): K1, **M1L**, k2, **M1L**, k to 3 sts before mA, **M1R**, k2, **M1R**, k1, smA, k1, **M1L**, k to 1 st before mB, **M1R**, k1, smB, k1, **M1L**, k2, **M1L**, k to 3 sts before mC, **M1R**, k2, **M1R**, k1, smC, k1, **M1L**, k to 1 st before mD, **M1R**, k1—12 sts inc (4 sts inc on each front and back, 2 sts inc on each sleeve).

Next Rnd (no inc): K to end, slipping markers as you go.

Rep these two rnds x (3, 3, 2, 2, 2, 2, 2, 3) times more for a total of x (4, 4, 3, 3, 3, 3, 3, 4).

Stitch Count Check-In

Front: x (118, 118, 118, 120, 124, 126, 132, 144)

Sleeves (ea): x (78, 80, 86, 86, 92, 94, 96, 102)

Back: x (118, 118, 118, 120, 124, 126, 132, 144)

Size M ONLY – Move ahead to **Divide for Sleeves**.

All Other Sizes Continue

Next Rnd (double extra inc): K1, **M1L**, [k2, **M1L**] twice, k to 5 sts before mA, **M1R**, [k2, **M1R**] twice, k1, smA, k1, **M1L**, k to 1 st before mB, **M1R**, k1, smB, k1, **M1L**, [k2, **M1L**] twice, k to 5 sts before mC, **M1R**, [k2, **M1R**] twice, k1, smC, k1, **M1L**, k to 1 st before mD, **M1R**, k1—16 sts inc (6 sts inc on each front and back, 2 sts inc on each sleeve).

Next Rnd (no inc): K to end, slipping markers as you go.

Rep these two rnds x (x, 1, 2, 3, 4, 2, 2, 2) time(s) more for a total of x (x, 2, 3, 4, 5, 3, 3, 3).

Stitch Count Check-In

Front: x (x, 130, 136, 144, 154, 144, 150, 162)

Sleeves (ea): x (x, 84, 92, 94, 102, 100, 102, 108)

Back: x (x, 130, 136, 144, 154, 144, 150, 162)

Sizes L, XL, 2X, and 3X ONLY – Move ahead to **Divide for Sleeves**.

All Other Sizes Continue

Next Rnd (triple extra inc): K1, **M1L**, [k2, **M1L**] 3 times, k to 7 sts before mA, **M1R**, [k2, **M1R**] 3 times, k1, smA, k1, **M1L**, k to 1 st before mB, **M1R**, k1, smB, k1, **M1L**, [k2, **M1L**] 3 times, k to 7 sts before mC, **M1R**, [k2, **M1R**] 3 times, k1, smC, k1, **M1L**, k to 1 st before mD, **M1R**, k1—20 sts inc (8 sts inc on each front and back, 2 sts inc on each sleeve).

Next Rnd (no inc): K to end of rnd, slipping markers as you go.

Rep these two rnds x (x, x, x, x, 1, 2, 2) time(s) more or a total of x (x, x, x, x, 2, 3, 3), then proceed to **Divide for Sleeves**.

Stitch Count Check-In

Front: x (x, x, x, x, x, 160, 174, 186)

Sleeves (ea): x (x, x, x, x, x, 104, 108, 114)

Back: x (x, x, x, x, x, 160, 174, 186)

Divide for Sleeves

Before separating the sleeves from the body, you should have the following number of sts:

Stitch Count Check-In

Front: 106 (118, 130, 136, 144, 154, 160, 174, 186)

Sleeves (ea): 72 (78, 84, 92, 94, 102, 104, 108, 114)

Back: 106 (118, 130, 136, 144, 154, 160, 174, 186)

Next Rnd: K to mA, remove mA, place next 72 (78, 84, 92, 94, 102, 104, 108, 114) sts onto waste yarn (loosely, so you can try it on later). Remove mB, CO 2 (2, 2, 4, 4, 4, 4, 4, 4) sts onto under arm using e-loop (backward loop) method worked tightly and join to back sts, then k to mC. Remove mC and place next 72 (78, 84, 92, 94, 102, 104, 108, 114) sts onto waste yarn (loosely). Remove mD, CO 2 (2, 2, 4, 4, 4, 4, 4, 4) sts under arm using e-loop (backward loop) method worked tightly.

> **Note:** Your new BOR is technically at the center of these final cast-on sts. However, you will move the BOR in the next section to simplify the placement of the lace panel under the arm. This will not affect the fit or look of your garment.

Your sleeves have now been separated from the yoke of your sweater. You will now transition to the Lower Body.

Stitch Count Check-In

216 (240, 264, 280, 296, 316, 328, 356, 380) sts in lower body

Lower Body

Next Rnd: K to end.

Next Rnd: K11, pmA, k86 (98, 110, 118, 126, 136, 142, 156, 168), pmB, k22, pmC, k86 (98, 110, 118, 126, 136, 142, 156, 168), pmD, stop. For the remainder of the lower body, this will be your new BOR. *You will begin the underarm lace panels as you start the next rnd and will need to work the panel with the last 11 sts of this rnd and the first 11 sts of the next rnd for this side.*

Next Rnd: Work Verbena Side Panel Chart (beginning with Rnd 1 of chart or written instructions, worked over 22 sts), smA, k to mB, smB, work Verbena Side Panel Chart (beginning with Rnd 1 of chart or written instructions, worked over 22 sts), smC, k to end.

Continue working the lower body in the rnd as established, repeating the lace chart rnds in order, until lower body measures approximately 11 (12, 12, 13, 13, 14, 14, 14, 14) in / 28 (30.5, 30.5, 33, 33, 35.5, 35.5, 35.5, 35.5) cm from underarm, ending after Rnd 4 of chart.

> **Note:** If you'd like your tee a little shorter or longer, simply work in pattern until you are about 3 in (7.75 cm) shorter than your desired length—this will account for 2 in (5 cm) of ribbing and growth with blocking.

Next Rnd: Remove BOR, k11, PM for new BOR (this is your original BOR location at the halfway point under the right sleeve).

Ribbing

Next Rnd: Using the same size needle (or one size smaller, if you prefer), [k2, p2] rep bet brackets to end.

Rep this rnd until your ribbed edge measures approximately 2 in (5 cm) in length. BO in pattern with medium tension (not too tight, not too loose—if the lower edge feels restrictive, BO more loosely).

Neckline

Before you work the neckline, use the tail left at the neckline join to weave the gap closed. With US 2 (3.25 mm) 16 in (40 cm) circular needle—*or one size smaller than used to achieve gauge*—pick up and knit every available st around the neckline, ending with a multiple of 4 sts. PM and join to work in the rnd.

Tip: You can adjust the size and feel of your neckline by doing one of the following: For a looser neckline, make sure you've picked up every available st and that your bind off is not too tight. If your neckline is too open (or your ribbing flares out), try picking up slightly fewer sts—such as 5 of every 6 available sts, and/or binding off a little more tightly. Necklines like this one are very easy to adjust with just a few simple changes to your technique.

Ribbing

Next Rnd: [K2, p2] rep bet brackets to end.

Rep this rnd until ribbed edge measures approximately 1 in (2.5 cm). BO in pattern with medium/loose tension.

Neckline Tip 1: If your neckline feels too tight, there are two possible reasons: 1) You did not pick up enough sts, 2) Your bind off is too tight.

Neckline Tip 2: If your neckline feels too loose, one likely culprit is that your initial cast-on at the neckline was too loose. Another possibility is that you may simply prefer a closer fit at the neckline. In either case, you can bring in the neckline by picking up approximately 5–10 percent fewer sts than you did initially. Then work the ribbing and bind off with slightly tighter tension to bring it in even further.

Sleeves

Beginning with either sleeve, and with US Size 3 (3.5 mm) needle—*or size needed to achieve gauge*—transfer the sleeve sts from waste yarn to your needles and pick up the sts cast on under arm—74 (80, 86, 96, 98, 106, 108, 112, 118) sts. When all sts are on your needle, PM at center of underarm and join to knit in the rnd.

Knit one rnd.

Dec Rnd: K2, k2tog, k to last 4 sts, ssk, k2—2 sts dec.

Continue working your sleeve in the rnd, decreasing every 1.25 (1, 1.5, 1.25, 1.5, 1.5, 1.25, 1.25, 1.5) in / 3.25 (2.75, 3.5, 3.25, 3.5, 3.5, 3.25, 3.25, 3.75) cm until you reach 52 (56, 68, 76, 80, 88, 88, 92, 100) sts and sleeve measures approximately 12.5 (12.5, 12.5, 12.5, 12.5, 12.5, 13, 13, 13) in / 31.75 (31.75, 31.75, 31.75, 31.75, 31.75, 33, 33, 33) cm.

Transition to US 2 (3.25 mm) circular needle or DPNs—*or one size smaller than needed to achieve gauge*—and k one rnd.

Ribbing

Next Rnd: [K2, p2] rep bet brackets to end.

Rep this rnd until ribbed edge measures 1.75 in (4.5 cm). BO in pattern with medium tension. (If your edge is too restrictive, BO again more loosely.)

Rep for second sleeve.

Finishing

Weave in ends on the WS and wet block for best results. Soak in lukewarm water with a splash of fiber wash for 20 minutes to gently cleanse and relax the fiber. Press out excess water, and pin the garment flat, pinning along the neckline, raglan seams, and sides. The recommended fiber in this pattern behaves nicely with regular pinning (unlike some plant-based blends), but do adjust your usage of pins, as necessary, to achieve the best results. Turn as needed for even drying.

Chart Written Directions

Rnd 1: K3, yo, k2, ssk, k2tog, k2, yo, k1, yo, k2, ssk, k2tog, k2, yo, k2.

Rnd 2 and all even rnds: K to end.

Rnd 3: K2, yo, k2, ssk, k2tog, k2, yo, k1, yo, k2, ssk, k2tog, k2, yo, k3.

verbena side detail tee chart

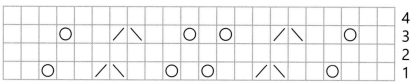

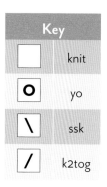

Key	
☐	knit
O	yo
\	ssk
/	k2tog

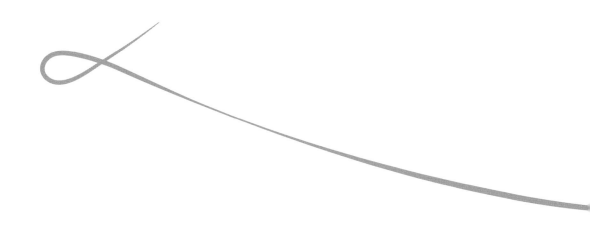

chamomile shimmer tee

There's nothing quite so cheerful as a spray of chamomile blooms; they're like tiny bursts of sunshine. I envisioned this design with an easy yet elevated look—like chamomile tea in a fancy teacup. The silk blend yarn and intricate texture dress up an otherwise simple concept that's perfect with jeans or over a sundress. This design is meant to be ever-so-slightly cropped for a flattering silhouette that hits just above the hip, but you can easily add length if you prefer a longer style. This is one of my personal favorites in this collection—and in my favorite color, too!

Skill Level
Intermediate

Construction
This highly textured, boxy-fit top is knit from the bottom up and worked in the round to the underarms. The front and back upper bodice sections are worked flat and smooth with shaped shoulders and a small, ribbed neckline. The drop-shoulder style is specifically constructed to fit with more ease than you might normally choose in a sweater—it's part of the design. Be cautious about sizing down; your sleeves and neckline may not fit properly if you do.

Sizes
S (M, L, XL, 2X, 3X, 4X, 5X, 6X)

Fit Advice
Designed to be worn with approximately 8–10 in (20–25 cm) positive ease.

Finished Measurements
A) Bust Circumference: 40 (45.25, 50.75, 53.25, 58.75, 61.25, 66.75, 72, 74.75) in / 100 (113.25, 126.75, 133.25, 146.75, 153.25, 166.75, 180, 186.75) cm – blocked

B) Drop Shoulder Depth: 6 (6.5, 7, 7.5, 7.5, 8, 8.5, 8.5, 9) in / 15.25 (16.5, 17.75, 19, 19, 20.25, 21.5, 21.5, 22.75) cm – prior to blocking

C) Underarm to Hem: 13 (13, 13, 14, 14, 15, 15, 15, 15) in / 33 (33, 33, 35.5, 35.5, 38, 38, 38, 38) cm – prior to blocking; expect 1.5–2 in (3.75–5 cm) growth with blocking

D) Sleeve Length: 7 in (17.75 cm) – unblocked

E) Back Neckline Width: 11.25 in (28.75 cm) – blocked

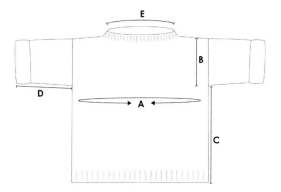

Abbreviations	
[ ]	brackets indicate a repeat
1/2RPC	1/2 right purl cross cable—slip 2 sts to cable needle and hold to back of work, k1 st, then p2 from cable needle
1/2LPC	1/2 left purl cross cable—slip 1 st to cable needle and hold to front of work, purl next 2 sts, then knit the st from the cable needle
bet	between
BO	bind off
BOR	beginning of row/round
CO	cast on
dec	decrease/decreases/decreased
inc	increase/increases/increased
k	knit
k2tog	knit two stitches together (dec 1)
M1L	make one stitch, left leaning (inc 1)
p	purl
p2tog	purl 2 sts together (dec 1)
PM	place marker
rep	repeat
rnd/s	round/rounds
RS	right side
ssk	slip one st knitwise, slip the next st knitwise, then return the two sts back to the left needle and knit the two together through the back loop (dec 1)
st/s	stitch/stitches
WS	wrong side
yo	yarn over (inc 1)
x	denotes sizes not represented in this line of instruction

Materials	
Yarn	Sport Weight	Malabrigo Susurro	50% Silk, 25% Merino, 25% Linen	325 yards (297 meters) in 3.5 oz (100 grams)	1029 (1111, 1199, 1295, 1399, 1511, 1632, 1763, 1904) yards / 941 (1016, 1096, 1184, 1279, 1381, 1492, 1612, 1740) meters	**Color:** Frank Ochre **Note:** Variations in yarn choice or row/round gauge may impact yarn consumption. If in doubt, round up to the nearest skein.
Needles	**Body:** US 4 (3.5 mm)* 24–40-in (60–100-cm) circular needle **Neckline:** US 3 (3.25 mm) 16-in (40-cm) circular needle **Sleeves:** US 4 (3.5 mm) 12-in (30-cm) circular needle or DPNs *Or size needed to achieve gauge. Adjust other needle sizes accordingly.*
Notions	Stitch markers (including locking markers) Waste yarn or spare needles, for holding stitches Blocking pins and mats Cable needle Darning needle to weave ends and seam shoulders
Gauge	27 sts and 36 rows/rounds in 4 in (10 cm) in lace pattern with largest needle, blocked 24 sts and 30 rows/rounds in 4 in (10 cm) in stockinette stitch with largest needle, blocked—*for both of these measurements, row gauge is less critical but may affect yarn consumption.*

chamomile shimmer tee pattern

With US Size 4 (3.5 mm) 24–40-in (60–100-cm) circular needle—*or size needed to obtain gauge*—CO 272 (308, 344, 360, 396, 416, 452, 488, 504) sts using cable cast-on method. Do not join in the rnd yet. (*Note: The cable cast-on begins your work immediately on the RS.*)

Set-Up Row (RS): [K2, p2] rep bet brackets to end, then PM and join to work in the rnd, being careful not to twist your sts.

Ribbing Rnd: [K2, p2] rep bet brackets to end. Rep this rnd until work measures approximately 2 in (5 cm).

Sizes S, M, L, 3X, 4X and 5X ONLY – Next Rnd: K one rnd, decreasing 2 (2, 2, x, x, 2, 2, 2, x) sts using k2tog—270 (306, 342, x, x, 414, 450, 486, x) sts.

Sizes XL, 2X, and 6X ONLY – Next Rnd: K to end.

Next Rnd: Work Chamomile Lace pattern (beginning with Rnd 1 of chart or written instructions, worked over 18 sts per repeat) to end.

Continue working the lower body in the rnd as established, repeating the lace chart rnds in order, until your work measures 13 (13, 13, 14, 14, 15, 15, 15, 15) in / 33 (33, 33, 35.5, 35.5, 38, 38, 38, 38) cm from cast-on edge, ending after an odd-numbered row. Remove BOR on the next row.

Upper Bodice

Going forward, you will separate the front and back bodice sections and work back and forth on each section, flat, beginning with the front. You will return to work the back afterward.

> **Tip:** As you begin working flat, be sure to keep your edges tidy. To do this, work the first st tighter than usual, then insert the tip of your needle into the second st, and pull the working yarn tight again to draw the first st a little tighter. Then proceed with the remainder of the row with normal tension. Do this at the start of every row (RS and WS) for nicer edges that will be easier to finish later.

Sizes S, M, L, 3X, 4X, and 5X ONLY – Next Rnd: K4, PM, K135 (153, 171, x, x, 207, 225, 243, x) sts, then stop. Slide remaining 135 (153, 171, x, x, 207, 225, 243, x) sts onto a long separate needle or waste yarn, including the first 4 sts you worked on this round. (This will shift the pattern placement so that it's relatively centered.)

Sizes XL, 2X, and 6X ONLY – Next Rnd: Kx (x, x, 180, 198, x, x, x, 252) sts, then stop. Slide remaining x (x, x, 180, 198, x, x, x, 252) sts onto a long separate needle or waste yarn.

Stitch Count Check-In

135 (153, 171, 180, 198, 207, 225, 243, 252)

Front

Next Row (WS): P2, k1, p to last 3 sts, k1, p2.

Next Row (RS): K2, p1, k to last 3 sts, p1, k2.

Rep these two rows until your flat section measures 6 (6.5, 7, 7.5, 7.5, 8, 8.5, 8.5, 9) in / 15.25 (16.5, 17.75, 19, 19, 20.25, 21.5, 21.5, 22.75) cm from where you began working flat, ending after a WS row (ready to work a RS).

Front Shoulder and Neckline Shaping

Next Row (RS): BO 7 (9, 10, 11, 13, 14, 15, 17, 18) sts knitwise, then k31 (38, 44, 48, 53, 57, 64, 71, 74) sts—this is the left front shoulder. BO next 59 (59, 63, 62, 66, 65, 67, 67, 68) sts knitwise for center front neckline. K38 (47, 54, 59, 66, 71, 79, 88, 92) sts to end—this is the right front shoulder.

Place the 31 (38, 44, 48, 53, 57, 64, 71, 74) sts of left front shoulder onto a holder or waste yarn; you will return to work them later. You will now work only on the right front shoulder and neckline dec as you proceed in this section.

Right Front Shoulder

Next Row (WS): BO 7 (9, 10, 11, 13, 14, 15, 17, 18) sts purlwise, p to end.

Next Row (RS): K1, ssk, k to end—1 st dec.

Next Row (WS): BO 7 (9, 10, 11, 13, 14, 15, 17, 18) sts purlwise, p to end.

Rep these two rows twice more (for a total of 3).

Next Row (RS): K1, ssk, BO remaining sts knitwise (including the first two).

Left Front Shoulder

Return to the left shoulder sts and place them back on your working needles. Position your yarn to begin a WS row.

Next Row (WS): P1, p2tog, p to end—1 st dec.

Next Row (RS): BO 7 (9, 10, 11, 13, 14, 15, 17, 18) sts knitwise, k to end.

Next Row (WS): P1, p2tog, p to end—1 st dec.

Rep these two rows twice more (for a total of 3).

Next Row (RS): BO remaining sts knitwise.

Back

Return back sts to needles and join working yarn, ready to work a RS row—135 (153, 171, 180, 198, 207, 225, 243, 252) sts on needle.

Next Row (RS): K2, p1, k to last 3 sts, p1, k2.

Next Row (WS): P2, k1, p to last 3 sts, k1, p2.

Rep these two rows until your flat section measures 6 (6.5, 7, 7.5, 7.5, 8, 8.5, 8.5, 9) in / 15.25 (16.5, 17.75, 19, 19, 20.25, 21.5, 22.75) cm and is the same length as the front (before you worked the first BO row). End after a WS row (ready to work a RS).

Back Shoulder Shaping

Next Row (RS): BO 7 (9, 10, 11, 13, 14, 15, 17, 18) sts knitwise, k to end.

Next Row (WS): BO 7 (9, 10, 11, 13, 14, 15, 17, 18) sts purlwise, p to end.

Rep these two rows 3 times more (for a total of 4).

Next Row (RS): BO remaining 79 (81, 91, 92, 94, 95, 105, 107, 108) sts knitwise for center back neckline.

Shoulder Finishing

Seam the shoulder sts together on each side to the neckline, ensuring that the front, back, and shoulder bind-off sections line up perfectly. See seaming and grafting tutorials on my website here: oliveknits.com/grafting.

Neckline

With US Size 3 (3.25 mm) 16 in (40 cm) circular needle—*or one size smaller than needed to achieve gauge*—pick up and k almost every available st around the neckline, ending with a multiple of 4. PM and join to work in the rnd.

Ribbing

Next Rnd: [K2, p2] rep bet brackets to end.

Repeat this rnd until ribbed edge measures approximately 1.25 in (3.25 cm) wide. BO in pattern with medium tension.

> **Tip:** You can adjust the size and feel of your neckline by doing one of the following: For a looser neckline, make sure you've picked up every available st and that your bind off is not too tight. If your neckline is too open (or your ribbing flares out), try picking up slightly fewer sts—such as 5 of every 6 available sts—and/or binding off a little more tightly. Necklines like this one are very easy to adjust with just a few simple changes to your technique.

Sleeves

Beginning with either armhole, and with US Size 4 (3.5 mm) 12 in (40 cm) circular needle or DPNs—*or size needed to achieve gauge*—pick up approximately 4 of every 5 sts around the first armhole opening, starting at the underarm. Jot down the number of sts you've picked up so you can match the same number on the other sleeve. Starting at the center of the underarm, PM, join working yarn and join to work in the rnd.

Next 13 Rnds: K to end of rnd.

Dec Rnd: K2, ssk, k to last 4 sts, k2tog, k2—2 sts dec.

Continue working sleeve in the rnd, decreasing every fifth rnd until sleeve measures approximately 10 in (25.5 cm) from pickup.

BO knitwise with medium tension (not too tight, not too loose). If the cuff edge is restrictive, BO again more loosely.

Rep for second sleeve.

Finishing

Weave in ends on the WS and wet block for best results. Soak in lukewarm water with a splash of fiber wash for 20 minutes to gently cleanse and relax the fiber. Press out excess water and lay flat, pinning into shape. Pin the sleeves flat for the first 24 hours, then fold each cuff up 1.5 in (3.75 cm) and fold them a second time (the same width). Press the folded cuffs flat and pin them so they will continue to dry folded. Turn as needed for even drying.

When dry, use matching yarn from your project to gently "tack" the cuff folds in two places each—once at the center of the underarm, and once at the center of the top of the arm. Be sure to stitch through all the layers. These sts should be relatively invisible and are necessary to keep the folded cuff in place. (Use a few more sts to secure your cuff, if needed.)

Chart Written Directions

Rnd 1: [K6, p5, k6, p1] rep bet brackets to end.

Rnd 2: [K3, 1/2RPC, p5, 1/2LPC, k3, p1] rep bet brackets to end.

Rnd 3: [K4, p9, k4, p1] rep bet brackets to end.

Rnd 4: [1/2LPC, k1, p1, (yo, p2tog) 4 times, k1, 1/2RPC, p1] rep bet brackets to end.

Rnd 5: [P2, k6, p1, k6, p3] to end.

Rnd 6: [P2, 1/2LPC, k3, p1, k3, 1/2RPC, p3] rep bet brackets to end.

Rnd 7: [P4, k4, p1, k4, p5] rep bet brackets to end.

Rnd 8: [(YO, p2tog) twice, k1, 1/2RPC, p1, 1/2LPC, k1, p1, (yo, p2tog) twice] rep bet brackets to end.

chamomile shimmer tee chart

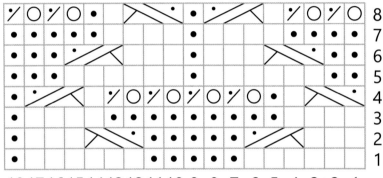

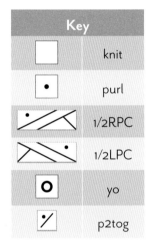

knit	
•	purl
⟋	1/2RPC
⟍	1/2LPC
O	yo
⟋	p2tog

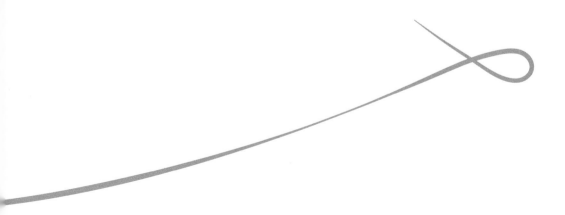

magnolia flutter sides top

I've always loved magnolias, but until I moved to the Pacific Northwest, I wasn't lucky enough to have them in my own yard; now I live in a neighborhood full of them. As it happens, there are many different varieties of magnolias; some are enormous, with magnificent blooms as big as a cantaloupe; others are delicate and slight. There's a Royal Star Magnolia near my garden with long thin petals that dance when the wind blows. I wait all year for those blooms, knowing they'll be here and gone in a blink of an eye. The billowy side shaping of this magnolia-inspired top is framed with statement lace panels to create a flattering, A-line fit with extra airflow around the waist and hips.

Skill Level
Advanced Beginner

Construction
This comfortable and stylish design is knit top-down in the round (in one seamless piece) with round yoke construction and evenly spaced increases to create the shape. The top and sleeves are worked all in one down to the underarm, then the sleeves are separated onto waste yarn while you complete the rest of the body. The lower body features A-line side panels worked in reverse stockinette stitch, framed on either side by a bold leafy lace design. The flared sides offer a forgiving fit—perfect for those who enjoy a little more room around the hips. The body is finished with picot edges along the bottom and three-quarter sleeves. The ribbed neckline is picked up and knit afterward, providing added structure, and giving you more control over the finished fit of the neckline.

Sizes
S (M, L, XL, 2X, 3X, 4X, 5X, 6X)

Fit Advice
Designed to be worn with about 2–3 in (5–7.5 cm) positive ease for a relaxed fit. There will be additional ease in the waist and hip area due to the flared shape.

Finished Measurements
A) Bust Circumference: 35.75 (39.75, 44.25, 48.75, 52, 55, 58.25, 62.25, 66.25) in / 89.5 (99.25, 110.5, 121.5, 130, 137.5, 145.5, 155.5, 165.5) cm – blocked

B) Lower Edge Circumference (with A-Line Flare): 50 (55, 59.5, 64.25, 68.75, 72.25, 75.5, 79.5, 83.5) in / 124.75 (137.5, 148.75, 160.75, 171.5, 180.75, 188.75, 198.75, 208.75) cm – blocked

C) Yoke Depth: 8 (8.75, 9, 10, 10.25, 11, 11.5, 12, 12.75) in / 20 (21.75, 22.25, 24.75, 26, 27.75, 28.75, 30, 31.75) cm – blocked

(Continued)

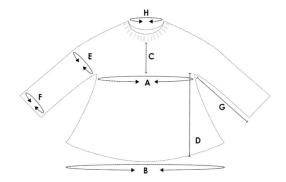

D) Underarm to Hem: 13 (14, 14, 15, 15, 16, 16, 16, 16) in / 33 (35.5, 35.5, 38, 38, 40.75, 40.75, 40.75, 40.75) cm – prior to blocking and picot edge

E) Sleeve Circumference: 11.5 (12.75, 14, 15, 16.75, 18, 19, 19.5, 19.5) in / 28.75 (32, 35.25, 37.5, 41.5, 45.25, 47.25, 48.75, 48.75) cm – blocked

F) Cuff Circumference: 9 (10.25, 11.5, 11.75, 13.5, 14, 14.75, 15.25, 15.25) in / 22.5 (25.5, 28.75, 29.5, 33.5, 34.75, 36.75, 38.5, 38.5) cm – blocked

G) Sleeve Length: 13 (13, 13, 13, 13, 14, 14, 14, 14) in / 32.5 (32.5, 32.5, 32.5, 32.5, 35, 35, 35, 35) cm – prior to blocking and picot edge

H) Neckline Circumference: Approximately 20 (20, 20.5, 20.5, 21.5, 21.5, 21.5, 21.5, 21.5) in / 50 (50, 51.5, 51.5, 53.5, 53.5, 53.5, 53.5, 53.5) cm in ribbing, with smaller needles – blocked

Abbreviations	
[ ]	brackets indicate a repeat
bet	between
BO	bind off
BOR	beginning of row/round
CO	cast on
dec	decrease/decreases/decreased
inc	increase/increases/increased
k	knit
k2tog	knit two stitches together (dec 1)
M1L	make one stitch, left leaning (inc 1)
M1P	make one st purlwise using e-loop (or backward loop) inc
mX	marker "X" denotes which marker (mA, mB, mC, etc...)
p	purl
p2tog	purl 2 stitches together (dec 1)
PM	place marker
pmX	place marker "X" denotes which marker (pmA, pmB, pmC, etc...)
rep	repeat
rnd/s	round/rounds
RS	right side
sl2-k1-p2sso	slip two stitches together as if to knit, knit the next stitch, then pass the two slipped stitches over the knit stitch; this is also known as a centered double decrease (dec 2)
smX	slip marker "X" denotes which marker (smA, smB, smC, etc...)
ssk	slip one st knitwise, slip the next st knitwise, then return the two sts back to the left needle and knit the two together through the back loop (dec 1)
st/s	stitch/stitches
WS	wrong side
x	denotes sizes not represented in this line of instruction
yo	yarn over (inc 1)

Materials	
Yarn	Fingering Weight	Purl Soho Linen Quill	50% Fine Highland Wool, 35% Alpaca, 15% Linen| 439 yards (410 meters) in 3.5 oz (100 grams)	1210 (1307, 1411, 1524, 1646, 1778, 1920, 2074, 2240) yards / 1106 (1195, 1290, 1393, 1505, 1625, 1755, 1896, 2048) meters	**Color:** Eggshell Blue **Note:** Variations in yarn choice or row/round gauge may impact yarn consumption. If in doubt, round up to the nearest skein.
Needles	**Body:** US 4 (3.5 mm)* 16–40-in (40–100-cm) circular needles **Neckline:** US 3 (3.25 mm) 16-in (40-cm) circular needles **Sleeves:** US 4 (3.5 mm) 12-in (30-cm) circular needles or DPNs *Or size needed to achieve gauge. Adjust other needle sizes accordingly.*
Notions	Stitch markers (including locking markers and several unique markers) Waste yarn or spare needles, for holding stitches Blocking pins and mats Darning needle to weave ends
Gauge	25 sts and 34 rows/rounds in 4 in (10 cm) in stockinette stitch with largest needle, blocked

magnolia flutter sides top pattern

With US Size 4 (3.5 mm) 16-in (40-cm) circular needle—*or one size smaller than used to achieve gauge*—CO 140 (140, 144, 144, 150, 150, 150, 150, 150) sts using cable cast-on method. Do not join in the rnd yet. (*Note: The cable cast-on begins your work immediately on the RS.*)

Set-Up Row (RS): K to end, PM and join to work in the rnd, being careful not to twist your sts.

Next 2 Rnds: K to end of rnd.

Next Rnd: K70 (70, 72, 72, 75, 75, 75, 75, 75) sts, place a side marker, k70 (70, 72, 72, 75, 75, 75, 75, 75) sts to end. Stop.

Short Rows

> **Tip:** If you prefer a different short row method, simply work 8 short rows in your preferred method, using these details as a guide for the turning point. Be sure to keep your BOR and side markers in place as you create the short rows.

Turn your work to the WS to begin 8 short rows using the Japanese short row method. You will need two locking markers for this technique.

Short Row 1 (WS): Slip first st to right needle (purlwise) without working it and place a locking marker on your working yarn (holding the marker to the WS of your work). P to the side marker. Stop and turn to RS.

Short Row 2 (RS): Slip first st to right needle (purlwise) without working it and place a locking marker on your working yarn (holding the marker to the WS of your work). K to the gap that is marked with locking marker. Using the marker to pull, draw up the marked yarn from the WS of your work and place it on the left needle as if a new st (adjusting the BOR marker, as needed, to work the short row, and then replacing it to its original location), then knit it together (k2tog) with the next st on the left needle (closing the gap) and remove locking marker. K1, stop, and turn to WS.

Short Row 3 (WS): Slip first st to right needle (purlwise) without working it and place a locking marker on the working yarn (holding the marker to the WS of your work). P to gap that is marked with locking marker. Slip the next st to the right needle purlwise without working it. Using the marker to pull, draw up the marked yarn from the WS of your work and place it on the left needle as if a new st (adjusting the side marker, as needed, to work the short row, and then replacing it to its original location). Place the st that you previously slipped back to the left needle and purl it together (p2tog) with the "new" st (closing the gap) and remove locking marker. P1, stop, and turn to RS.

Short Row 4 (RS): Slip the first st to right needle (purlwise) without working it, place a locking marker on the working yarn (held at the WS of your work). K to gap that is marked with locking marker. Using the marker to pull, draw up the marked yarn from the WS of your work and place it on the left needle as if a new st, then knit it together (k2tog) with the next st on the left needle (closing the gap) and remove locking marker. K1, stop, and turn to WS.

Short Rows 5–8: Rep Short Rows 3 and 4 twice more. Do not turn work to WS after final repeat of Short Row 4.

Continue on RS, and work in pattern to end of rnd until you are one st before the final gap. Slip this st to your right needle purlwise without working it, then, using the marker to pull, draw up the marked yarn from the WS of your work and place it on the left needle as if a new st. Place the st that you previously slipped back to the left needle and knit it together (k2tog) with the "new" st (closing the gap) and remove the locking marker. Knit to end of rnd. Your short rows have been completed and your gaps should be closed.

K one rnd.

Pattern Begins

Inc #1 – Next Rnd: [K7 (7, 6, 6, 6, 6, 6, 6, 6), M1L, PM] rep bet brackets to end of rnd—20 (20, 24, 24, 25, 25, 25, 25, 25) sts inc.

Work 4 rnds even in established stockinette.

Inc #2 – Next Rnd: [K to m, M1L, sm] rep bet brackets to end—20 (20, 24, 24, 25, 25, 25, 25, 25) sts inc.

Work 4 rnds even in established stockinette.

Inc #3 – Next Rnd: [K to m, M1L, sm] rep bet brackets to end—20 (20, 24, 24, 25, 25, 25, 25, 25) sts inc.

Work 4 rnds even in established stockinette.

Stitch Count Check-In

200 (200, 216, 216, 225, 225, 225, 225, 225)

Note: Transition to longer circular needle when necessary for sts to move comfortably.

Inc #4 – Next Rnd: [K to m, M1L, sm] rep bet brackets to end—20 (20, 24, 24, 25, 25, 25, 25, 25) sts inc.

Work 4 rnds even in established stockinette.

Inc #5 – Next Rnd: [K to m, M1L, sm] rep bet brackets to end—20 (20, 24, 24, 25, 25, 25, 25, 25) sts inc.

Work 4 rnds even in established stockinette.

Inc #6 – Next Rnd: [K to m, M1L, sm] rep bet brackets to end—20 (20, 24, 24, 25, 25, 25, 25, 25) sts inc.

Work 4 rnds even in established stockinette.

Stitch Count Check-In
260 (260, 288, 288, 300, 300, 300, 300, 300)

Inc #7 – Next Rnd: [K to m, M1L, sm] rep bet brackets to end—20 (20, 24, 24, 25, 25, 25, 25, 25) sts inc.

Work 4 rnds even in established stockinette.

Inc #8 – Next Rnd: [K to m, M1L, sm] rep bet brackets to end—20 (20, 24, 24, 25, 25, 25, 25, 25) sts inc.

Work 4 rnds even in established stockinette.

Inc #9 – Next Rnd: [K to m, M1L, sm] rep bet brackets to end—20 (20, 24, 24, 25, 25, 25, 25, 25) sts inc.

Work 4 rnds even in established stockinette.

Inc #10 – Next Rnd: [K to m, M1L, sm] rep bet brackets to end—20 (20, 24, 24, 25, 25, 25, 25, 25) sts inc.

Work 4 rnds even in established stockinette.

Inc #11 – Next Rnd: [K to m, M1L, sm] rep bet brackets to end—20 (20, 24, 24, 25, 25, 25, 25, 25) sts inc.

Work 4 rnds even in established stockinette.

Stitch Count Check-In
360 (360, 408, 408, 425, 425, 425, 425, 425)

Note: As you proceed you will see an "x" as a placeholder for sizes that are no longer represented on that rnd.

Size S ONLY – Move ahead to **Divide for Sleeves** on page 70.

All Other Sizes Continue

Inc #12 – Next Rnd: [K to m, M1L, sm] rep bet brackets to end—x (20, 24, 24, 25, 25, 25, 25, 25) sts inc.

Work 4 rnds even in established stockinette.

Size L ONLY – Inc #13 – Next Rnd: [K to m, sm, k to m, M1L, sm] rep bet brackets to end—x (x, 12, x, x, x, x, x, x) sts inc.

Sizes M, XL, 2X, 3X, 4X, 5X, and 6X ONLY – Inc #13 – Next Rnd: [K to m, M1L, sm] rep bet brackets to end—x (20, x, 24, 25, 25, 25, 25, 25) sts inc.

Work 4 rnds even in established stockinette.

Sizes M and L ONLY – Move ahead to **Divide for Sleeves** on page 70.

All Other Sizes Continue

Inc #14 – Next Rnd: [K to m, M1L, sm] rep bet brackets to end—x (x, x, 24, 25, 25, 25, 25, 25) sts inc.

Work 4 rnds even in established stockinette.

Size XL ONLY – Move ahead to **Divide for Sleeves** on page 70.

All Other Sizes Continue

Stitch Count Check-In
x (x, x, x, 500, 500, 500, 500, 500)

Inc #15 – Next Rnd: [K to m, M1L, sm] rep bet brackets to end—x (x, x, x, 25, 25, 25, 25, 25) sts inc.

Work 4 rnds even in established stockinette.

Size 2X ONLY – Move ahead to **Divide for Sleeves** on page 70.

All Other Sizes Continue

Inc #16 – Next Rnd: [K to m, M1L, sm] rep bet brackets to end—x (x, x, x, 25, 25, 25, 25) sts inc.

Work 4 rnds even in established stockinette.

Size 3X ONLY – Move ahead to **Divide for Sleeves** on page 70.

All Other Sizes Continue

Inc #17 – Next Rnd: [K to m, M1L, sm] rep bet brackets to end—x (x, x, x, x, x, 25, 25, 25) sts inc.

Work 4 rnds even in established stockinette.

Inc #18 – Next Rnd: [K to m, M1L, sm] rep bet brackets to end—x (x, x, x, x, x, 25, 25, 25) sts inc.

Work 4 rnds even in established stockinette.

Size 4X ONLY – Move ahead to **Divide for Sleeves** on page 70.

Inc #19 – Next Rnd: [K to m, M1L, sm] rep bet brackets to end—x (x, x, x, x, x, x, 25, 25) sts inc.

Work 4 rnds even in established stockinette.

Size 5X ONLY – Move ahead to **Divide for Sleeves** on page 70.

Size 6X ONLY – Continue

Inc #20 – Next Rnd: [K to m, M1L, sm] rep bet brackets to end—x (x, x, x, x, x, x, 25) sts inc.

Work 4 rnds even in established stockinette, then move on to **Divide for Sleeves** on page 70.

Divide for Sleeves

You should have the following number of sts: 360 (400, 444, 480, 525, 550, 600, 625, 650) sts.

For all sizes, before you divide for sleeves, knit 9 (5, 7, 11, 10, 13, 6, 5, 2) rnds more, removing all but BOR marker as you go.

Next Rnd: K35 (39, 43, 45, 51, 54, 59, 60, 60), PM (*Note: This marker is to save your spot for the edge of your right sleeve, which you will come back to as you complete this round.*), k110 (122, 136, 150, 161, 167, 182, 193, 205) sts—this is the front of the body. Place next 70 (78, 86, 90, 102, 108, 118, 120, 120) sts onto waste yarn (loosely, so you can try it on later)—this is the left sleeve. CO 2 (2, 2, 2, 2, 5, 0, 2, 2) sts under arm using e-loop (backward loop) method worked tightly and place a marker at the center of this underarm. (**Size 3X ONLY:** Since you have an odd number, place the marker so that 2 sts are before the marker and 3 after.) Join to back sts. K110 (122, 136, 150, 160, 167, 182, 192, 205) sts—this is the back. Place next 70 (78, 86, 90, 102, 108, 118, 120, 120) sts onto waste yarn (loosely)—this is the right sleeve. CO 2 (2, 2, 2, 2, 5, 0, 2, 2) sts under arm and place a marker at the center of this underarm (**Size 3X ONLY:** Since you have an odd number, place the marker so that 2 sts are before the marker and 3 after.)—end of rnd. This will be the start of each rnd going forward.

Your sleeves have now been separated from the yoke of your sweater. You will now transition to the Lower Body.

Stitch Count Check-In (Lower Body)

224 (248, 276, 304, 325, 344, 364, 389, 414) sts in lower body

Lower Body

Next Rnd: K to side m, sm, k to end.

Next Rnd: P2, M1P, pmA, work Magnolia Lace Chart 1 (beginning with Rnd 1 of chart or written instructions, worked over 17 sts), pmB, k to 19 sts before next marker, pmC, work Magnolia Lace Chart 2 (beginning with Rnd 1 of chart or written instructions, worked over 17 sts), pmD, M1P, p2, remove side marker, p2, M1P, pmE, work Magnolia Lace Chart 1 (beginning with Rnd 1 of chart or written instructions, worked over 17 sts), pmF, k to 19 sts before end of rnd, pmG, work Magnolia Lace Chart 2 (beginning with Rnd 1 of chart or written instructions, worked over 17 sts), pmH, M1P, p2—4 sts inc.

Next Rnd: P to mA, smA, work Magnolia Lace Chart 1 (next rnd), smB, k to mC, smC, work Magnolia Lace Chart 2 (next rnd), smD, p to mE, smE, work Magnolia Lace Chart 1 (next rnd), smF, k to mG, smG, work Magnolia Lace Chart 2 (next rnd), smH, p to end.

Next Rnd (inc): P to mA, M1P, smA, work Magnolia Lace Chart 1 (next rnd), smB, k to mC, smC, work Magnolia Lace Chart 2 (next rnd), smD, M1P, p to mE, M1P, smE, work Magnolia Lace Chart 1 (next rnd), smF, k to mG, smG, work Magnolia Lace Chart 2 (next rnd), smH, M1P, p to end—4 sts inc.

Work 4 rnds even in established pattern.

Rep these five rnds, repeating the lace chart rnds in order, until lower body measures approximately 13 (14, 14, 15, 15, 16, 16, 16, 16) in / 33 (35.5, 35.5, 38, 38, 40.75, 40.75, 40.75, 40.75) cm from underarm, ending after Rnd 12.

Lower Edging

If you maintain a consistent round gauge through-out, you should have approximately 312 (348, 376, 404, 425, 452, 472, 497, 522) sts on your needles when you reach the correct length. The length is more important than your final st count, so be sure you reach the correct length regardless. (The stitch count for the lower edge isn't critical.)

Next Rnd: BO using the picot bind-off method as follows—[CO 2 sts using the knitted cast-on method at the beginning of this rnd. BO 4 sts. Slide the remaining st from the right needle to the left needle.] Rep the process in brackets to the end of the rnd. For sizes 2X and 5X, BO the final st. Draw thread through final st.

Neckline

With US 3 (3.25 mm) 16 in (40 cm) circular needle—*or one size smaller than needed to achieve gauge*—pick up approximately every available st around the neckline, ending with a multiple of 4 sts. For best results, I recommend starting your neckline ribbing rnd near either shoulder (rather than in the front or back).

Ribbing

Next Rnd: [K2, p2] rep bet brackets to end.

Rep this rnd until ribbed edge measures approximately 1.25 in (3.25 cm). BO in pattern with medium tension.

Tip: You can adjust the size and feel of your neckline by doing one of the following: For a looser neckline, make sure you've picked up every available st and that your bind off is not too tight. If your neckline is too open (or your ribbing flares out), try picking up slightly fewer sts—such as 5 of every 6 available sts—and/or binding off a little more tightly. Necklines like this one are very easy to adjust with just a few simple changes to your technique.

Sleeves

Beginning with either sleeve and with US Size 4 (3.75 mm) needles—*or size needed to achieve gauge*—transfer the sleeve sts from waste yarn to your needles and pick up the sts cast on under arm—72 (80, 88, 92, 104, 113, 118, 122, 122) sts. When all sts are on your needle, PM at center of underarm and join to work in the rnd.

Work your sleeve in the rnd in stockinette st (knitting every rnd) for 1 in (2.5 cm).

Dec Rnd: K2, k2tog, k to last 4 sts, ssk, k2—2 sts dec.

Continue working the sleeve in the rnd, decreasing every 1.5 (1.5, 1.5, 1.25, 1, 1, 1, 1, 1) in / 3.75 (3.75, 3.75, 3.25, 2.5, 2.5, 2.5, 2.5, 2.5) cm until you reach 56 (64, 72, 74, 84, 87, 92, 96, 96) sts and sleeve measures approximately 13 (13, 13, 13, 13, 14, 14, 14, 14) in / 32.5 (32.5, 32.5, 32.5, 32.5, 35, 35, 35, 35) cm from underarm. BO using the picot bind-off method (same as for lower body). For size 3X, BO the final st.

Rep for second sleeve.

Chart 1 Written Directions

Rnd 1: K1, k2tog, yo, k4, sl2-k1-p2sso, k4, yo, k1, yo, ssk, yo.

Rnd 2 and all even-numbered rounds: Knit.

Rnd 3: K1, k2tog, yo, k3, sl2-k1-p2sso, (k3, yo) twice, ssk, yo.

Rnd 5: K1, k2tog, yo, k2, sl2-k1-p2sso, k2, yo, k5, yo, ssk, yo.

Rnd 7: K1, k2tog, yo, k1, sl2-k1-p2sso, k1, yo, k7, yo, ssk, yo.

Rnd 9: K1, k2tog, yo, sl2-k1-p2sso, yo, k9, yo, ssk, yo.

Rnd 11: K1, sl2-k1-p2sso, yo, k11, yo, ssk, yo. (*Note: The double decrease on this row does not align with the others on previous rows; this is intentional.*)

Finishing

Weave in ends on the WS. Wet block. Soak in lukewarm water with a splash of fiber wash for 20 minutes to gently cleanse and relax the fiber. Press out excess water and pin in place, drawing the side panels out from the center (they should fan out sideways) so they lay flat out to the sides. Pin around the neckline, lower picot edges, and gently around the side folds to enhance the lace and let rest until nearly dry. Before fully dry, remove the pins along the sides of the lower body and fold the side panels inward so they rest in layers (the reverse stockinette should be folded inside the garment). This will soften the edges and enhance the waves when they are dry.

Chart 2 Written Directions

Rnd 1: Yo, k2tog, yo, k1, yo, k4, sl2-k1-p2sso, k4, yo, ssk, k1.

Rnd 2 and all even-numbered rounds: Knit.

Rnd 3: Yo, k2tog, (yo, k3) twice, sl2-k1-p2sso, k3, yo, ssk, k1.

Rnd 5: Yo, k2tog, yo, k5, yo, k2, sl2-k1-p2sso, k2, yo, ssk, k1.

Rnd 7: Yo, k2tog, yo, k7, yo, k1, sl2-k1-p2sso, k1, yo, ssk, k1.

Rnd 9: Yo, k2tog, yo, k9, yo, sl2-k1-p2sso, yo, ssk, k1.

Rnd 11: Yo, k2tog, yo, k11, yo, sl2-k1-p2sso, k1. (*Note: The double decrease on this row does not align with the others on previous rows; this is intentional.*)

magnolia flutter sides top chart 1

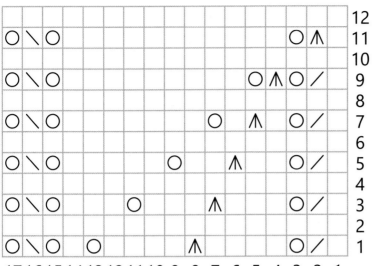

																			12
O	\	O												O	∧		11
																		10
O	\	O								O	∧	O	/				9
																		8
O	\	O						O		∧		O	/				7
																		6
O	\	O				O			∧			O	/				5
																		4
O	\	O			O				∧			O	/				3
																		2
O	\	O		O				∧				O	/				1

17 16 15 14 13 12 11 10 9 8 7 6 5 4 3 2 1

Key

☐	knit
∧	sl2 (knitwise), k1, p2sso
O	yo
\	ssk
/	k2tog

magnolia flutter sides top chart 2

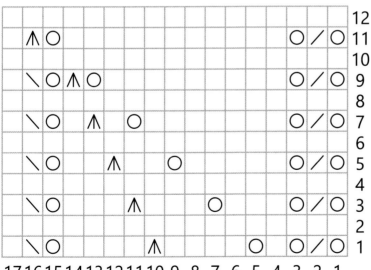

																			12
	∧	O										O	/	O			11
																		10
\	O	∧	O									O	/	O			9
																		8
\	O		∧		O							O	/	O			7
																		6
\	O			∧		O						O	/	O			5
																		4
\	O				∧		O					O	/	O			3
																		2
\	O					∧					O		O	/	O		1

17 16 15 14 13 12 11 10 9 8 7 6 5 4 3 2 1

Key

☐	knit
O	yo
/	k2tog
∧	sl2 (knitwise), k1, p2sso
\	ssk
•	purl

violet eyelet tee

When I first sat down with the idea for this design, lace seemed an obvious choice. Maybe it's because violets have those gorgeous lacy centers, or perhaps because the words *violet* and *eyelet* are fun to say together. (Sometimes inspiration is a silly thing.) Traditional raglan shaping is a bit sporty on its own, but the addition of lace details and an elegant yarn work together to elevate the otherwise casual shape and make it suitable for a nice evening. The drape and stitch definition of the recommended yarn coordinate beautifully, and the fabric makes it wearable most of the year. If you love the look of a cropped sweater over a summer dress, you can shorten the length or make it an extra long tunic to wear with leggings. The top-down, seamless style makes it easy to modify for the look you want.

Skill Level
Advanced Beginner

Construction
This lightweight, short sleeve tee is knit top-down in the round (in one seamless piece). The yoke is knit with raglan construction, which begins by working flat to shape the rounded neckline (without the need for short rows) and is then joined to work in the round. The yoke increases are worked at even intervals (on either side of the raglan "seams," which are not really seamed at all, but are rather a result of partnered increases). For all but the smallest size, these increases accelerate in pace near the sleeve divide to allow for a raglan shape that has a flattering and comfortable fit, regardless of the size you make. The top and sleeves are worked all in one down to the underarm, then the sleeves are separated onto waste yarn while you complete the rest of the body. Lace details are worked around the circumference of the lower body, finished off with ribbing. The rolled neckline offers a quick and easy finish.

Sizes
S (M, L, XL, 2X, 3X, 4X, 5X, 6X)

Fit
Designed for a casual fit with approximately 2–4 in (5–10 cm) positive ease.

Finished Measurements

A) Bust Circumference: 35 (39.25, 41.5, 45.75, 48, 52.25, 54.5, 61, 65.5) in / 87.25 (98.25, 103.75, 114.5, 120, 131, 136.25, 152.75, 163.75) cm – blocked

B) Yoke Depth: 8.5 (9.75, 10.25, 11.25, 11.5, 12.75, 12.75, 12.75, 13) in / 21 (24.5, 25.75, 28.25, 28.75, 31.5, 31.5, 32, 32.5) cm – blocked

C) Underarm to Hem: 12.5 (13.5, 13.5, 14.5, 14.5, 15.5, 15.5, 15.5, 15.5) in / 31.75 (34.25, 34.25, 36.75, 36.75, 39.25, 39.25, 39.25, 39.25) cm – prior to blocking

D) Sleeve Circumference: 12 (13.75, 14.5, 16, 16.25, 17.75, 18.25, 18.5, 19) in / 30 (34.5, 36.25, 40, 41, 44.5, 45.5, 46.25, 47.25) cm – blocked

E) Cuff Circumference: 10.25 (12.25, 13, 14.5, 15.25, 16.75, 16.75, 16.75, 17.5) in / 25.5 (31, 32.75, 36.25, 38.25, 41.75, 41.75, 41.75, 43.75) cm – blocked

F) Sleeve Length: 6.75 in (17.25 cm) – prior to blocking

G) Neck Circumference: 18 (18, 18.5, 19.75, 20, 20, 20, 21.25, 22.5) in / 45.75 (45.75, 47, 50.25, 50.75, 50.75, 50.75, 54, 57.25) cm – blocked

Abbreviations	
[ ]	brackets indicate a repeat
bet	between
BO	bind off
BOR	beginning of row/round
CO	cast on
dec	decrease/decreases/decreased
ea	each
inc	increase/increases/increased
k	knit
k2tog	knit two stitches together (dec 1)
mX	marker "X" denotes which marker (mA, mB, mC, etc...)
M1L	make one stitch, left leaning (inc 1)
M1R	make one stitch, right leaning (inc 1)
p	purl
PM	place marker
pmX	place marker "X" denotes which marker (pmA, pmB, pmC, etc...)
rep	repeat
rnd/s	round/rounds
RS	right side
smX	slip marker "X" denotes which marker (smA, smB, smC, etc...)
ssk	slip one st knitwise, slip the next st knitwise, then return the two sts back to the left needle and knit the two together through the back loop (dec 1)
st/s	stitch/stitches
WS	wrong side
x	denotes sizes not represented in this line of instruction
yo	yarn over (inc 1)

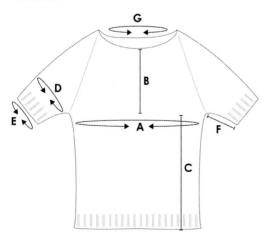

Materials	
Yarn	Sport Weight | Rylie by Skacel | 50% Baby Alpaca, 25% Mulberry Silk, 25% Linen | 274 yards (251 meters) in 3.5 oz (100 grams) | 750 (795, 843, 893, 947, 1004, 1064, 1128, 1195) yards / 686 (726, 770, 816, 865, 918, 973, 1031, 1092) meters | **Color:** Thistle **Note:** Variations in yarn choice or row/round gauge may impact yarn consumption. If in doubt, round up to the nearest skein.
Needles	**Body:** US 4 (3.5 mm)* 16–40-in (40–100-cm) circular needle **Neckline Finish:** US 3 (3.25 mm) 16-in (40-cm) circular needle **Sleeves:** US 4 (3.5 mm) 12-in (30-cm) circular needle or DPNs **Or size needed to achieve gauge. Adjust other needle sizes accordingly.*
Notions	Stitch markers (including locking markers and several unique markers) Waste yarn or spare needles, for holding stitches Blocking pins and mats Darning needle to weave in ends **A note about markers:** Markers are labeled to make them easier to differentiate. Markers A, B, C, and D will mark the raglan "seams" or increase sections that separate the front, sleeves, and back. Unique markers will be placed later to denote special details (like lace panels).
Gauge	22 sts and 28 rows/rounds in 4 in (10 cm) with largest needle in stockinette stitch, blocked

violet eyelet tee pattern

With US Size 4 (3.5 mm) 16-in (40-cm) circular needle—*or size needed to achieve gauge*—CO 70 (70, 74, 80, 86, 86, 86, 92, 98) sts using cable cast-on method. Do not join in the rnd yet. (*Note: The cable cast-on begins your work immediately on the RS.*)

Note: You will work the pattern flat for a few rows to create the shaped neckline (This is a technique I "unvented" many years ago—as Elizabeth Zimmerman would say—in order to create a beautifully shaped neckline without short rows.); the pattern will indicate when to join in the rnd to continue your work. You will shape the neckline with new sts cast on at the start of each row until the shaping is complete. You will then join your sts to work in the rnd and will reposition your working yarn as indicated when the time comes.

Set-Up Row (RS): K2, pmA, k12 (12, 14, 16, 18, 18, 18, 20, 22), pmB, k42 (42, 42, 44, 46, 46, 46, 48, 50), pmC, k12 (12, 14, 16, 18, 18, 18, 20, 22), pmD, k2.

Set-Up Row (WS): P to end, slipping markers as you go.

Row 1 (RS): CO 2 sts, using cable cast-on method worked knitwise (tightly)*, k to 1 st before mA, **YO****, k1, smA, k1, **YO**, k to 1 st before mB, **YO**, k1, smB, k1, **YO**, k to 1 st before mC, **YO**, k1, smC, k1, **YO**, k to 1 st before mD, **YO**, k1, smD, k1, **YO**, k to end—8 sts inc + 2 sts CO.

Row 2 (WS): CO 2 sts using cable cast-on method worked purlwise (tightly)*, p to end, slipping markers as you go—2 sts CO.

> ***Note:** Going forward, all sts cast on at the start of a row will be worked using the cable cast-on method, either knitwise or purlwise, depending on the row. Keep your cast-on sts nice and tight to ensure a tidy neckline (it will make for easier finishing as well). Always work the new sts in pattern after casting them on.
>
> ****Note:** The YOs in this pattern serve as both inc AND decorative elements. Take care not to work them too loosely to prevent the holes from being too large.

Row 3 (RS): CO 4 sts, k to 1 st before mA, **YO**, k1, smA, k1, **YO**, k to 1 st before mB, **YO**, k1, smB, k1, **YO**, k to 1 st before mC, **YO**, k1, smC, k1, **YO**, k to 1 st before mD, **YO**, k1, smD, k1, **YO**, k to end—8 sts inc + 4 sts CO.

Row 4 (WS): CO 4 sts, p to end, slipping markers as you go—4 sts CO.

Stitch Count Check-In

Fronts (ea): 10 (10, 10, 10, 10, 10, 10, 10, 10)

Sleeves (ea): 16 (16, 18, 20, 22, 22, 22, 24, 26)

Back: 46 (46, 46, 48, 50, 50, 50, 52, 54)

Row 5 (RS): CO 4 sts, k to 1 st before mA, **YO**, k1, smA, k1, **YO**, k to 1 st before mB, **YO**, k1, smB, k1, **YO**, k to 1 st before mC, **YO**, k1, smC, k1, **YO**, k to 1 st before mD, **YO**, k1, smD, k1, **YO**, k to end row—8 sts inc + 4 sts CO.

Row 6 (WS): CO 4 sts, p to end, slipping markers as you go—4 sts CO.

Row 7 (RS): CO 4 (4, 4, 4, 4, 4, 4, 6, 6) sts, k to 1 st before mA, **YO**, k1, smA, k1, **YO**, k to 1 st before mB, **YO**, k1, smB, k1, **YO**, k to 1 st before mC, **YO**, k1, smC, k1, **YO**, k to 1 st before mD, **YO**, k1, smD, k1, **YO**, k to end—8 sts inc + 4 (4, 4, 4, 4, 4, 4, 6, 6) sts CO.

Row 8 (WS): CO 4 (4, 4, 4, 4, 4, 4, 6, 6) sts, p to end, slipping markers as you go—4 (4, 4, 4, 4, 4, 4, 6, 6) sts CO.

Row 9 (RS): CO 10 (10, 10, 12, 14, 14, 14, 12, 14) sts, k to 1 st before mA, **YO**, k1, smA, k1, **YO**, k to 1 st before mB, **YO**, k1, smB, k1, **YO**, k to 1 st before mC, **YO**, k1, smC, k1, **YO**, k to 1 st before mD, **YO**, k1, smD, k1, **YO**, k to end—8 sts inc + 10 (10, 10, 12, 14, 14, 14, 12, 14) sts CO.

Neckline Join

The neckline shaping is complete. Cut the working yarn, leaving a tail. Bring your needles together to form a circle and find mD. This will be your new BOR. Slide the sts after mD to the left needle so they are ready to be worked and rejoin the working yarn at mD to begin your new rnd. (This will reposition the start of your rnd at mD.) Be sure to check that your sts are all positioned correctly and are not twisted (this is one of the few things that's impossible to fix later, so it's worth checking). You will initially have a small gap where you've joined at the front neckline; don't worry! You'll weave it closed when you finish the neckline later.

Next Rnd (no inc): Starting at your new BOR (at mD), k to end, slipping markers as you go.

Stitch Count Check-In

Front: 52 (52, 52, 54, 56, 56, 56, 58, 60)

Sleeves (ea): 22 (22, 24, 26, 28, 28, 28, 30, 32)

Back: 52 (52, 52, 54, 56, 56, 56, 58, 60)

Next Rnd (inc): K1, **YO**, k to 1 st before mA, **YO**, k1, smA, k1, **YO**, k to 1 st before mB, **YO**, k1, smB, k1, **YO**, k to 1 st before mC, **YO**, k1, smC, k1, **YO**, k to 1 st before mD, **YO**, k1—8 sts inc.

Next Rnd (no inc): K to end, slipping markers as you go.

Rep these two rnds until you reach the following number of sts and have just completed a "no inc" rnd.

> **Note:** Transition to a longer circular needle when necessary for sts to move comfortably.

Stitch Count Check-In

Front: 94 (102, 100, 106, 106, 112, 110, 108, 104)

Sleeves (ea): 64 (72, 72, 78, 78, 84, 82, 80, 76)

Back: 94 (102, 100, 106, 106, 112, 110, 108, 104)

Size S ONLY – Move ahead to **Divide for Sleeves** on page 80.

> **Note:** As you proceed you will see an "x" as a placeholder for sizes that are no longer represented on that rnd.

All Other Sizes Continue

Next Rnd (extra inc): K1, **YO**, k2, **M1L**, k to 3 sts before mA, **M1R**, k2, **YO**, k1, smA, k1, **YO**, k to 1 st before mB, **YO**, k1, smB, k1, **YO**, k2, **M1L**, k to 3 sts before mC, **M1R**, k2, **YO**, k1, smC, k1, **YO**, k to 1 st before mD, **YO**, k1—12 sts inc (4 sts inc on each front and back, 2 sts inc on each sleeve).

Next Rnd (no inc): K to end, slipping markers as you go.

Rep these two rounds x (0, 2, 2, 2, 2, 2, 1, 3) time(s) more (for a total of x (1, 3, 3, 3, 3, 3, 2, 4).

Stitch Count Check-In

Front: x (106, 112, 118, 118, 124, 122, 116, 120)

Sleeves (ea): x (74, 78, 84, 84, 90, 88, 84, 84)

Back: x (106, 112, 118, 118, 124, 122, 116, 120)

Sizes M and L ONLY – Move ahead to **Divide for Sleeves** on page 80.

All Other Sizes Continue

Next Rnd (double extra inc): K1, **YO**, [k2, **M1L**] twice, k to 5 sts before mA, [**M1R**, k2] twice, **YO**, k1, smA, k1, **YO**, k to 1 st before mB, **YO**, k1, smB, k1, **YO**, [k2, **M1L**] twice, k to 5 sts before mC, [**M1R**, k2] twice, **YO**, k1, smC, k1, **YO**, k to 1 st before mD, **YO**, k1—16 sts inc (6 sts inc on each front and back, 2 sts inc on each sleeve).

Next Rnd (no inc): K to end, slipping markers as you go.

Rep these two rnds x (x, x, 0, 1, 2, 3, 3, 3) time(s) more (for a total of x (x, x, 1, 2, 3, 4, 4, 4).

Stitch Count Check-In

Front: x (x, x, 124, 130, 142, 146, 140, 144)

Sleeves (ea): x (x, x, 86, 88, 96, 96, 92, 92)

Back: x (x, x, 124, 130, 142, 146, 140, 144)

Sizes XL, 2X, 3X, and 4X ONLY – Move ahead to **Divide for Sleeves**.

All Other Sizes Continue

Next Rnd (triple extra inc): K1, **YO**, [k2, **M1L**] 3 times, k to 7 sts before mA, [**M1R**, k2] 3 times, **YO**, k1, smA, k1, **YO**, k to 1 st before mB, **YO**, k1, smB, k1, **YO**, [k2, **M1L**] 3 times, k to 7 sts before mC, [**M1R**, k2] 3 times, **YO**, k1, smC, k1, **YO**, k to 1 st before mD, **YO**, k1—20 sts inc (8 sts inc on each front and back, 2 sts inc on each sleeve).

Next Rnd (no inc): K to end, slipping markers as you go.

Rep these two rnds x (x, x, x, x, x, x, 2, 3) times more (for a total of x (x, x, x, x, x, x, 3, 4), then proceed to **Divide for Sleeves**.

Stitch Count Check-In

Front: x (x, x, x, x, x, x, 164, 176)

Sleeves (ea): x (x, x, x, x, x, x, 98, 100)

Back: x (x, x, x, x, x, x, 164, 176)

Divide for Sleeves

Before separating the sleeves from the body, you should have the following number of sts:

Stitch Count Check-In

Front: 94 (106, 112, 124, 130, 142, 146, 164, 176)

Sleeves (ea): 64 (74, 78, 86, 88, 96, 96, 98, 100)

Back: 94 (106, 112, 124, 130, 142, 146, 164, 176)

Next Rnd: K to mA, remove marker, place next 64 (74, 78, 86, 88, 96, 96, 98, 100) sts onto waste yarn (loosely, so you can try it on later). Remove mB, CO 2 (2, 2, 2, 2, 2, 4, 4, 4) sts under arm using e-loop (backward loop) method worked tightly and join to back sts, then k to mC. Remove mC and place next 64 (74, 78, 86, 88, 96, 96, 98, 100) sts onto waste yarn (loosely). Remove mD, CO 2 (2, 2, 2, 2, 2, 4, 4, 4) sts under arm using e-loop (backward loop) method worked tightly. Place your new BOR marker at the center of these newly cast-on sts—this will be the start of each rnd going forward.

Your sleeves have now been separated from the yoke of your sweater. You will now transition to the Lower Body.

Stitch Count Check-In

192 (216, 228, 252, 264, 288, 300, 336, 360) sts in lower body

Lower Body

Work the lower body in stockinette st (knitting every rnd) until body measures 1.5 (2, 2, 2.5, 3, 3, 3.5, 4, 4) in / 3.75 (5, 5, 6.25, 7.5, 7.5, 8.75, 10, 10) cm from underarm join.

On the next rnd, begin Violet Lace Chart (beginning with Rnd 1 of chart or written instructions, worked over 12 sts per repeat) to end.

Continue knitting the lower body in the rnd, repeating the lace chart rnds in order, until your lower body measures approximately 11 (12, 12, 13, 13, 14, 14, 14, 14) in / 28 (30.5, 30.5, 33, 33, 35.5, 35.5, 35.5, 35.5) cm from underarm, ideally **ending after completing a Rnd 6 or 12** of the chart.

Transition to US 3 (3.25 mm) needle—*or one size smaller than needed to achieve gauge*—and k one rnd.

Ribbing
Next Rnd: [K2, p2] rep bet brackets to end.

Rep this rnd until ribbed edge measures about 1.5 in (3.75 cm) in length. BO in pattern with medium tension (not too tight, but not too loose—if the lower edge feels restrictive, BO more loosely).

Neckline
Before you work the neckline, use the tail left at the neckline join to weave the gap closed. With US 3 (3.25 mm) 16 in (40 cm) circular needle—*or one size smaller than needed to achieve gauge*—pick up and knit approximately 6 of every 7 available sts for sizes S–XL, and 5 of every 6 available sts for sizes 2XL–6XL. PM and join to work in the rnd. Knit four rnds, then BO knitwise.

Tip: You can adjust the size and feel of your neckline by doing one of the following: For a looser neckline, pick up every available st and ensure that your bind off is not too tight. If your neckline is too open, try picking up slightly fewer sts and/or binding off a little more tightly. Necklines like this one are very easy to adjust with just a few simple changes to your technique.

Sleeves
Beginning with either sleeve, and with US Size 4 (3.5 mm) needle—*or size needed to achieve gauge*—transfer the sleeve sts from waste yarn to your needles and pick up the sts cast on under arm—66 (76, 80, 88, 90, 98, 100, 102, 104) sts. When all sts are on your needle, PM at center of underarm and join to knit in the rnd.

Knit one rnd.

Dec Rnd: K2, k2tog, k to last 4 sts, ssk, k2—2 sts dec.

Next Rnds: Work in stockinette st in the rnd for 1 in (2.5 cm).

Continue working your sleeve in the rnd, decreasing every 1 in (2.5 cm) until you reach 56 (66, 70, 78, 80, 88, 90, 92, 94) sts and your sleeve measures approximately 5 in (12.5 cm) from underarm.

Sizes S, 2X, 3X, and 5X ONLY – Move ahead to **All Sizes Continue** before the **Ribbing** on page 82.

Sizes M, L, XL, 4X, and 6X ONLY – Work one more dec rnd: x (64, 68, 76, x, x, 88, x, 92) sts.

Transition to US 3 (3.25 mm) circular needle or DPNs—*or one size smaller than needed to achieve gauge*—and knit one rnd.

All Sizes Continue

Ribbing

Next Rnd: [K2, p2] rep bet brackets to end of rnd.

Rep this rnd until ribbed edge measures 1.5 in (3.75 cm). BO in pattern with medium tension (not too tight, not too loose). If the cuff edge is restrictive, BO again more loosely.

Rep for second sleeve.

Finishing

Weave in ends on the WS and wet block for best results. Soak in lukewarm water with a splash of fiber wash for about 20 minutes to gently cleanse and relax the fiber. Press out excess water, lay flat, and pin along the neckline, raglan seams, and sides. The recommended fiber in this pattern behaves nicely with regular pinning (unlike some plant-based blends), but do adjust your usage of pins as necessary to achieve the best results. Turn as needed for even drying.

Chart Written Directions

Rnd 1: [K3, k2tog, k1, yo, k6] rep bet brackets to end.

Rnd 2: [K2, k2tog, k1, yo, k7] rep bet brackets to end.

Rnd 3: [K1, k2tog, k1, yo, k8] rep bet brackets to end.

Rnd 4: [K2tog, k1, yo, k9] rep bet brackets to end.

Rnds 5–6: Knit to end.

Rnd 7: [K6, yo, k1, ssk, k3] rep bet brackets to end.

Rnd 8: [K7, yo, k1, ssk, k2] rep bet brackets to end.

Rnd 9: [K8, yo, k1, ssk, k1] rep bet brackets to end.

Rnd 10: [K9, yo, k1, ssk] rep bet brackets to end.

Rnds 11–12: Knit to end.

violet eyelet tee chart

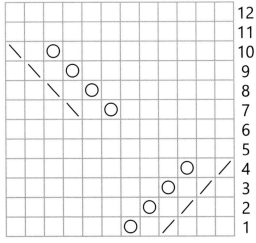

Key	
☐	knit
/	k2tog
O	yo
\	ssk

thistle sleeveless tunic

Thistles are rugged and beautiful in a practical sort of way, and I think they're a bit underrated. They're an important flower for pollinators and birds, so I'm always happy to see them in the wild. I'm especially fond of the Wavyleaf Thistle, which is native to some areas in Oregon, where I live. The hardiness of the humble thistle inspired this design—after all, what is style, if not an opportunity to make practicality beautiful? The mindless, rhythmic stitch detail of this tunic is perfect for a long-haul project; you can pick it up and put it down without worrying about losing your place or missing an increase. The effortless shape makes it a wardrobe staple you'll wear for years to come.

Skill Level
Advanced Beginner

Construction
This allover lace textured tunic is knit from the bottom up and worked in one flat piece to the underarms. The upper bodice is worked flat in sections with lightly shaped shoulders. The overall shape is a long, lean rectangle—and there are no sleeves, so it's perfect to slip right over whatever else you're wearing. Finishing is minimal; just seam the shoulders, knit your edgings, weave in your ends, and block! The open-front style doesn't close—it's not meant to—which makes it an easy fit for a range of sizes.

Sizes
1 (2, 3)

Fit Advice
Designed to fit 32–42 (42–52, 52–62) in / 81.25–106.75 (106.75–132, 132–157.5) cm bust circumference.

Finished Measurements
A) **Width Across Back:** 24.5 (30, 35.5) in / 61.25 (75, 88.75) cm – blocked

B) **Drop Shoulder Depth:** 9 (11, 12) in / 22.75 (28, 30.5) cm – prior to blocking

C) **Underarm to Hem:** 17 (18, 19) in / 43.25 (45.75, 48.25) cm – prior to blocking

D) **Back Neckline Width:** 4.5 (6.25, 8.25) in / 11.25 (16, 20.5) cm – blocked (should fit snug at back neck to help it stay on due to the open front)

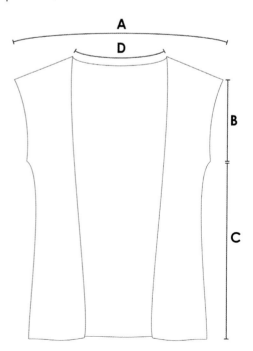

Abbreviations	
[ ]	brackets indicate a repeat
bet	between
BO	bind off
CO	cast on
dec	decrease/decreases/decreased
inc	increase/increases/increased
k	knit
k2tog	knit two stitches together (dec 1)
p	purl
PM	place marker
rep	repeat
rnd/s	round/rounds
RS	right side
sl2-k1-p2sso	slip two stitches together as if to knit, knit the next stitch, then pass the two slipped stitches over the knit stitch; this is also known as a centered double decrease (dec 2)
sm	slip marker
ssk	slip one st knitwise, slip the next st knitwise, then return the two sts back to the left needle and knit the two together through the back loop (dec 1)
st/s	stitch/stitches
WS	wrong side
yo	yarn over (inc 1)

Materials	
Yarn	Fingering Weight | Schoppel Cotton Ball | 100% Long Staple Greek Cotton | 459 yards (420 meters) in 3.5 oz (100 grams) | 1100 (1200, 1300) yards / 1005 (1097, 1188) meters | **Color:** Natural **Note:** Variations in yarn choice or row/round gauge may impact yarn consumption. If in doubt, round up to the nearest skein.
Needles	**Body:** US Size 4 (3.5 mm)* 32–40-in (80–100-cm) circular needle **Ribbing/Trim:** US Size 3 (3.25 mm) 60-in (150-cm) circular needle **Sleeve Edge:** US Size 3 (3.25 mm) 12–16-in (30–40-cm) circular needle or DPNs *Or size needed to achieve gauge. Adjust other needle sizes accordingly.*
Notions	Stitch markers (including locking markers) Waste yarn or spare needles, for holding stitches Blocking pins and mats Darning needle, to weave ends and seam shoulders
Gauge	22 sts and 28 rows in 4 in (10 cm) in lace pattern on largest needle, blocked—*because this is knit bottom-up, row gauge is less critical but may affect yarn consumption.*

Tip: Since this entire garment is worked flat and has minimal finishing, you'll want to make sure to keep your edges tidy. To do this, work the first st tighter than usual, then insert the tip of your needle into the second st and pull the working yarn tight again to draw the first st a little tighter. Then proceed with the remainder of the row with normal tension. Do this at the start of every row (RS and WS) for nicer edges that will be easier to finish later.

thistle sleeveless tunic pattern

With US Size 4 (3.5 mm) 32–40-in (80–100-cm) circular needle—*or size needed to achieve gauge*—CO 245 (295, 345) sts using cable cast-on method. Do not join. (*Note: The cable cast-on begins your work immediately on the RS.*)

Set-Up Row (RS): K55 (65, 75), PM, k135 (165, 195), PM, k55 (65, 75) to end.

Set-Up Row (WS): P to end, slipping markers as you go.

Pattern Row 1 (RS): K3, [(yo, ssk) twice, k1, (k2tog, yo) twice, k1] rep bet brackets to 2 sts before marker, k2, sm, k3, [(yo, ssk) twice, k1, (k2tog, yo) twice, k1] rep bet brackets to 2 sts before marker, k2, sm, k3, [(yo, ssk) twice, k1, (k2tog, yo) twice, k1] rep bet brackets to last 2 sts, k2.

Pattern Row 2 (WS): P to end, slipping markers as you go.

Pattern Row 3 (RS): K4, [yo, ssk, yo, sl2-k1-p2sso, yo, k2tog, yo, k3] rep bet brackets to 1 st before marker, k1, sm, k4, [yo, ssk, yo, sl2-k1-p2sso, yo, k2tog, yo, k3] rep bet brackets to 1 st before marker, k1, sm, k4, [yo, ssk, yo, sl2-k1-p2sso, yo, k2tog, yo, k3] rep bet brackets to last st, k1.

Pattern Row 4 (WS): P to end, slipping markers as you go.

Rep Pattern Rows 1–4 to establish pattern until the body of your tunic measures 17 (18, 19) in / 43.25 (45.75, 48.25) cm from cast-on edge, and you have **just completed a Pattern Row 4** (ready to start Row 1).

Upper Bodice

Next Row (RS): K3, [(yo, ssk) twice, k1, (k2tog, yo) twice, k1] rep bet brackets to 2 sts before m, k2, stop—this will be the right front. Slide these 55 (65, 75) sts onto a long separate needle or waste yarn; you'll come back to work them later. K3, [(yo, ssk) twice, k1, (k2tog, yo) twice, k1] rep bet brackets to 2 sts before m, k2, stop—this is the back.

Slide remaining 55 (65, 75) sts onto a long separate needle or waste yarn—this is the left front. You will work back and forth (flat) on the back section (only) for now. Markers can be removed on this row.

Back

Next Row (WS): P to end.

Next Row (RS): K4, [yo, ssk, yo, sl2-k1-p2sso, yo, k2tog, yo, k3] rep bet brackets to last 1 st, k1.

Next Row (WS): P to end.

Next Row (RS): K3, [(yo, ssk) twice, k1, (k2tog, yo) twice, k1] rep bet brackets to last 2 sts, k2.

Next Row (WS): P to end.

Rep these four rows until your flat section measures approximately 9 (11, 12) in / 22.75 (28, 30.5) cm from where you separated it from the other sections, ending after a WS row (ready to work a RS).

Back Shoulder and Neckline Shaping

Note: Keep in mind that you may not be able to work full lace repeats as you BO on the back shoulders, neckline, and front sections (next page). To avoid ending up with an extra inc or dec, if you cannot work the inc/dec pair together, simply switch to stockinette st for those sections.

Next Row (RS): BO 13 (16, 18) sts knitwise, work in pattern to end.

Next Row (WS): BO 13 (16, 18) sts purlwise, p to end.

Rep these two rows twice more (for a total of 3).

Next Row (RS): BO 16 (17, 21) sts knitwise, work in pattern to end.

Next Row (WS): BO 16 (17, 21) sts, p to end.

BO remaining sts knitwise for center back neckline.

Left Front

Return left front to your needles and rejoin working yarn ready to work a RS row.

Next Row (RS): K3, [(yo, ssk) twice, k1, (k2tog, yo) twice, k1] rep bet brackets to last 2 sts, k2.

Next Row (WS): P to end.

Next Row (RS): K4, [yo, ssk, yo, sl2-k1-p2sso, yo, k2tog, yo, k3] rep bet brackets to last st, k1.

Next Row (WS): P to end.

Rep these four rows until your flat section measures approximately 9 (11, 12) in / 22.75 (28, 30.5) cm from where you separated it from the other sections and is the same length as the back piece, ending after a WS row (ready to work a RS).

Left Shoulder Shaping

Next Row (RS): BO 13 (16, 18) sts knitwise, then work in established lace pattern to end.

Next Row (WS): P to end.

Rep these two rows twice more (for a total of 3).

Next Row (RS): BO remaining 16 (17, 21) sts knitwise.

Right Front

Return right front sts to your needles and rejoin working yarn, ready to work a WS row.

Next Row (WS): P to end.

Next Row (RS): K4, [yo, ssk, yo, sl2-k1-p2sso, yo, k2tog, yo, k3] rep bet brackets to last st, k1.

Next Row (WS): P to end.

Next Row (RS): K3, [(yo, ssk) twice, k1, (k2tog, yo) twice, k1] rep bet brackets to last 2 sts, k2.

Rep these four rows until your flat section measures approximately 9 (11, 12) in / 22.75 (28, 30.5) cm from where you separated it from the other sections and is the same length as the other two pieces, ending after a RS row (ready to work a WS).

Right Shoulder Shaping

Next Row (RS): Work in established pattern to end.

Next Row (WS): BO 13 (16, 18) purlwise, then p to end.

Rep these two rows twice more (for a total of 3).

Next Row (RS): BO remaining 16 (17, 21) sts purlwise.

Shoulder Finishing

Seam the shoulder stitches together on each side to the neckline, ensuring that the front, back, and shoulder bind-off sections line up perfectly. See seaming and grafting tutorials on my website here: oliveknits.com/grafting.

Trim

With US 3 (3.25 mm) circular needle—*or one size smaller than needed to achieve gauge*—and starting at the bottom edge of the right front, pick up and knit approximately 5 of every 6 available sts (counting from rows along the front edges and sts across back neck) around the front. You will pick up along the RS all the way up to the neckline, around the back neck, and back down the left front.

Next Row (WS): P to end.

Next Row (RS): K to end.

Rep these two rows once more (for a total of 2).

BO in pattern with medium tension.

Armhole Edge

Beginning with either armhole and with US Size 3 (3.25 mm) 12–16 in (30–40 cm) circular needle or DPNs—*or one size smaller than needed to achieve gauge*—pick up and knit approximately 7 of every 8 available sts around the first armhole edge, starting at the underarm. PM and join to work in the rnd.

Next Rnd: K to end.

Rep this rnd 3 times more.

BO knitwise with medium tension.

Rep for second armhole.

Finishing

Weave in ends on the WS and wet block for best results. Soak in lukewarm water with a splash of fiber wash for 20 minutes to gently cleanse and relax the fiber. Press out excess water, and lay flat, drawing the sides and length out taut, and pinning into shape along the shoulders and front panels to enhance the lace. Even in cotton yarn (which doesn't always play well with blocking pins), some pinning—even minimal—is beneficial for this design. (For stellar results with your ribbed edges, use comb-style pins along the ribbing where it meets the body of your work, rather than along the outer edge. This will create smooth ribbing transitions that lay beautifully flat when you wear your garment.)

texture & color

I could write a whole book about texture and color; they're my two favorite things about knitting. But in this section, I've leaned into texture and color in a way that makes one or the other the central feature of the design—except for Yarrow (page 107), which features a distinct effect using both texture *and* color.

When it comes to color, I've stayed away from complex patterns like Fair Isle, which can be a challenge with plant-based yarns. Their unforgiving nature can make colorwork look messy and uneven, and the more colors you use, the higher your risk of seeing colors bleed together—something more likely to happen when working with plant-based yarn. Instead, I've chosen color-blocking and stripes—see Bluebell (page 93) and Wild Iris (page 125)—which make it easy to add color to your project without a lot of fuss.

Graphic textures, like the bold front details of Water Lily (page 133) or the allover texture of Windflower (page 101), add visual interest and keep things exciting on your needles. You'll find that both the texture and color sequences are relatively steady, making it easy to follow along without babysitting the patterns too closely. *But please note:* Your choice of color and fiber content will make a difference in these designs, so choose carefully—and don't forget to block your swatches (especially in multiple colors) to check for color transfer before you begin.

bluebell striped tee

There's nothing I love more than stripes—if you were to peek in my closet, you might think they're all I wear. In fact, I once participated in a style course that asked us to identify our fashion "power piece," or the thing in our closet that makes us feel our absolute best. For me, it's stripes. They're smart, stylish, and easy to mix and match with other staple pieces; I always feel put together when I can throw stripes in the mix. In this pattern, I've paired classic stripes with the modern silhouette of a batwing top to create a winning combination for casual wear. This relaxed fit, drop-shoulder style tee is ultra comfy and would be perfect with linen pants and strappy sandals for a day out.

Skill Level
Advanced Beginner

Construction
This sporty striped top is knit bottom-up in the round to the underarms with paced increases as you near the underarm to create the batwing shape. Color changes throughout the lower body keep the knitting interesting—even in stockinette stitch. The upper bodice is worked flat in sections (front and back) in a solid color, and the shoulders are seamed along the top. The sleeves are knit right into the design as it's worked, so just add the cuffs and you're good to go!

It's worth noting that the lower body is meant to be slightly cropped—possibly more than you might normally wear. This is part of the batwing shape and ensures a proper fit. I don't recommend adding much length (the design will swallow you if you do), but if you prefer a little more length, you can squeeze in an extra inch or two just after the lower ribbing (before you begin the increases). Lower body length IS determined by your row gauge, however, so keep this in mind when measuring your swatch. Note that the sizing for this design is unique compared to traditional shapes; when in doubt, start with your hip measurement. (The shape of the upper body is quite forgiving of bellies and busts!)

Sizes
S (M, L, XL/2X, 3X, 4/5X, 6X)

Fit Advice
Designed for 32–34 (36–38, 40–42, 44–46, 48–50, 52–54, 56–58) in / 80–85 (90–95, 100–105, 110–115, 120–125, 130–135, 140–145) cm bust.

Finished Measurements

A) Hip Circumference: 40 (44.25, 48, 52.25, 56, 59, 64) in / 100 (110.75, 120, 130.75, 140, 147.75, 160) cm – blocked

B) Wingtip to Wingtip (Including Cuff Ribbing): 24.5 (25.5, 26.5, 27.75, 29, 30.5, 33) in / 61.5 (63.75, 66.25, 69.25, 72.25, 76.25, 82.25) cm – blocked

C) Armhole Depth: 6.25 (6.75, 7, 7.25, 7.5, 7.75, 7.75) in / 16 (17.25, 17.75, 18.5, 19, 19.75, 19.75) cm – prior to blocking

D) Underarm to Hem: 13.25 (13.25, 13.5, 13.5, 13.5, 14.5, 14.5) in / 33.75 (33.75, 34.25, 34.25, 34.25, 36.75, 36.75) cm – prior to blocking

E) Cuff Circumference (Hits at Elbow): 12.5 (13.5, 14, 14.5, 15, 15.5, 15.5) / 32 (34.5, 35.5, 37, 38, 39.5, 39.5) cm – blocked

F) Back Neckline Width (with Ribbing): 7 (7, 7.5, 7.5, 7.5, 7.75, 7.75) in / 17.75 (17.75, 18.5, 18.5, 18.5, 19.25, 19.25) cm – blocked

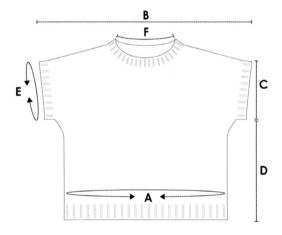

Abbreviations	
[ ]	brackets indicate a repeat
bet	between
BO	bind off
BOR	beginning of row/round
CC	contrast color
CO	cast on
dec	decrease/decreases/decreased
inc	increase/increases/increased
k	knit
m	marker/markers
M1L	make one stitch, left leaning (inc 1)
M1R	make one stitch, right leaning (inc 1)
MC	main color
p	purl
p2tog	purl two stitches together (dec 1)
PM	place marker
rep	repeat
rnd/s	round/rounds
RS	right side
sm	slip marker/s
ssk	slip one st knitwise, slip the next st knitwise, then return the two sts back to the left needle and knit the two together through the back loop (dec 1)
st/s	stitch/stitches
WS	wrong side

Materials	
Yarn	Fingering Weight | Knit Picks Comfy Fingering | 75% Pima Cotton, 25% Acrylic | 218 yards (199 meters) in 1.76 oz (50 grams) | **Colors:** White & Clarity **Note:** Variations in yarn choice or row/round gauge may impact yarn consumption. If in doubt, round up to the nearest skein. **MC (White):** 617 (667, 719, 777, 839, 907, 979) yards / 564 (610, 657, 710, 767, 829, 895) meters **CC (Clarity):** 412 (444, 480, 518, 560, 604, 653) yards / 377 (406, 439, 474, 512, 552, 597) meters **Yarn Color Note:** This easy summer top features two-color stripes through the lower body; feel free to use more or less contrast, depending on your preference. High contrast colors may present a higher risk of color bleeding when you wet block your garment (especially in cotton), so please take care when selecting yarn for your project. Be sure to swatch (and wet block your swatch) with both colors to test for colorfastness before you begin.
Needles	**Body:** US Size 3 (3.25 mm)* 24–40 in (60–100 cm) circular needle **Lower Ribbing:** US Size 2 (2.75 mm) 24–40-in (60–100-cm) circular needle **Neckline:** US Size 2 (2.75 mm) 16-in (40-cm) circular needle **Sleeve Ribbing:** US Size 2 (2.75 mm) 12-in (30-cm) circular needle or DPNs *Or size needed to achieve gauge. Adjust other needle sizes accordingly.*
Notions	Stitch markers (including locking markers) Waste yarn or spare needles, for holding stitches Blocking mats Darning needle to weave ends and seam shoulders
Gauge	26 st and 34 rows/rounds in 4 in (10 cm) in stockinette stitch with largest needle, blocked

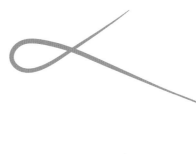

bluebell striped tee pattern

With US Size 2 (2.75 mm) 24–40-in (60–100-cm) circular needle—or one size smaller than needed to achieve gauge—and MC, CO 260 (288, 312, 340, 364, 384, 416) sts using cable cast-on method. Do not join in the rnd yet. (*Note: The cable cast-on begins your work immediately on the RS.*)

Set-Up Row (RS): [K2, p2] rep bet brackets to end, then PM and join to work in the rnd, being careful not to twist your sts.

Ribbing Rnd: [K2, p2] rep bet brackets to end.

Rep this rnd until work measures 2 in (5 cm) from cast-on edge.

Transition to US Size 3 (3.25 mm) 24–40 in (60–100 cm) circular needle—or *size needed to achieve gauge*—and k one rnd.

Next Rnd: Join CC and work Bluebell Stripes Chart (beginning with Rnd 1) to end. (*Note: The chart shows stripes over 8 sts for the sake of visibility, but it can be worked over any number of sts.*)

Continue working the lower body in the rnd as established, repeating the stripe chart rnds in order (carrying the alternate colors along the inside as you go) until lower body measures approximately 10 (11, 11.75, 12.5, 13, 14, 14) in / 25.5 (28, 29.75, 31.75, 33, 35.5, 35.5) cm from cast-on edge.

Next Rnd: Continuing with established stripe sequence, k130 (144, 156, 170, 182, 192, 208) sts, PM, k to end. Remain in stripe sequence until otherwise indicated.

Next Rnd: K2, M1L, k to 2 sts before next m, M1R, k2, sm, k2, M1L, k to last 2 sts, M1R, k2— 4 sts inc.

Next Rnd: K to end.

Rep these two rnds 14 (10, 7, 4, 2, 2, 2) times more—320 (332, 344, 360, 376, 396, 428) sts. Do not worry about finishing the last chart repeat—just stop wherever you are when you read the correct stitch count. You will cut your CC and transition to the MC from this point forward.

Upper Bodice

Going forward, you will separate the front and back bodice sections, and will work back and forth on each section, flat, beginning with the front section. You will return to work the back section afterward.

> **Tip:** As you begin working flat, be sure to keep your edges tidy. To do this, work the first st tighter than usual, then insert the tip of your needle into the second st, and pull the working yarn tight again to draw the first st a little tighter. Then proceed with the remainder of the row with normal tension. Do this at the start of every row (RS and WS) for nicer edges that will be easier to finish later.

Next Row (RS): With MC, k to side marker, stop.

Slide remaining 160 (166, 172, 180, 188, 198, 214) sts onto a long separate needle or waste yarn. You will work back and forth (flat) on the front section (only) for now.

Front

Next Row (WS): With MC, p to end.

Next Row (RS): With MC, k to end.

Next Row (WS): With MC, p to end.

Rep these two rows until your flat section measures approximately 6.25 (6.75, 7, 7.25, 7.5, 7.75, 7.75) in / 16 (17.25, 17.75, 18.5, 19, 19.75, 19.75) cm from where you began working flat, ending after a WS row (ready to work a RS).

Front Neckline and Shoulder Shaping

Next Row (RS): With MC, BO 6 (5, 5, 5, 5, 5, 6) sts knitwise, then k56 (60, 62, 66, 70, 74, 81) sts—this is the left front shoulder. BO next 36 (36, 38, 38, 38, 40, 40) sts knitwise for the center front neckline. K62 (65, 67, 71, 75, 79, 87) sts to end—this is the right front shoulder.

Place the 56 (60, 62, 66, 70, 74, 81) sts of the left front shoulder onto a holder or waste yarn—you will return to work them later. You will now work only on the right front shoulder and neckline dec as you proceed in this section.

Right Front Shoulder

Next Row (WS): Continuing with MC, BO 6 (5, 5, 5, 5, 5, 6) sts purlwise, p to end.

Next Row (RS): K1, ssk, k to end—1 st dec.

Rep these two rows 7 (8, 9, 9, 9, 10, 10) times more for a total of 8 (9, 10, 10, 10, 11, 11)—6 (11, 7, 11, 15, 13, 10) sts.

Next Row (WS): BO remaining sts purlwise.

Left Front Shoulder

Return left front shoulder sts to your needles and rejoin working yarn in MC, ready to work a WS row.

Next Row (WS): P1, p2tog, p to end—1 st dec.

Next Row (RS): BO 6 (5, 5, 5, 5, 5, 6) sts knitwise, k to end.

Rep these two rows 6 (7, 8, 8, 8, 9, 9) times more for a total of (7 (8, 9, 9, 9, 10, 10)—7 (12, 8, 12, 16, 14, 11) sts.

Next Row (WS): P1, p2tog, p to end—1 st dec.

Next Row (RS): BO remaining 6 (11, 7, 11, 15, 13, 10) sts knitwise.

Back

Return back sts to needles and join MC, ready to work a RS row—160 (166, 172, 180, 188, 198, 214).

Next Row (RS): With MC, k to end.

Next Row (WS): P to end.

Rep these two rows with MC until your flat section measures approximately 6.25 (6.75, 7, 7.25, 7.5, 7.75, 7.75) in / 16 (17.25, 17.75, 18.5, 19, 19.75, 19.75) cm and is the same length as the front section from where you began working flat. End after a WS row (ready to work a RS).

Back Shoulder Shaping
Next Row (RS): BO 6 (5, 5, 5, 5, 5, 6) sts knitwise, k to end.

Next Row (WS): BO 6 (5, 5, 5, 5, 5, 6) sts purlwise, p to end.

Rep these two rows 4 times more (for a total of 5)—100 (116, 122, 130, 138, 148, 154) sts.

Next Row (RS): BO 6 (5, 5, 5, 5, 5, 6) sts knitwise, k21 (30, 32, 36, 40, 44, 46)—this is the right back shoulder. BO the next 46 (46, 48, 48, 48, 50, 50) sts knitwise for center back neckline. K27 (35, 37, 41, 45, 49, 52) sts to end—this is the left back shoulder. Place the 21 (30, 32, 36, 40, 44, 46) sts for right back shoulder onto a separate needle or holder—you will return to work these sts later. You will now work only on the left back shoulder and neckline dec as you proceed in this section.

Left Back Shoulder
Next Row (WS): BO 6 (5, 5, 5, 5, 5, 6) sts purlwise, p to end.

Next Row (RS): K1, ssk, k to end—1 st dec.

Rep these two rows 7 (8, 9, 9, 9, 10, 10) times more (for a total of 8 (9, 10, 10, 10, 11, 11)—6 (11, 7, 11, 15, 13, 10) sts.

Next Row (WS): BO remaining sts purlwise.

Right Back Shoulder
Return the sts for the right back shoulder to your needle, and rejoin working yarn, ready to work a WS row.

Next Row (WS): P1, p2tog, p to end—1 st dec.

Next Row (RS): BO 6 (5, 5, 5, 5, 5, 6) sts knitwise, k to end.

Rep these two rows 6 (7, 8, 8, 8, 9, 9) times more (for a total of (7 (8, 9, 9, 9, 10, 10)—7 (12, 8, 12, 16, 14, 11) sts.

Next Row (WS): P1, p2tog, p to end—1 st dec.

Next Row (RS): BO remaining 6 (11, 7, 11, 15, 13, 10) sts knitwise.

Shoulder Finishing
Seam the shoulder sts together on each side to the neckline, ensuring that the front, back, and shoulder bind-off sections line up perfectly. See seaming and grafting tutorials on my website here: oliveknits.com/grafting.

Neckline
With US Size 2 (2.75 mm) 16 in (40 cm) circular needle—or one size smaller than needed to achieve gauge—and using MC, pick up and knit approximately every available st around the neckline, ending with a multiple of 4. PM and join to work in the rnd. (You can control the fit and look of your neckline by picking up slightly fewer sts, if you prefer.)

Ribbing
Next Rnd: [K2, p2] rep bet brackets to end.

Rep this rnd until ribbed edge measures approximately 1.25 in (3.25 cm). BO in pattern with medium tension.

Tip: You can adjust the size and feel of your neckline by doing one of the following: For a looser neckline, make sure you've picked up every available st and that your bind off is not too tight. If your neckline is too open (or your ribbing flares out), try picking up slightly fewer sts—such as 5 of every 6 available sts—and/or binding off a little more tightly. Necklines like this one are very easy to adjust with just a few simple changes to your technique.

Armhole Ribbing

Beginning with either armhole, with US Size 2 (2.75 mm) 12 in (30 cm) circular needle or DPNs—*or one size smaller than needed to achieve gauge*—and using MC, pick up and knit approximately 4 of every 5 available sts around the first armhole opening, starting at the underarm and ending with a multiple of 4. Jot down the number of sts you've picked up so you can match the same number on the other sleeve. Starting at the center of the underarm, PM and join to work in the rnd.

Ribbing

Next Rnd: [K2, p2] rep bet brackets to end.

Rep this rnd until ribbed edge measures approximately 1.25 in (3.25 cm). BO in pattern with medium tension.

Rep for second armhole.

Tip: If your sleeve ribbing flares out, it means you've either picked up slightly too many sts or have worked your ribbing too loosely. If this happens, try again with 8 fewer sts and/or go down another needle size to work your ribbing more tightly.

Finishing

Weave in ends on the WS, taking care to weave ends in sections of the same color to prevent interruptions to the stripe details. Wet block for best results, soaking in lukewarm water with a splash of fiber wash for 20 minutes to gently cleanse and relax the fiber. Press out excess water, and lay flat, patting into shape to ensure it dries evenly. Pin around the neckline where the ribbing meets the stockinette and along the cuffs where the ribbing meets the stockinette. No other pinning should be needed if you smooth your tee out flat and even. Turn as needed for even drying. Due to the fiber content, excessive pinning is not recommended, but adjust as needed for best results.

bluebell striped tee chart

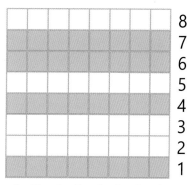

Key	
☐	RS: knit WS: purl
☐	MC
▨	CC

windflower loose rib top

This design began as something entirely different, but—as with so many of my patterns—it can be a winding road from the first sprout of an idea to the final design. Fisherman's rib creates an irresistibly squishy fabric that feels somehow abundant and breezy at the same time. It looks a bit like brioche but is far simpler to knit. The allover texture and minimalist shape create a top that looks utterly stunning when you put it on. It was one of my surprise favorites from this whole collection. I intentionally chose a fiber blend that is soft enough to wear right against your skin—no need to layer it over a camisole or tank unless you want to. I love this top with a pair of jeans and clogs.

Skill
Advanced Beginner

Construction
This loose-fitting, drop-shoulder style top is knit bottom-up with allover fisherman's rib texture. The body is worked in the round to the underarms, then the upper bodice is worked flat to the shoulders. There is minimal seaming at the shoulders (see a tutorial here: oliveknits.com/grafting), and the sleeve edges are finished simply with a quick knit edge. There's no finishing needed for the neckline. This design is meant to have an easy, relaxed fit.

Sizes
S (M, L, XL, 2X, 3X, 4X, 5X, 6X)

Fit Advice
Designed to fit bust sizes 30–32 (34–36, 38–40, 42–44, 46–48, 50–52, 54–56, 58–60, 62–64) in / 75–80 (85–90, 95–100, 105–110, 115–120, 125–130, 135–140, 145–150, 155–160) cm.

Note: This design is intended to be worn with approximately 6–8 in (15–20 cm) positive ease. Be careful about sizing down for less ease, as it may cause issues with the fit in your sleeves and shoulders.

Finished Measurements
A) **Bust Circumference:** 38.5 (42.75, 45.75, 50.25, 54.5, 58.75, 61.75, 66.25, 70.5) in / 96 (106.75, 114.75, 125.25, 136, 146.75, 154.75, 165.25, 176) cm – blocked

B) **Armhole Depth:** 6 (6.5, 7, 7.5, 7.5, 8, 8.5, 8.5, 9) in / 15.25 (16.5, 17.75, 19, 19, 20.25, 21.5, 21.5, 22.75) cm – prior to blocking

(Continued)

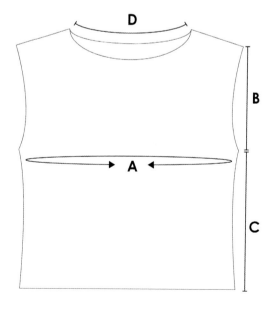

C) Underarm to Hem: 12 (12, 13, 13, 14, 14, 14, 15, 15) in / 30.5 (30.5, 33, 33, 35.5, 35.5, 35.5, 38, 38) cm – prior to blocking

D) Back Neckline Width: 9 (9, 9.5, 9.5, 9.5, 10.25, 10.25, 10.25, 10.25) in / 22.75 (22.75, 24, 24, 24, 25.25, 25.25, 25.25, 25.25) cm – blocked

Abbreviations	
[ ]	brackets indicate a repeat
bet	between
BO	bind off
BOR	beginning of row/rnd
CO	cast on
dec	decrease/decreases/decreased
k	knit
k1b	knit one below—knit into the st below the next st on your left needle
p	purl
p1b	purl one below—purl into the st below the next st on your left needle
p2tog	purl two stitches together (dec 1)
PM	place marker
rep	repeat
rnd/s	round/rounds
RS	right side
sm	slip marker/s
ssk	slip one st knitwise, slip the next st knitwise, then return the two sts back to the left needle and knit the two together through the back loop (dec 1)
st/s	stitch/stitches
WS	wrong side

Materials	
Yarn	Sport Weight | Scheepjes Stonewashed | 78% Cotton, 22% Acrylic | 142 yards (130 meters) in 1.76 oz (50 grams) | 769 (818, 870, 922, 978, 1036, 1098, 1164, 1234) yards / 703 (748, 795, 843, 894, 947, 1004, 1064, 1128) | **Color:** Corundum Ruby **Note:** Variations in yarn choice or row/round gauge may impact yarn consumption. If in doubt, round up to the nearest skein.
Needles	**Body:** US Size 5 (3.75 mm)* 24–40-in (60–100-cm) circular needle **Sleeve Edges:** US Size 3 (3.25 mm) 12-in (30-cm) circular needle or DPNs *Or size needed to achieve gauge. Adjust other needle sizes accordingly.*
Notions	Stitch markers Waste yarn or spare needles, for holding stitches Blocking pins and mats Darning needle to weave ends and seam shoulders
Gauge	15 sts and 28 rows/rounds in 4 in (10 cm) in fisherman's rib on largest needle, blocked—*row gauge is less critical but may affect yarn consumption. Be careful not to stretch your swatch too much.*

windflower loose rib top pattern

With US Size 5 (3.75 mm) circular needle—*or size needed to achieve gauge*—CO 144 (160, 172, 188, 204, 220, 232, 248, 264) sts using cable cast-on method. Do not join in the rnd yet. (*Note: The cable cast-on begins your work immediately on the RS.*)

Set-Up Row (RS): [K1, p1] rep bet brackets to end. PM and join to work in the rnd, being careful not to twist your sts.

Rnd 1: [K1b, p1] rep bet brackets to end.

Rnd 2: [K1, p1b] rep bet brackets to end.

Continue working the lower body in the rnd as established, repeating these two rnds in order until your lower body measures approximately 12 (12, 13, 13, 14, 14, 14, 15, 15) in / 30.5 (30.5, 33, 33, 35.5, 35.5, 35.5, 38, 38) cm from the cast-on edge, **ending after Rnd 2.** Be careful when measuring, and don't pull your work to make it reach; fisherman's rib can be deceiving. For best results, measure flat without stretching your work.

Upper Bodice
Going forward, you will separate the front and back bodice sections and work back and forth on each section, flat, beginning with the front section. You will return to work the back section afterward.

Tip: As you begin working flat, be sure to keep your edges tidy. To do this, work the first st tighter than usual, then insert the tip of your needle into the second st and pull the working yarn tight again to draw the first st a little tighter. Then proceed with the remainder of the row with normal tension. Do this at the start of every row (RS and WS) for nicer edges that will be easier to finish later.

Next Rnd: Work in established pattern for 72 (80, 86, 94, 102, 110, 116, 124, 132) sts, stop.

Slide remaining 72 (80, 86, 94, 102, 110, 116, 124, 132) sts onto a long separate needle or holder. You will work back and forth (flat) on the front section (only) for now.

Front
Next Row (WS): P1, [p1, k1b] rep bet brackets to last st, p1.

Next Row (RS): K1, [p1, k1b] rep bet brackets to last st, k1.

Rep these two rows until your flat section measures approximately 6 (6.5, 7, 7.5, 7.5, 8, 8.5, 8.5, 9) in / 15.25 (16.5, 17.75, 19, 19, 20.25, 21.5, 21.5, 22.75) cm from where you began working flat, ending after a WS row (ready to work a RS).

Front Shoulder and Neckline Shaping

Next Row (RS): BO 5 (6, 6, 7, 9, 10, 11, 12, 13) sts knitwise, then work 17 (20, 22, 25, 27, 29, 31, 34, 37) sts in established pattern—this is the left front shoulder. BO next 28 (28, 30, 30, 30, 32, 32, 32, 32) sts for the center front neckline—**be sure to bind these off loosely for best results (but do not use a stretchy BO).** Work 22 (26, 28, 32, 36, 39, 42, 46, 50) sts in established pattern to end—this is the right front shoulder.

Place the 17 (20, 22, 25, 27, 29, 31, 34, 37) sts of the left front shoulder onto a holder; you will return to work them later. You will now work only on the right front shoulder and neckline dec as you proceed in this section.

Right Front Shoulder

Next Row (WS): BO 5 (6, 6, 7, 9, 10, 11, 12, 13) sts purlwise, work in established pattern to end.

Next Row (RS): K1, ssk, work in established pattern to end—1 st dec.

Next Row (WS): BO 5 (6, 6, 7, 9, 10, 11, 12, 13) sts purlwise, work in established pattern to end.

Rep these two rows once more (for a total of 2).

Next Row (RS): K1, ssk, BO remaining sts knit-wise (including the first two).

Left Front Shoulder

Return to the left shoulder sts and place them back on your working needles. Position your yarn to begin a WS row.

Next Row (WS): P1, p2tog, work in established pattern to end—1 st dec.

Next Row (RS): BO 5 (6, 6, 7, 9, 10, 11, 12, 13) sts knitwise, work in established pattern to end.

Rep these two rows once more (for a total of 2).

Next Row (WS): P1, p2tog, BO purlwise to end (including the first 2 sts).

Back

Return back sts to needles and join working yarn, ready to work a RS row—72 (80, 86, 94, 102, 110, 116, 124, 132) sts on needle.

Next Row (RS): K1, [p1, k1b] rep bet brackets to last st, k1.

Next Row (WS): P1, [p1, k1b] rep bet brackets to last st, p1.

Rep these two rows until your flat section measures approximately 6 (6.5, 7, 7.5, 7.5, 8, 8.5, 8.5, 9) in / 15.25 (16.5, 17.75, 19, 19, 20.25, 21.5, 21.5, 22.75) cm and is the same length as the front section from where you began working flat. End after a WS row (ready to work a RS).

Back Shoulder Shaping

Next Row (RS): BO 5 (6, 6, 7, 9, 10, 11, 12, 13) sts knitwise, work in established pattern to end.

Next Row (WS): BO 5 (6, 6, 7, 9, 10, 11, 12, 13) sts purlwise, work in established pattern to end.

Rep these two rows twice more (for a total of 3)—42 (44, 50, 52, 48, 50, 50, 52, 54) sts.

Next Row (RS): BO 4 (5, 7, 8, 6, 6, 6, 7, 8) sts knitwise, work in established pattern to end.

Next Row (WS): BO 4 (5, 7, 8, 6, 6, 6, 7, 8) sts purlwise, work in established pattern to end.

BO remaining 34 (34, 36, 36, 36, 38, 38, 38, 38) sts knitwise for center back neckline—be sure to bind these off loosely for best results.

Shoulder Finishing

Seam the shoulder sts together on each side to the neckline, ensuring that the front, back and shoulder bind-off sections line up perfectly. See seaming and grafting tutorials on my website here: oliveknits.com/grafting.

Neckline

There is no additional neckline finishing. The width, fit, and look of your neckline will depend on the quality of the BO you previously worked.

Armhole Finishing

With US 3 (3.25 mm) 12 in (30 cm) circular needle or DPNs—*or two sizes smaller than needed to achieve gauge*—pick up and knit 4 of every 5 sts (approximately) around the arm opening. PM and join to work in the rnd. K just one rnd, then BO knitwise with medium tension. Adjust your pickup and/or bind off, as needed, for best results.

Rep for second armhole.

> **Tip:** If your sleeve edge flares out, it means you've either picked up slightly too many sts or have worked your bind off too loosely. If this happens, try again with 4–5 fewer sts and/or go down another needle size to work your edge round more tightly.

Finishing

Weave in ends on the WS. Wet block for best results, soaking in lukewarm water with a splash of fiber wash for 20 minutes to gently cleanse and relax the fiber. Press out excess water, and lay flat, patting gently into shape. Take care not to stretch the fabric too much (fisherman's rib will stretch forever if you encourage it). Turn as needed for even drying.

> **Tip:** The fabric will be prone to significant stretching while it's wet, but this tendency will resolve when the garment is dry.

yarrow color-pop tee

Texture and color are endlessly inspiring, and I never shy away from an opportunity to bring them together in a smart and balanced way. I used a stitch pattern called "granite stitch" in this design to add raised bands of color that stand out on a background of smooth fabric. The result is a casual, slightly sporty top that reminds me of a favorite pinstripe twin set from my youth. The use of color here is playful but restrained, with just a hint of nautical charm. Pair it with denim and bright sandals for an afternoon by the sea—or *anywhere*.

Skill Level
Advanced Beginner

Construction
This lightweight tee is knit top-down in the round beginning with the neckline ribbing. It has a circular yoke, with increases spaced evenly to create the shape. The top and sleeves are worked all in one down to the underarm, then the sleeves are separated onto waste yarn while you complete the rest of the body. There are short rows just under the initial ribbing to gently shape the back of the neckline for a comfortable fit. Contrast colors are used to create textured stripes around the yoke, body, and sleeves at evenly spaced intervals, which vary between sizes. The sleeves fall somewhere between three-quarter and bracelet length and are worked last.

Sizes
S (M, L, XL, 2X, 3X, 4X, 5X, 6X)

Fit Advice
Made to fit bust sizes 31–34 (35–37, 38–41, 42–46, 47–49, 50–53, 54–56, 57–59, 60–63) in / 77.5–85 (87.5–92.5, 95–102.5, 105–115, 117.5–122.5, 125–132.5, 135–140, 142.5-147.5, 150-157.5) cm.

Designed for a classic fit with approximately 2–3 in (5–7.5 cm) positive ease. If you are right on the line between sizes, you may prefer to size up for comfort.

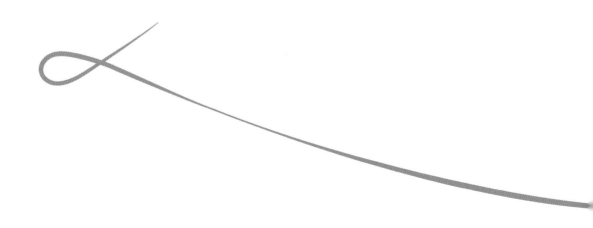

Finished Measurements

A) Bust Circumference: 34.75 (38.25, 42.5, 46.5, 50.75, 54, 57.5, 60.75, 64.75) in / 87 (95.75, 106, 116.5, 127, 134.75, 144.25, 152.25, 161.75) cm – blocked

B) Yoke Depth (from Center Front Neckline Below Ribbing): 8.75 (9.75, 10.25, 10.5, 11.75, 11.75, 13.25, 13.25, 13.5) in / 22.25 (24.25, 25.75, 26.5, 29.25, 29.75, 32.75, 32.75, 34.25) cm – blocked

C) Underarm to Hem: 12.5 (13.5, 13.5, 14.5, 14.5, 15.5, 15.5, 15.5, 15.5) in / 31.75 (34.25, 34.25, 36.75, 36.75, 39.25, 39.25, 39.25, 39.25) cm – prior to blocking

D) Sleeve Circumference: 11.25 (12.75, 14, 15.75, 16, 16.25, 17, 18, 18.5) in / 27.75 (32.25, 34.75, 39.25, 40, 40.75, 42.5, 45.25, 46) cm – blocked

E) Cuff Circumference: 9.75 (11.25, 12.25, 13.5, 14.25, 14.25, 15, 16, 16.25) in / 24.25 (27.75, 30.5, 34, 35.75, 35.75, 37.5, 40, 40.75) cm – blocked

F) Sleeve Length: 13.5–15 in (34.25–38 cm) – prior to blocking

G) Neck Circumference: 20.75 (20.75, 20.75, 20.75, 22.25, 22.25, 22.25, 22.25, 22.25) in / 52.25 (52.25, 52.25, 52.25, 55.75, 55.75, 55.75, 55.75, 55.75) cm – blocked

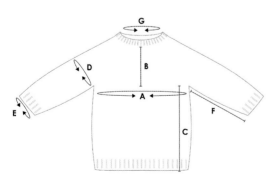

Abbreviations	
[ ]	brackets indicate a repeat
bet	between
BO	bind off
BOR	beginning of row/round
CC	contrast color
CO	cast on
dec	decrease/decreases/decreased
inc	increase/increases/increased
k	knit
k2tog	knit two stitches together (dec 1)
kfb	knit into the front and back of the same stitch (inc 1)
M1L	make one stitch, left leaning (inc 1)
MC	main color
p	purl
p2tog	purl two stitches together (dec 1)
PM	place marker
rep	repeat
rnd/s	round/rounds
RS	right side
ssk	slip one st knitwise, slip the next st knitwise, then return the two sts back to the left needle and knit the two together through the back loop (dec 1)
st/s	stitch/stitches
WS	wrong side
x	denotes sizes not represented in this line of instruction

Materials

Yarn	Heavy Sport / Light DK | HiKoo Twisp | 70% Pima Cotton, 20% Bamboo Viscose, 10% Hemp | 164 yards (150 meters) in 1.76 oz (50 grams) | 1029 (1111, 1199, 1295, 1399, 1511, 1632, 1763, 1904) yards / 941 (1016, 1096, 1184, 1279, 1381, 1492, 1612, 1740) meters | **Colors:** Natural, Fuchsia, Lagoon

Note: Variations in yarn choice or row/round gauge may impact yarn consumption. If in doubt, round up to the nearest skein.

Colors

Natural (MC): 823 (889, 959, 1036, 1119, 1209, 1306, 1410, 1523) yards / 752 (813, 877, 947, 1023, 1105, 1194, 1289, 1392) meters

Fuchsia (CC1): 103 (111, 120, 130, 140, 151, 163, 176, 190) yards / 94 (101, 110, 119, 128, 138, 149, 161, 174) meters

Lagoon (CC2): 103 (111, 120, 130, 140, 151, 163, 176, 190) yards / 94 (101, 110, 119, 128, 138, 149, 161, 174) meters

Yarn Color Note: I recommend a light neutral for your main color so that the "color pops" can be the eye-catching feature of your project. However, keep in mind that strong contrast can sometimes lead to colors that bleed into each other when they get wet. Please take care when selecting yarn for your project (especially when working with plant fiber). Test your colors in your swatch and wet block it before you begin to be sure. |

Needles	**Body:** US 5 (3.75 mm) 16–40-in (40–100-cm) circular needle*

Lower Ribbing: US 4 (3.5 mm) 24–40-in (60–100-cm) circular needle

Neckline: US 3 (3.25 mm) 16-in (40-cm) circular needle

Sleeves: US 5 (3.75 mm) 12-in (30-cm) circular needle or DPNs

Sleeve Cuffs: US 3 (3.25 mm) 12-in (30-cm) circular needle or DPNs

Or size needed to achieve gauge. Adjust other needle sizes accordingly. |
| Notions | Stitch markers (including locking markers and several unique markers)

Waste yarn or spare needles, for holding stitches

Blocking pins and mats

Darning needle, to weave ends |
| Gauge | 23 sts and 28 rnds in 4 in (10 cm) in stockinette stitch with largest needle, blocked |

yarrow color-pop tee pattern

With US Size 3 (3.25 mm) 16-in (40-cm) circular needle, CO 120 (120, 120, 120, 128, 128, 128, 128, 128) sts using cable cast-on method. Do not join in the rnd yet. (*Note: The cable cast-on begins your work immediately on the RS.*)

Set-Up Row (RS): [K2, p2] rep bet brackets to end. PM and join to work in the rnd, being careful not to twist your sts.

Ribbing Rnd: [K2, p2] rep bet brackets to end. Rep this rnd until neckline ribbing measures 1.25 in (3.25 cm)—*or slightly longer, if desired.*

Next Rnd: With US Size 5 (3.75) mm circular needle, k one rnd to begin the upper yoke.

Next Rnd: K60 (60, 60, 60, 64, 64, 64, 64, 64) sts, place a side marker, k60 (60, 60, 60, 64, 64, 64, 64, 64) sts to end. Stop.

Turn your work to the wrong side to begin 8 short rows using the Japanese short row method. You will need two locking markers for this technique.

Short Rows

> **Tip:** If you prefer a different short row method, simply work 8 short rows in your preferred method, using these details as a guide for the turning point. Be sure to keep your BOR and side markers in place as you create the short rows.

Short Row 1 (WS): Slip first st to right needle (purlwise) without working it and place a locking marker on your working yarn (holding the marker to the WS of your work). P to the side marker. Stop and turn to RS.

Short Row 2 (RS): Slip first st to right needle (purlwise) without working it and place a locking marker on your working yarn (holding the marker to the WS of your work). K to the gap that is marked with the locking marker. Using the marker to pull, draw up the marked yarn from the WS of your work and place it on the left needle as if a new st (adjusting the BOR marker, as needed, to work the short row, and then replacing it to its original location), then knit it together (k2tog) with the next st on the left needle (closing the gap) and remove the locking marker. K1, stop, and turn to WS.

Short Row 3 (WS): Slip first st to right needle (purlwise) without working it and place a locking marker on the working yarn (holding the marker to the WS of your work). P to gap that is marked with locking marker. Slip the next st to the right needle purlwise without working it (adjusting the side marker, as needed, to work the short row, and then replacing it to its original location). Using the locking marker to pull, draw up the marked yarn from the WS of your work and place it on the left needle as if a new st. Place the st that you previously slipped back to the left needle and purl it together (p2tog) with the "new" st (closing the gap) and remove locking marker. P1, stop, and turn to RS.

Short Row 4 (RS): Slip the first st to right needle (purlwise) without working it, place a locking marker on the working yarn (held at the WS of your work). K to gap that is marked with the locking marker. Using the marker to pull, draw up the marked yarn from the WS of your work and place it on the left needle as if a new st, then knit it together (k2tog) with the next st on the left needle (closing the gap) and remove locking marker. K1, stop, and turn to WS.

Short Rows 5–8: Rep Short Rows 3 and 4 twice more. Do not turn work to WS after final repeat of Short Row 4.

Continue on RS, and work in pattern to end of rnd until you are one st before the final gap. Slip this st to your right needle purlwise without working it, then, using the marker to pull, draw up the marked yarn from the WS of your work and place it on the left needle as if a new st. Place the st that you previously slipped back to the left needle and knit it together (k2tog) with the "new" st (closing the gap) and remove the locking marker. Knit to end of rnd. Your short rows have been completed and your gaps should be closed.

K one rnd.

Inc #1 – Next Rnd: [K3, M1L] rep bet brackets to last 0 (0, 0, 0, 2, 2, 2, 2, 2) sts, k to end—40 (40, 40, 40, 42, 42, 42, 42, 42) sts inc.

Stitch Count Check-In
160 (160, 160, 160, 170, 170, 170, 170, 170)

K7 (6, 5, 4, 5, 4, 4, 4, 4) rnds.

Note: Transition to longer circular needle when necessary for sts to move comfortably.

Color Pop A: Join CC1—do not cut MC.

Next Rnd: With CC1, k to end.

Next Rnd: With CC1, [p2tog] rep bet brackets to end—cut CC1 and continue with MC only—do not count sts this rnd.

Next Rnd: With MC, [kfb] rep bet brackets to end (st count should return to normal at the end of this rnd).

Next Rnd: K to end.

Inc #2 – Next Rnd: [K4, M1L] rep bet brackets to last 0 (0, 0, 0, 2, 2, 2, 2, 2) sts, k to end—40 (40, 40, 40, 42, 42, 42, 42, 42) sts inc.

Stitch Count Check-In
200 (200, 200, 200, 212, 212, 212, 212, 212)

K7 (6, 5, 4, 5, 4, 4, 4, 4) rnds.

Color Pop B: Join CC2—do not cut MC.

Next Rnd: With CC2, k to end.

Next Rnd: With CC2, [p2tog] rep bet brackets to end—cut CC2 and continue with MC only—do not count sts this rnd.

Next Rnd: With MC, [kfb] rep bet brackets to end (st count should return to normal at the end of this rnd).

Next Rnd: K to end.

Inc #3 – Next Rnd: [K5, M1L] rep bet brackets to last 0 (0, 0, 0, 2, 2, 2, 2, 2) sts, k to end—40 (40, 40, 40, 42, 42, 42, 42, 42) sts inc.

Stitch Count Check-In
240 (240, 240, 240, 254, 254, 254, 254, 254)

K7 (6, 5, 4, 5, 4, 4, 4, 4) rnds.

Color Pop A: Join CC1—do not cut MC.

Next Rnd: With CC1, k to end.

Next Rnd: With CC1, [p2tog] rep bet brackets to end—cut CC1 and continue with MC only—do not count sts this rnd.

Next Rnd: With MC, [kfb] rep bet brackets to end (st count should return to normal at the end of this rnd).

Next Rnd: K to end.

Inc #4 – Next Rnd: [K6, M1L] rep bet brackets to last 0 (0, 0, 0, 2, 2, 2, 2, 2) sts, k to end—40 (40, 40, 40, 42, 42, 42, 42, 42) sts inc.

Stitch Count Check-In
280 (280, 280, 280, 296, 296, 296, 296, 296)

K7 (6, 5, 4, 5, 4, 4, 4, 4) rnds.

Color Pop B: Join CC2—do not cut MC.

Next Rnd: With CC2, k to end.

Next Rnd: With CC2, [p2tog] rep bet brackets to end—cut CC2 and continue with MC only—do not count sts this rnd.

Next Rnd: With MC, [kfb] rep bet brackets to end (st count should return to normal at the end of this rnd).

Next Rnd: K to end.

Inc #5 – Next Rnd: [K7, M1L] rep bet brackets to last 0 (0, 0, 0, 2, 2, 2, 2, 2) sts, k to end—40 (40, 40, 40, 42, 42, 42, 42, 42) sts inc.

> **Note:** As you proceed you will see an "x" as a placeholder for sizes that are no longer represented on that rnd.

Stitch Count Check-In
320 (320, 320, 320, 338, 338, 338, 338, 338)

Size S ONLY – Move ahead to **Divide for Sleeves** on page 114.

All Other Sizes Continue

K x (6, 5, 4, 5, 4, 4, 4, 4) rnds.

Color Pop A: Join CC1—do not cut MC.

Next Rnd: With CC1, k to end.

Next Rnd: With CC1, [p2tog] rep bet brackets to end—cut CC1 and continue with MC only—do not count sts this rnd.

Next Rnd: With MC, [kfb] rep bet brackets to end (st count should return to normal at the end of this rnd).

Next Rnd: K to end.

Inc #6 – Next Rnd: [K8, M1L] rep bet brackets to last x (0, 0, 0, 2, 2, 2, 2, 2) sts, k to end—x (40, 40, 40, 42, 42, 42, 42, 42) sts inc.

Stitch Count Check-In

x (360, 360, 360, 380, 380, 380, 380, 380)

Size M ONLY – Move ahead to **Divide for Sleeves** on page 114.

All Other Sizes Continue

K x (x, 5, 4, 5, 4, 4, 4, 4) rnds.

Color Pop B: Join CC2—do not cut MC.

Next Rnd: With CC2, k to end.

Next Rnd: With CC2, [p2tog] rep bet brackets to end—cut CC2 and continue with MC only—do not count sts this rnd.

Next Rnd: With MC, [kfb] rep bet brackets to end (st count should return to normal at the end of this rnd).

Next Rnd: K to end.

Inc #7 – Next Rnd: [Kx (x, 10, 9, 9, 9, 9, 9, 9, M1L] rep bet brackets to last x (x, 0, 0, 2, 2, 2, 2, 2) sts, k to end—x (x, 36, 40, 42, 42, 42, 42, 42) sts inc.

Stitch Count Check-In

x (x, 396, 400, 422, 422, 422, 422, 422)

Size L ONLY – Move ahead to **Divide for Sleeves** on page 114.

All Other Sizes Continue

K x (x, x, 4, 5, 4, 4, 4, 4) rnds.

Color Pop A: Join CC1—do not cut MC.

Next Rnd: With CC1, k to end.

Next Rnd: With CC1, [p2tog] rep bet brackets to end—cut CC1 and continue with MC only—do not count sts this rnd.

Next Rnd: With MC, [kfb] rep bet brackets to end (st count should return to normal at the end of this rnd).

Next Rnd: K to end.

Inc #8 – Next Rnd: [Kx (x, x, 10, 11, 16, 10, 10, 10), M1L] rep bet brackets to last x (x, x, 0, 4, 6, 2, 2, 2) sts, k to end—x (x, x, 40, 38, 26, 42, 42, 42) sts inc.

Stitch Count Check-In

x (x, x, 440, 460, 448, 464, 464, 464)

Sizes XL and 2X ONLY – Move ahead to **Divide for Sleeves** on page 114.

All Other Sizes Continue

K 4 rnds.

Color Pop B: Join CC2—do not cut MC.

Next Rnd: With CC2, k to end.

Next Rnd: With CC2, [p2tog] rep bet brackets to end—cut CC2 and continue with MC only—do not count sts this rnd

Next Rnd: With MC, [kfb] rep bet brackets to end (st count should return to normal at the end of this rnd).

Next Rnd: K to end.

Inc #9 – Next Rnd: [Kx (x, x, x, x, 13, 19, 11, 11), M1L] rep bet brackets to last x (x, x, x, x, 6, 8, 2, 2) sts, k to end—x (x, x, x, x, 34, 24, 42, 42) sts inc.

Stitch Count Check-In
x (x, x, x, x, 482, 488, 506, 506)

Size 3X ONLY – Move ahead to **Divide for Sleeves**.

All Other Sizes Continue

K 4 rnds.

Color Pop A: Join CC1—do not cut MC.

Next Rnd: With CC1, k to end.

Next Rnd: With CC1, [p2tog] rep bet brackets to end—cut CC1 and continue with MC only—do not count sts this rnd.

Next Rnd: With MC, [kfb] rep bet brackets to end (st count should return to normal at the end of this rnd).

Next Rnd: K to end.

Inc #10 – Next Rnd: [Kx (x, x, x, x, x, 20, 14, 12), M1L] rep bet brackets to last x (x, x, x, x, x, 8, 2, 2) sts, k to end—x (x, x, x, x, x, 24, 36, 42) sts inc.

Stitch Count Check-In
x (x, x, x, x, x, 512, 542, 548)

Sizes 4X and 5X ONLY – Move ahead to **Divide for Sleeves**.

Size 6X Continue

K 4 rnds.

Color Pop B: Join CC2—do not cut MC.

Next Rnd: With CC2, k to end.

Next Rnd: With CC2, [p2tog] rep bet brackets to end—cut CC2 and continue with MC only—do not count sts this rnd.

Next Rnd: With MC, [kfb] rep bet brackets to end (st count should return to normal at the end of this rnd).

Next Rnd: K to end.

Inc #11 – Next Rnd: [Kx (x, x, x, x, x, x, x, 27), M1L] rep bet brackets to last x (x, x, x, x, x, x, x, 8) sts, k to end—x (x, x, x, x, x, x, x, 20) sts inc.

Stitch Count Check-In
x (x, x, x, x, x, x, x, 568)

Size 6X – Move ahead to **Divide for Sleeves**.

Divide for Sleeves
Before separating the sleeves from the body, you should have the following number of sts: 320 (360, 396, 440, 460, 482, 510, 542, 568).

Next Rnd: K31 (36, 39, 44, 44, 45, 47, 50, 51) PM (*Note: This marker is to save your spot for the edge of your right sleeve, which you will come back to as you finish this round.*), k98 (108, 120, 132, 142, 151, 162, 171, 182)—this is the front of the body. Place the next 62 (72, 78, 88, 88, 90, 94, 100, 102) sts onto waste yarn (loosely, so you can try it on later)—this is the left sleeve. CO 2 (2, 2, 2, 4, 4, 4, 4, 4) sts under arm using e-loop (or backward loop) method worked tightly and join to back sts. K98 (108, 120, 132, 142, 151, 162, 171, 182) sts—this is the back, place next 62 (72, 78, 88, 88, 90, 94, 100, 102) sts onto waste yarn (loosely) for the right sleeve. CO 2 (2, 2, 2, 4, 4, 4, 4, 4) under arm using e-loop (backward loop) method worked tightly—end of rnd. Place your new BOR marker at the center of these newly cast-on sts—this will be the start of each rnd going forward.

Your sleeves have now been separated from the yoke of your sweater. You will now transition to the Lower Body.

Stitch Count Check-In
200 (220, 244, 268, 292, 310, 332, 350, 372) sts in lower body

Lower Body
Continue working the lower body in the rnd, continuing the Color Pop sequences by working the same intervals of stockinette st (in the MC) between Color Pops and alternating Color Pop A and B until lower body measures approximately 11 (12, 12, 13, 13, 14, 14, 14, 14) in / 28 (30.5, 30.5, 33, 33, 35.5, 35.5, 35.5, 35.5) cm from underarm. End with a MC section—you will finish the lower ribbing in the MC.

Sizes S, M, L, XL, 2X, 4X, and 6X ONLY:

Next Rnd: Transition to US Size 4 (3.5 mm) needle—*or one size smaller than needed to achieve gauge*—and k one rnd.

Sizes 3X and 5X ONLY:

Next Rnd: Transition to US Size 4 (3.5 mm) needle—*or one size smaller than needed to achieve gauge*—and dec 2 sts evenly using k2tog.

All Sizes Continue

Ribbing
Next Rnd: [K2, p2] rep bet brackets to end.

Rep this rnd until ribbed edge measures 1.5 in (3.75 cm) in length. BO in pattern with medium tension (not too tight, but not too loose—if the lower edge feels restrictive, BO more loosely).

Sleeves
Beginning with either sleeve, and with US Size 5 (3.75 mm) needle—*or size needed to achieve gauge*—transfer the sleeve sts from waste yarn to your needles and pick up the sts cast on under arm—64 (74, 80, 90, 92, 94, 98, 104, 106) sts. When all sts are on your needle, PM at center of underarm and join to knit in the rnd.

Note: You will work the sleeve primarily with the MC, alternating Color Pop sections to match the ones you worked on the body.

Next Rnd: With MC, k to end.

Dec Rnd: K2, k2tog, k to last 4 st, ssk, k2—2 st dec.

Work in pattern to next Color Pop sequence (to match the spacing on the body), then proceed as follows:

Sleeve Pattern Sequence

Next 3 Rnds: Work the next Color Pop sequence, as established.

With MC, work in stockinette st to next Color Pop sequence (maintaining the spacing, as established).

Next 3 Rnds: Work the next Color Pop sequence, as established.

Next Rnd: With MC, k to end.

Next Rnd (dec): With MC, k1, k2tog, k to last 3 sts, ssk, k1—2 sts dec.

With MC, work in stockinette st to next Color Pop sequence (maintaining the spacing, as established).

Repeat the Sleeve Pattern sequence until you reach 56 (64, 70, 78, 82, 82, 86, 92, 94) sts and your sleeve measures approximately 11.5–13 in (28.75–32.5 cm) from underarm.

> **Note:** If you reach the round/st count in the middle of a Color Pop sequence, finish the sequence before you continue.

Cut contrast colors and continue with MC only.

Sizes S, M, and 5X ONLY – Move ahead to **All Sizes Continue**.

Sizes L, XL, 2X, 3X, 4X, and 6X ONLY – Next Rnd: Work one more Dec Rnd—x (x, 68, 76, 80, 80, 84, x, 92) sts.

All Sizes Continue

Transition to US 3 (3.25 mm) 12 in (30 cm) circular needle or DPNs—*or two sizes smaller than needed to achieve gauge*—and knit one rnd.

Ribbing: [K2, p2] rep bet brackets to end of rnd.

Rep this rnd until ribbed edge measures 1.75 in (4.5 cm). BO in pattern with medium tension (not too tight, not too loose). If the cuff edge is restrictive, BO again more loosely.

Rep for second sleeve.

Finishing

Weave in ends and wet block for best results. Soak in lukewarm water with a splash of fiber wash for about 20 minutes to gently cleanse and relax the fiber. Press out excess water and lay the garment flat, smoothing the sides, sleeves, and edges and pinning around the neckline (where the ribbing meets the stockinette). In the recommended yarn (or similar), the sleeves and lower body should dry nicely without pinning, but adjust as needed for best results. Turn as needed for even drying.

forget-me-not rolled neck tee

I've always loved flowers, but as a teen, I was especially fond of pressing them in the pages of my favorite books. I don't know what it is about forget-me-nots, but that's how I always think of them: pressed flat and tucked away for safe-keeping. It's that pressed flower imagery that inspired this design, but with an abstract and somewhat retro feel. The eyelets sit flat against a background of subtle texture, in a similar way that flowers might be pressed flat on a type-filled page. This mod top shines in a linen rayon blend that lends drape and elegance for a night out. I love this one for days when the weather is just starting to turn—still warm, but with a whisper that fall is on the way.

Skill
Advanced Beginner

Construction
This textured tee is knit bottom-up in the round to the underarms and features eyelet details on a body of reverse stockinette stitch. The upper bodice is worked flat to the shoulders, which are seamed afterward using horizontal mattress stitch. The neckline features a short, rolled funnel with elegant drape to dress up the design. The fit is relaxed—you don't want it to cling. The eyelet details are prominent in the recommended fabric, so you may want to wear this over a camisole or tank.

Sizes
S (M, L, XL, 2X, 3X, 4X, 5X, 6X)

Fit Advice
Designed to be worn with approximately 3–4 in (7.5–10 cm) positive ease.

Finished Measurements
A) Bust Circumference: 34.5 (38.5, 42.25, 46, 51.75, 55.75, 59.5, 63.25, 67.25) in / 86.5 (96, 105.5, 115.25, 129.5, 139.25, 148.75, 158.5, 168) cm – blocked

B) Armhole Depth: 6.5 (7, 7, 7.5, 7.5, 8, 8.5, 8.5, 9) in / 16.5 (17.75, 17.75, 19, 19, 20.25, 21.5, 21.5, 22.75) cm – prior to blocking

C) Underarm to Hem: 13 (13, 13, 14, 14, 15, 15, 15, 15) in / 33 (33, 33, 35.5, 35.5, 38, 38, 38, 38) cm – prior to blocking

D) Back Neckline Width: 10 (10, 10, 10.5, 10.5, 10.5, 11, 11, 11) in / 24.75 (24.75, 24.75, 26.5, 26.5, 26.5, 27.25, 27.25, 27.25) cm – blocked

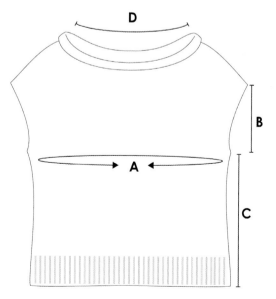

Abbreviations	
[ ]	brackets indicate a repeat
bet	between
BO	bind off
BOR	beginning of row/round
CO	cast on
dec	decrease/decreases/decreased
inc	increase/increases/increased
k	knit
k2tog	knit two stitches together (dec 1)
p	purl
PM	place marker
p2tog	purl two stitches together (dec 1)
rep	repeat
rnd/s	round/rounds
RS	right side
ssk	slip one st knitwise, slip the next st knitwise, then return the two sts back to the left needle and knit the two together through the back loop (dec 1)
st/s	stitch/stitches
WS	wrong side
yo	yarn over (inc 1)

Materials	
Yarn	DK Weight | Erika Knight Studio Linen | 85% Rayon, 15% Linen | 131 yards (120 meters) in 1.76 oz (50 grams) | 810 (859, 910, 965, 1042, 1125, 1215, 1312, 1417) yards / 740 (785, 832, 882, 952, 1028, 1111, 1199, 1295) meters | **Color:** Pomegranate **Note:** Variations in yarn choice or row/round gauge may impact yarn consumption. If in doubt, round up to the nearest skein.
Needles	**Body:** US 5 (3.75 mm)* 24–40-in (60–100-cm) circular needle **Lower Ribbing:** US 4 (3.5 mm) 24–40-in (60–100-cm) circular needle **Neckline:** US 4 (3.5 mm) 16-in (40-cm) circular needle *Or size needed to achieve gauge. Adjust other needle sizes accordingly.*
Notions	Stitch markers (including locking markers) Waste yarn or spare needles, for holding stitches Blocking mats Darning needle, to weave ends and seam shoulders
Gauge	25 sts and 32 rows/rounds in 4 in (10 cm) in texture pattern with largest needle, blocked—*row gauge is less critical but may affect yarn consumption.*

forget-me-not rolled neck tee pattern

With US Size 4 (3.5 mm) 24–40-in (60–100-cm) circular needle—*or one size smaller than needed to achieve gauge*—CO 216 (240, 264, 288, 324, 348, 372, 396, 420) sts using cable cast-on method. Do not join in the rnd yet. (*Note: The cable cast-on begins your work immediately on the RS.*)

Set-Up Row (RS): [K1, p1] rep bet brackets to end. PM and join to work in the rnd, being careful not to twist your sts.

Ribbing Rnd: [K1, p1] rep bet brackets to end. Rep this rnd until work measures 3 in (7.5 cm) from cast-on edge.

Transition to US Size 5 (3.75 mm) needle—*or size needed to achieve gauge*—and p 2 rnds.

Next Rnd: Work Forget-Me-Not Chart (beginning with Rnd 1 of chart or written instructions, worked over 6 sts per repeat) to end.

Continue working the lower body in the rnd as established, repeating the lace chart rnds in order, until your work measures approximately 13 (13, 13, 14, 14, 15, 15, 15, 15) in / 33 (33, 33, 35.5, 35.5, 38, 38, 38, 38) cm from cast-on edge, ending with an even-numbered right.

Upper Bodice
Going forward, you will separate the front and back bodice sections and work back and forth on each section, flat, beginning with the front. You will return to work the back afterward.

Tip: As you begin working flat, be sure to keep your edges tidy. To do this, work the first st tighter than usual, then insert the tip of your needle into the second st, and pull the working yarn tight again to draw the first st a little tighter. Then proceed with the remainder of the row with normal tension. Do this at the start of every row (RS and WS) for nicer edges that will be easier to finish later.

Lace Note (Working Flat): Because of the way the pattern splits to work flat, you may not have enough sts to work the full lace repeats to the selvedge. If you cannot complete the full inc/dec of the lace repeat, work that portion in reverse stockinette st instead.

Next Row (RS): Work 108 (120, 132, 144, 162, 174, 186, 198, 210) sts in established pattern, stop.

Slide remaining 108 (120, 132, 144, 162, 174, 186, 198, 210) sts onto a long separate needle or waste yarn. You will work back and forth (flat) on the front section (only) for now.

Front
Next Row (WS): P2, work in established pattern to last 2 sts, p2.

Next Row (RS): K2, work in established pattern to last 2 sts, k2.

Rep these two rows continuing in established pattern until your flat section measures approximately 6.5 (7, 7, 7.5, 7.5, 8, 8.5, 8.5, 9) in / 16.5 (17.75, 17.75, 19, 19, 20.25, 21.5, 21.5, 22.75) cm from where you began working flat, ending after a WS row (ready to work a RS).

Front Shoulder and Neckline Shaping

Next Row (RS): BO 4 (5, 6, 7, 8, 9, 10, 11, 12) sts knitwise, then work 27 (32, 37, 40, 48, 53, 58, 62, 67) sts in established pattern—this is the left front shoulder. BO next 46 (46, 46, 50, 50, 50, 50, 52, 52) sts knitwise for center front neckline. Work 31 (37, 43, 47, 56, 62, 68, 73, 79) sts in established pattern to end—this is right front shoulder.

Place the first 27 (32, 37, 40, 48, 53, 58, 62, 67) sts of left front shoulder sts onto a holder; you will return to work them later. You will now work only on the right front shoulder and neckline dec as you proceed in this section.

Right Front Shoulder

Next Row (WS): BO 4 (5, 6, 7, 8, 9, 10, 11, 12) sts purlwise, work in established pattern to end.

Next Row (RS): K1, ssk, work in established pattern to end—1 st dec.

Rep these two rows 4 times more (for a total of 5)—6 (7, 8, 7, 11, 12, 13, 13, 14) sts.

Next Row (RS): BO remaining sts knitwise.

Left Front Shoulder

Return left front shoulder sts to your needles and rejoin working yarn, ready to work a WS row.

Next Row (WS): P1, p2tog, work in established pattern to end—1 st dec.

Next Row (RS): BO 4 (5, 6, 7, 8, 9, 10, 11, 12) sts knitwise, work in established pattern to end.

Rep these two rows 3 times more (for a total of 4)—7 (8, 9, 8, 12, 13, 14, 14, 15) sts.

Next Row (WS): P1, p2tog, BO remaining sts in purl (including the first two sts).

Back

Return back sts to needles and join working yarn, ready to work a RS row—108 (120, 132, 144, 162, 174, 186, 198, 210) sts.

Next Row (RS): K2, work in established pattern to last 2 sts, k2.

Next Row (WS): P2, work in established pattern to last 2 sts, p2.

Rep these two rows until your flat section measures 6.5 (7, 7, 7.5, 7.5, 8, 8.5, 8.5, 9) in / 16.5 (17.75, 17.75, 19, 19, 20.25, 21.5, 21.5, 22.75) cm and is the same length as the front section from where you began working flat. End after a WS row (ready to work a RS).

Back Shoulder Shaping

> **Note:** As you BO, transition to reverse stockinette (and skip the lace pattern) when you are within 12 sts of the bind-off edge of the row.

Next Row (RS): BO 4 (5, 6, 7, 8, 9, 10, 11, 12) sts knitwise, work in established pattern to end.

Next Row (WS): BO 4 (5, 6, 7, 8, 9, 10, 11, 12) sts purlwise, work in established pattern to end.

Rep these two rows 5 times more (for a total of 6)—60 (60, 60, 60, 66, 66, 66, 66, 66) sts.

Next Row (RS): BO remaining sts knitwise.

Shoulder Finishing

Seam the shoulder sts together on each side to the neckline, ensuring that the front, back, and shoulder bind-off sections line up perfectly. See seaming and grafting tutorials on my website here: oliveknits.com/grafting.

Neckline

With US Size 4 (3.5 mm) 16 in (40 cm) circular needle—*or one size smaller than needed to achieve gauge*—pick up and knit all available sts around the neckline. PM and join to work in the rnd.

Next Rnds: Work 3 in (7.5 cm) in stockinette stitch, then BO knitwise on the next rnd. (If you prefer a shorter rolled edge, simply work fewer rnds until it's the length you prefer.)

> **Tip:** You can adjust the size and feel of your neckline by doing one of the following: For a looser neckline, pick up available st and ensure that your bind off is not too tight. If your neckline is too loose or open, try picking up slightly fewer sts—such as 5 of every 6 available sts—and/or binding off a little more tightly. Necklines like this one are very easy to adjust with just a few simple changes to your technique.

Sleeves

There is no finishing necessary for the sleeves.

Finishing

Weave in ends and wet block for best results, soaking in lukewarm water with a splash of fiber wash for 20 minutes to gently cleanse and relax the fiber. Press out excess water, and lay flat, patting the garment into place (rather than pinning). Draw the edges taut and ensure that the neckline is pulled gently upward and patted flat to dry. (It will drape like a loose, rolled funnel when it's dry.) In the recommended yarn, pinning is not advised; it's likely to snag the fiber. Turn as needed for even drying.

Chart Written Directions (Rnd)

Rnd 1: [P4, yo, k2tog] rep bet brackets to end.

Rnd 2: P to end.

Rnds 3–6: [P4, k1, p1] rep bet brackets to end.

Rnd 7: [P1, yo, k2tog, p3] rep bet brackets to end.

Rnd 8: P to end.

Rnds 9–12: [P1, k1, p4] rep bet brackets to end.

Chart Written Directions (Flat)

Row 1 (RS): [P4, yo, k2tog] rep bet brackets to end.

Row 2 (WS): K to end.

Row 3 (RS): [P4, k1, p1] rep bet brackets to end.

Row 4 (WS): [K1, p1, k4] rep bet brackets to end.

Rows 5–6: Rep Rows 3–4.

Row 7 (RS): [P1, yo, k2tog, p3] rep bet brackets to end.

Row 8 (WS): K to end.

Row 9 (RS): [P1, k1, p4] rep bet brackets to end.

Row 10 (WS): [K4, p1, k1] rep bet brackets to end.

Rows 11-12: Rep Rows 9–10.

forget-me-not rolled neck tee chart

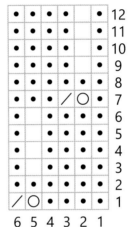

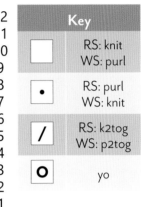

Key		
☐	RS: knit WS: purl	
•	RS: purl WS: knit	
/	RS: k2tog WS: p2tog	
O	yo	

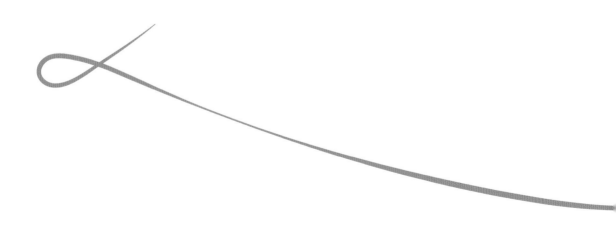

wild iris striped tank

As a girl, I thought irises were very fancy. I would ride my bike around the neighborhood and stop to smell them whenever they were within reach. I might have even snipped a few and secreted them away to take home. Now the neighbor kids swing by to snip ours, so the circle of life continues. This bold striped top is something between a vest and a tank top. The boxy shape frames a series of two-color stripes, with a set-in sleeve rib that keeps the silhouette closer to the body. It's perfect for sunny afternoons, neighborhood walks, and flower picking, and the style is so classic that you'll wear it for years to come.

Skill Level
Advanced Beginner

Construction
This top is knit bottom-up in the round to the underarms, then worked flat to the shoulders. The shoulders are seamed with horizontal mattress stitch and finished with a ribbed neckline. The armholes are minimally shaped by binding off a few stitches at the underarm on each side as you make the transition to the upper body. When you've finished the body and neckline, you'll add ribbing around the armhole edge, tacking it down at the underarm where the stitches are set in.

Sizes
S (M, L, XL, 2X, 3X, 4X, 5X, 6X)

Fit Advice
Made to fit bust sizes 32–34 (36–38, 40–42, 44–46, 48–50, 52–54, 56–58, 60–62, 64–66) in / 80–85 (90–95, 100–105, 110–115, 120–125, 130–135, 140–145, 150–155, 160–165) cm.

Designed to be worn with approximately 2–4 in (5–10 cm) positive ease.

Finished Measurements
A) **Bust Circumference:** 35.25 (39.25, 43.25, 47.25, 51.25, 55.25, 59.25, 63.25, 67.25) in / 88.25 (98.25, 108.25, 118.25, 128.25, 138.25, 148.25, 158.25, 168.25) cm – blocked

B) **Armhole Depth:** 8 (8.5, 9, 9.5, 9.5, 10, 10.5, 10.5, 11) in / 20.25 (21.5, 22.75, 24.25, 24.25, 25.5, 26.75, 26.75, 28) cm – prior to blocking

C) **Underarm to Hem:** 13 (13, 13, 14, 14, 15, 15, 15, 15) in/ 33 (33, 33, 35.5, 35.5, 38, 38, 38, 38) cm – prior to blocking (should grow approximately 1 in [2.5 cm] in recommended yarn)

D) **Back Neckline Width:** 9.25 (9.25, 9.25, 9.75, 9.75, 10.25, 10.25, 10.25, 10.25) in / 23.25 (23.25, 23.25, 24.25, 24.25, 25.75, 25.75, 25.75, 25.75) cm – blocked, not including ribbing

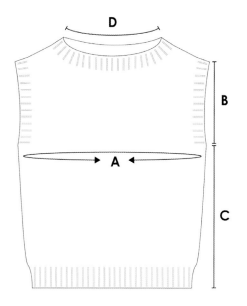

Abbreviations	
[ ]	brackets indicate a repeat
bet	between
BO	bind off
BOR	beginning of row/round
CO	cast on
CC	contrast color
dec	decrease/decreases/decreased
k	knit
k2tog	knit two stitches together (dec 1)
MC	main color
p	purl
p2tog	purl two stitches together (dec 1)
PM	place marker
rep	repeat
rnd/s	round/rounds
RS	right side
ssk	slip one st knitwise, slip the next st knitwise, then return the two sts back to the left needle and knit the two together through the back loop (dec 1)
st/s	stitch/stitches
WS	wrong side

Materials

Yarn	Sport / Light DK Weight | Elemental Affects Coastal | 50% Shaniko Wool, 25% Belgian Flax, 25% Mulberry Silk | 205 yards (187 meters) in 2 oz (57 grams) | **Colors:** Blueberry & Natural

Note: Variations in yarn choice or row/round gauge may impact yarn consumption. If in doubt, round up to the nearest skein.

MC (Blueberry): 617 (667, 719, 777, 839, 907, 979, 1058, 1142) yards / 564 (610, 657, 710, 767, 829, 895, 967, 1044) meters

CC (Natural): 500 (540, 583, 630, 680, 735, 793, 857, 925) yards / 457 (494, 533, 576, 622, 672, 725, 783, 846) meters

Yarn Color Note: This easy summer tank is knit from the bottom up and features two-color stripes throughout; feel free to use more or less contrast, depending on your preference. High contrast colors may present a higher risk of color bleeding when you wet block your garment, so please take care when selecting yarn for your project. Be sure to swatch (and wet block your swatch) with both colors to test for colorfastness before you begin. |

Needles	**Body:** US Size 5 (3.75 mm)* 24–40-in (60–100-cm) circular needle **Lower Body Ribbing:** US Size 3 (3.25 mm) 24–40-in (60–100-cm) circular needle **Neckline Finishing:** US Size 3 (3.25 mm) 16-in (40-cm) circular needle *Or size needed to achieve gauge. Adjust other needle sizes accordingly.*
Notions	Stitch markers Waste yarn or spare needles, for holding stitches Blocking pins and mats Darning needle to weave ends, seam shoulders, and tack down ribbing
Gauge	24 sts and 32 rows/rounds in 4 in (10 cm) in stockinette stitch with largest needle, blocked—*row gauge is less critical but may affect yarn consumption.*

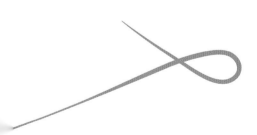

wild iris striped tank pattern

With US Size 3 (3.25 mm) 24–40-in (60–100-cm) circular needle—*or two sizes smaller than needed to achieve gauge*—and MC, CO 212 (236, 260, 284, 308, 332, 356, 380, 404) sts using cable cast-on method. Do not join in the rnd yet. (*Note: The cable cast-on begins your work immediately on the RS.*)

Set-Up Row (RS): [K2, p2] rep bet brackets to end, then PM and join to work in the rnd, being careful not to twist your sts.

Ribbing Rnd: [K2, p2] rep bet brackets to end.

Rep this rnd until work measures 2 in (5 cm).

Transition to US Size 5 (3.75 mm) 24–40-in (60–100-cm) circular needle—*or size needed to achieve gauge*—and k 3 rnds with MC.

Next Rnd: Join CC and work Wild Iris Stripes Chart (beginning with Rnd 1) to end. (*Note: The chart shows stripes over 6 sts for the sake of visibility, but it can be worked over any number of sts.*)

Continue working the lower body in the rnd as established, repeating the stripe chart rnds in order (carrying the alternate colors along the inside as you go) until lower body measures approximately 13 (13, 13, 14, 14, 15, 15, 15, 15) in / 33 (33, 33, 35.5, 35.5, 38, 38, 38, 38) cm from cast-on edge, **ending after Rnd 1, 2, 3, or 4 of chart.**

Upper Bodice

Going forward, you will separate the front and back bodice sections and work back and forth on each section, flat, beginning with the front. You will return to work the back afterward.

> **Tip:** As you begin working flat, be sure to keep your edges tidy. To do this, work the first st tighter than usual, then insert the tip of your needle into the second st, and pull the working yarn tight again to draw the first st a little tighter. Then proceed with the remainder of the row with normal tension. Do this at the start of every row (RS and WS) for nicer edges that will be easier to finish later.
>
> Keep in mind that you will frequently need to work two WS rows or two RS rows back to back (switching to the opposite color and working across the row) to maintain the stripe sequence; this will prevent having to cut and rejoin yarn on sections with a single stripe row.

Next Row (RS): Continuing in established stripe sequence, BO 6 sts knitwise, k100 (112, 124, 136, 148, 160, 172, 184, 196) sts, stop.

Slide remaining 106 (118, 130, 142, 154, 166, 178, 190, 202) sts onto a long separate needle or waste yarn. You will work back and forth (flat) on the front section (only) for now.

Front

Next Row (WS): Continuing in established stripe sequence, BO 6 sts purlwise, then p to end—94 (106, 118, 130, 142, 154, 166, 178, 190) sts.

Next Row (RS): Continuing in established stripe sequence, k to end.

Next Row (WS): Continuing in established stripe sequence, p to end.

Rep these two rows, continuing in established stripe sequence, until your flat section measures approximately 8 (8.5, 9, 9.5, 9.5, 10, 10.5, 10.5, 11) in / 20.25 (21.5, 22.75, 24.25, 24.25, 25.5, 26.75, 26.75, 28) cm from where you began working flat, ending after a WS row (ready to work a RS).

Front Shoulder and Neckline Shaping

Next Row (RS): Continuing in stripe sequence, BO 4 (6, 7, 9, 10, 11, 13, 14, 16) sts knitwise, then k19 (23, 28, 31, 36, 39, 43, 48, 52) sts—this is left front shoulder. BO next 48 (48, 48, 50, 50, 54, 54, 54, 54) sts knitwise for center front neckline. K1, ssk, k20 (26, 32, 37, 43, 47, 53, 59, 65) to end—this is right front shoulder.

Place the 19 (23, 28, 31, 36, 39, 43, 48, 52) sts of left front shoulder section onto a holder; you will return to work them later. You will now work only on the right front shoulder and neckline dec as you proceed in this section.

Right Front Shoulder

Note: As you BO, there may be times that you'll need to cut and rejoin a color in the stripe sequence in order to stay in pattern.

Next Row (WS): Continuing in established stripe sequence, BO 4 (6, 7, 9, 10, 11, 13, 14, 16) sts purlwise, then p to end.

Next Row (RS): Continuing in established stripe sequence, k1, ssk, k to end—1 st dec.

Next Row (WS): Continuing in established stripe sequence, BO 4 (6, 7, 9, 10, 11, 13, 14, 16) sts purlwise, then p to end.

Rep these two rows once more (for a total of 2).

Next Row (RS): Continuing in established stripe sequence, k1, ssk, k to end—1 st dec.

Next Row (WS): Using the same color used for the previous row, BO remaining 7 (7, 10, 9, 12, 13, 13, 16, 16) sts purlwise.

Left Front Shoulder

Return left front shoulder sts to your needles and rejoin working yarn in color necessary to continue stripe sequence, ready to work a WS row.

Next Row (WS): Continuing in established stripe sequence, p1, p2tog, p to end—1 st dec.

Next Row (RS): Continuing in established stripe sequence, BO 4 (6, 7, 9, 10, 11, 13, 14, 16) sts knitwise, then k to end.

Rep these two rows once more (for a total of 2).

Next Row (WS): Continuing in established stripe sequence, p1, p2tog, p to end—1 st dec.

Next Row (RS): Using the same color used for the previous row BO remaining sts knitwise to last 3 sts, k2tog, BO this st, then BO final st.

Back

Return back sts to needles and join working yarn (to continue the stripe sequence), ready to work a RS row—106 (118, 130, 142, 154, 166, 178, 190, 202) sts.

Next Row (RS): Continuing in established stripe sequence, BO 6 sts knitwise, k100 (112, 124, 136, 148, 160, 172, 184, 196) sts to end.

Next Row (WS): Continuing in established stripe sequence, BO 6 sts purlwise, then p to end— 94 (106, 118, 130, 142, 154, 166, 178, 190) sts.

Next Row (RS): Continuing in established stripe sequence k to end.

Next Row (WS): Continuing in established stripe sequence p to end.

Rep these two rows continuing in established stripe sequence until your flat section measures approximately 8 (8.5, 9, 9.5, 9.5, 10, 10.5, 10.5, 11) in / 20.25 (21.5, 22.75, 24.25, 24.25, 25.5, 26.75, 26.75, 28) cm and is the same length as the front section from where you began working flat. End after a WS row (ready to work a RS).

Back Shoulder Shaping

Next Row (RS): Continuing in established stripe sequence, BO 4 (6, 7, 9, 10, 11, 13, 14, 16) sts knitwise, k to end.

Next Row (WS): Continuing in established stripe sequence, BO 4 (6, 7, 9, 10, 11, 13, 14, 16) sts purlwise, p to end.

Rep these two rows twice more (for a total of 3).

Next Row (RS): Continuing in established stripe sequence, BO 7 (7, 10, 9, 12, 13, 13, 16, 16) sts knitwise, k to end.

Next Row (WS): Continuing in established stripe sequence, BO 7 (7, 10, 9, 12, 13, 13, 16, 16) sts purlwise, p to end.

BO remaining sts knitwise for center back neckline.

Shoulder Finishing

Seam the shoulder sts together on each side to the neckline, ensuring that the front, back, and shoulder bind-off sections line up perfectly. See seaming and grafting tutorials on my website here: oliveknits.com/grafting .

Neckline

With US Size 3 (3.25 mm) 16-in (40-cm) circular needle—*or two sizes smaller than needed to achieve gauge*—and MC, pick up and knit almost every available st around the neckline, ending with a multiple of 4. PM and join to work in the rnd.

> **Tip:** You can adjust the size and feel of your neckline by doing one of the following: For a looser neckline, pick up every available st and ensure that your bind off is not too tight. If your neckline is too open (or your ribbing flares out), try picking up slightly fewer sts—such as 5 of every 6 available sts—and/or binding off a little more tightly. Necklines like this one are very easy to adjust with just a few simple changes to your technique.

Ribbing

Next Rnd: [K2, p2] rep bet brackets to end.

Repeat this rnd until ribbed edge measures approximately 1.25 in (3.25 cm). BO in pattern with medium tension.

> **Tip:** If you prefer a smaller neckline, you may adjust the width by picking up approximately 8–12 fewer sts and/or working your ribbing more tightly.

Armhole Ribbing

Beginning with either armhole, and with US Size 3 (3.25 mm) 12-in (30-cm) circular needle or DPNs—*or needle two sizes smaller than needed to achieve gauge*—and MC, pick up and knit sts at a rate of approximately 4 of every 5 sts along the sleeve edge, starting perpendicular to the 6 sts you bound off and ending with a multiple of 4 +2. Jot down the number of sts you've picked up so you can match the same number on the other sleeve. When you complete your ribbing, it should line up with the 6 sts you bound off at the underarm. You will tack it down along that lower edge when you finish. Do not join in the rnd. The sleeve ribbing will be worked back and forth, flat.

Ribbing

Row 1 (WS): P2, [k2, p2] rep bet brackets to end.

Row 2 (RS): K2, [p2, k2] rep bet brackets to end.

Rep these two rows until ribbed edge equals the width of the 6 sts you bound off at the underarm, approximately 1–1.25 in (2.5–3.75 cm). BO in pattern with medium tension.

Rep for second armhole.

> **Tip:** If your sleeve ribbing flares out, it means you've either picked up slightly too many sts or have worked your ribbing too loosely. If this happens, try again with slightly fewer sts and/or go down another needle size to work your ribbing more tightly.

Finishing

Weave in ends on the WS and use a strand of your MC to tack down the bottom edges of the sleeve ribbing (to close the flap) at the bottom of each sleeve (in all four places, two under each arm). Wet block for best results, soaking in lukewarm water with a splash of fiber wash for 20 minutes to gently cleanse and relax the fiber. Press out excess water, and lay flat, pinning into shape, especially around the ribbed areas where the ribbing meets the stockinette stitch. Turn as needed for even drying.

wild iris striped tank chart

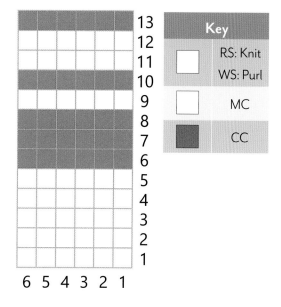

Key

RS: Knit
WS: Purl

MC

CC

water lily silk pullover

Some patterns begin with the design idea, while others begin with the yarn; this one was the latter. Silk isn't technically a plant-based yarn, but because it behaves in a similar way, I think it deserves a spot in this book. The luxuriously soft (yet strong) fabric created with mulberry silk results in an almost ethereal, lustrous sheen; it reminds me of the soft pink glow of water lilies in a koi pond. I wanted to capture that lovely, dreamlike quality in the way the sheen of the fabric dances with the gentle wave of the stitch pattern. Knit in a different type of fiber, this would be an entirely different—decidedly more casual—tee. Yarn makes such a difference!

Skill

Intermediate

Construction

This top-down, seamless tee is knit with unique shoulder and arm shaping—a style I developed as a way to create a more tailored fit (especially in the shoulders) while staying within the bounds of the top-down, seamless construction I love. The result is not a raglan or a circular yoke; instead, it's something along the lines of a contiguous sleeve shape with a built-in shoulder saddle. While it may feel unusual as you're knitting it (especially at first!), the result is a beautifully smart shape that cradles your shoulders and resembles a set-in sleeve. The design features a contemporary panel of knits and purls down the center, a simple neckline, and half sleeves. Both the sleeves and the neckline are finished with garter stitch ridges to match the center panel. The lower body is finished with standard ribbing. If 100% silk isn't your cup of tea (or isn't in your budget), other plant blends—or even a more traditional superwash merino—would work as well.

Sizes

32 (34, 36, 38, 40, 42, 44), 46 (48, 50, 52, 54, 56, 58, 60)

Fit Advice

Designed to be worn with approximately 2–3 in (5–7.5 cm) positive ease. Choose the size that most closely matches your full bust circumference; the appropriate ease is already included.

Finished Measurements

A) Bust Circumference: 34.5 (37.5, 39.5, 41.25, 42.5, 45, 46.75), 48.5 (51, 53, 55.5, 56.5, 59, 61, 63) in / 86.25 (93.75, 98.5, 103, 106.25, 112.25, 117), 121.5 (127.75, 132.25, 138.5, 141.5, 147.75, 152.25, 157.75) cm – blocked

B) Yoke Depth: 9.25 (9.25, 9.75, 10.25, 10.5, 10.5, 10.75), 11.25 (11.75, 12, 12.25, 12.5, 13, 13.25, 13.5) in / 22.75 (22.75, 23.5, 24.5, 25, 25, 26), 27.25 (28.25, 28.5, 29.5, 30, 31.25, 32, 32.5) cm – blocked

(Continued)

C) Underarm to Hem: 14–16 in (35.5–40.5 cm) – prior to blocking

D) Sleeve Circumference: 11.75 (12, 12.5, 14.25, 14.5, 14.75, 15.5), 16 (16.5, 17, 17.5, 17.75, 18.5, 18.75, 19) in / 29.25 (30, 31.5, 35.5, 36.25, 37, 38.5), 40 (41.5, 42.25, 43.75, 44.5, 46.25, 47, 47.75) cm – blocked

E) Cuff Circumference: 9.5 (9.75, 10.25, 11.75, 12.25, 12.5, 13), 13 (13.75, 14, 14.5, 14.75, 15.5, 15.5, 15.5) in / 23.75 (24.5, 26, 29.75, 30.25, 31, 32.5), 32.5 (34, 34.75, 36.25, 37, 38.5, 38.5, 38.5) cm – blocked (worked at a slightly tighter gauge than the rest with the smaller needle)

F) Sleeve Length: 7 in (17.5 cm) – prior to blocking

G) Neck Circumference: 17.5 (17.5, 16.75, 18, 18, 18.5, 20.5), 20.5 (21, 22.75, 23.5, 24.75, 25.75, 25.75, 25.75) in / 44.5 (44.5, 42.5, 45.75, 45.75, 47, 52), 52 (53.25, 57.75, 59.75, 62.75, 65.5, 65.5, 65.5) cm – blocked

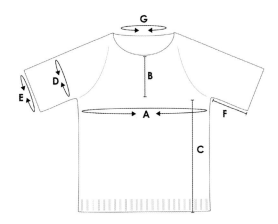

Abbreviations	
[ ]	brackets indicate a repeat
bet	between
BO	bind off
CO	cast on
dec	decrease/decreases/decreased
inc	increase/increases/increased
k	knit
k2tog	knit two stitches together (dec 1)
m	marker
mX	marker A (B, C, D, etc...), "x" denotes which marker
M1L	make one stitch, left leaning (inc 1)
M1R	make one stitch, right leaning (inc 1)
p	purl
PM	place marker
pmX	place marker A (B, C, D, etc...), "x" denotes which marker
rep	repeat
rnd/s	round/rounds
RS	right side
sm	slip marker
smX	slip marker A (B, C, D, etc...), "x" denotes which marker
ssk	slip one st knitwise, slip the next st knitwise, then return the two sts back to the left needle and knit the two together through the back loop (dec 1)
st/s	stitch/stitches
WS	wrong side
x	denotes sizes not represented in this line of instruction

Materials	
Yarn	Fingering Weight | Treasure Goddess Pure Silk Riches | 100% Pure Mulberry Silk | 436 yards (398 meters) in 3.5 oz (100 grams) | 1012 (1100, 1196, 1300, 1404, 1516, 1638), 1736 (1806, 1878, 1953, 2031, 2112, 2197, 2285) yards / 925 (1005, 1093, 1188, 1283, 1386, 1497), 1587 (1651, 1717, 1785, 1857, 1931, 2008, 2089) meters | **Color:** Perfect Shell **Note:** Variations in yarn choice or row/round gauge may impact yarn consumption. If in doubt, round up to the nearest skein.
Needles	**Body:** US Size 3 (3.25 mm)* 24–32-in (60–80-cm) circular needle **Body Ribbing:** US Size 2 (2.75 mm) 24–32-in (60–80-cm) circular needle **Neckline:** US Size 1 (1.25 mm) 16-in (40-cm) circular needle **Sleeves:** US Size 3 (3.25 mm) 12-in (30-cm) circular or DPNs *Or size needed to achieve gauge. Adjust other needle sizes accordingly.*
Notions	Stitch markers Waste yarn or spare needles, for holding stitches Blocking mats Darning needle to weave ends
Gauge	26 sts and 32 rows/rounds in 4 in (10 cm) in stockinette stitch with largest needle, blocked

water lily silk pullover pattern

With US Size 3 (3.25 mm) 24–32-in (60–80-cm) circular needle, CO 72 (72, 86, 98, 98, 102, 116), 116 (120, 130, 134, 142, 146, 146, 146) sts using cable cast-on method, worked tightly. Do not join to work in the rnd.

Note: You will work the pattern flat for a few rows to create the shaped neckline (This is a technique I "unvented" many years ago—as Elizabeth Zimmerman would say—in order to create a beautifully shaped neckline without short rows.). The pattern will indicate when to join in the rnd to continue your work. You will shape the neckline with new sts cast on at the start of each row until the shaping is complete. You will then join your sts to work in the rnd and will reposition your working yarn as indicated when the time comes.

Set-Up Row (RS): K1—this will become the left edge of the front section once the neckline shaping is complete. PmA, k8 (8, 12, 18, 18, 20, 24), 24 (26, 28, 28, 30, 30, 30, 30)—this will become the left sleeve. PmB, k54 (54, 60, 60, 60, 60, 66), 66 (66, 72, 76, 80, 84, 84, 84)—this will become the back section. PmC, k8 (8, 12, 18, 18, 20, 24), 24 (26, 28, 28, 30, 30, 30, 30)—this will become the right sleeve. PmD, k1—this will become the right edge of the front section once the neckline shaping is complete.

Set-Up Row (WS): P to end, slipping markers as you go.

Row 1 (RS): CO 2 sts using knitted cast-on worked knitwise (tightly)*, k to mA, smA, k to mB, smB, **M1L**, k2, **M1L**, k to 2 sts before mC, **M1R**, k2, **M1R**, smC, k to mD, smD, k to end—4 sts inc + 2 sts CO.

Row 2 (WS): CO 2 sts using knitted cast-on worked purlwise (tightly)*, purl to end, slipping markers as you go—2 sts CO.

*Note:** Going forward, all sts cast on at the start of a row will be worked using the cable cast-on method, either knitwise or purlwise, depending on the row. Keep your cast-on sts nice and tight to ensure a tidy neckline (it will make for nicer finishing, as well). Always work the new sts in pattern after casting them on.

Row 3 (RS): CO 3 sts, k to mA, smA, k to mB, smB, **M1L**, k2, **M1L**, k to 2 sts before mC, **M1R**, k2, **M1R**, smC, k to mD, smD, k to end—4 sts inc + 3 sts CO.

Row 4 (WS): CO 3 sts, p to end, slipping markers as you go—3 sts CO.

Row 5 (RS): CO 5 (5, 5, 5, 5, 5, 5), 5 (5, 5, 7, 7, 7, 7, 7) sts, k to mA, smA, k to mB, smB, **M1L**, k2, **M1L,** k to 2 sts before mC, **M1R**, k2, **M1R**, smC, k to mD, smD, k to end—4 sts inc + 5 (5, 5, 5, 5, 5, 5), 5 (5, 5, 7, 7, 7, 7) sts CO.

Row 6 (WS): CO 5 (5, 5, 5, 5, 5, 5), 5 (5, 5, 7, 7, 7, 7, 7) sts, p to end, slipping markers as you go— 5 (5, 5, 5, 5, 5, 5), 5 (5, 5, 7, 7, 7, 7, 7) sts CO.

Note: On the next few RS rows, you will be staggering a series of inc across the top of the sleeves (between mA and mB, and between mC and mD).

Row 7 (RS): CO 5 (5, 9, 9, 9, 9, 9), 9 (9, 9, 7, 7, 7, 7, 7) sts , k to mA, smA, k1, **M1L**, k2, **M1L**, k to 3 sts before mB, **M1R**, k2, **M1R**, k1, smB, k to mC, smC, k1, **M1L**, k2, **M1L**, k to 3 sts before mD, **M1R**, k2, **M1R**, k1, smD, k to end—4 sts inc on each sleeve + 5 (5, 9, 9, 9, 9, 9), 9 (9, 9, 7, 7, 7, 7, 7) sts CO, no inc on back).

Row 8 (WS): CO 5 (5, 9, 9, 9, 9, 9), 9 (9, 9, 7, 7, 7, 7, 7) sts, p to end, slipping markers as you go— 5 (5, 9, 9, 9, 9, 9), 9 (9, 9, 7, 7, 7, 7, 7) sts CO.

Stitch Count Check-In

Fronts (ea): 16 (16, 20, 20, 20, 20, 20), 20 (20, 20, 20, 20, 20, 20, 20)

Sleeves (ea): 12 (12, 16, 22, 22, 24, 28), 28 (30, 32, 32, 34, 34, 34, 34)

Back: 66 (66, 72, 72, 72, 72, 78), 78 (78, 84, 88, 92, 96, 96, 96)

Row 9 (RS): CO 9 sts, k to mA, smA, k1, **M1L**, k2, **M1L**, k to 3 sts before mB, **M1R**, k2, **M1R**, k1, smB, k to mC, smC, k1, **M1L**, k2, M1L, k to 3 sts before mD, **M1R**, k2, **M1R**, k1, smD, k to end— 4 sts inc on each sleeve + 9 sts CO, no inc on back.

Row 10 (WS): CO 9 sts, p to end, slipping markers as you go—9 sts CO.

Sizes 32, 34, and 36 ONLY – Row 11 (RS): CO 16 (16, 14, x, x, x, x), x (x, x, x, x, x, x, x) sts, k to mA, smA, k1, **M1L**, k to 1 st before mB, **M1R**, k1, smB, k to mC, smC, k1, **M1L**, k to 1 st before mD, **M1R**, k1, smD, k to end—4 sts inc + 16 (16, 14, x, x, x, x), x (x, x, x, x, x, x, x) sts CO. (*Note: You will be working two inc on each sleeve and no inc on front/back until otherwise noted.*) Move ahead to **Neckline Join.**

Sizes 38, 40, 42, 44, 46, and 48 ONLY – Row 11 (RS): CO x (x, x, 14, 14, 14, 20), 20 (20, x, x, x, x, x, x) sts, k to mA, smA, k1, **M1L**, k2, **M1L**, k to 3 sts before mB, **M1R**, k2, **M1R**, k1, smB, k to mC, smC, k1, **M1L**, k2, **M1L**, k to 3 sts before mD, **M1R**, k2, **M1R**, k1, smD, k to end—8 sts inc + x (x, x, 14, 14, 14, 20), 20 (20, x, x, x, x, x, x) sts CO. (*Note: You will be working two inc on each sleeve and no inc on front/back until otherwise noted.*) Move ahead to **Neckline Join.**

Sizes 50, 52, 54, 56, 58, and 60 ONLY – Row 11 (RS): CO x (x, x, x, x, x, x), x (x, 9, 9, 9, 10, 10, 10) sts, k to mA, smA, k1, **M1L**, k2, **M1L**, k to 3 sts before mB, **M1R**, k2, **M1R**, k1, smB, k to mC, smC, k1, **M1L**, k2, **M1L**, k to 3 sts before mD, **M1R**, k2, **M1R**, k1, smD, k to end—4 sts inc on each sleeve + x (x, x, x, x, x, x), x (x, 9, 9, 9, 10, 10, 10) sts CO, no inc on back.

Row 12 (WS): CO x (x, x, x, x, x, x), x (x, 9, 9, 9, 10, 10, 10) sts, p to end, slipping markers as you go—x (x, x, x, x, x, x), x (x, 9, 9, 9, 10, 10, 10) sts CO.

Row 12 (RS): CO x (x, x, x, x, x, x), x (x, 8, 12, 16, 18, 18, 18) sts , k to mA, smA, k1, **M1L**, k2, **M1L**, k to 3 sts before mB, **M1R**, k2, **M1R**, k1, smB, k to mC, smC, k1, **M1L**, k2, **M1L**, k to 3 sts before mD, **M1R**, k2, **M1R**, k1, smD, k to end—8 sts inc + x (x, x, x, x, x, x), x (x, 8, 12, 16, 18, 18, 18) sts CO. Move ahead to **Neckline Join.**

Neckline Join

The neckline shaping is complete. Cut the working yarn, leaving a tail. Bring your needles together to form a circle and find mD. This will be your new BOR. Slide the sts after mD to the left needle so they are ready to be worked and join the working yarn at mD to begin your new rnd. Be sure to check that your sts are all positioned correctly and are not twisted (this is one of the few things that's impossible to fix later, so it's worth checking). You will initially have a small gap where you've joined at the front neckline; don't worry! You'll weave it closed when you finish the neckline later.

Next Rnd: K to end, slipping markers as you go. (You will be knitting across the two front sections as you do this, and they will be joined as one front piece at the conclusion of this rnd.)

Sizes 32, 34, and 36 ONLY – Next Rnd: K to mA, smA, k2, **M1L**, k to 2 sts before mB, **M1R**, k2, smB, k to mC, smC, k2, **M1L**, k to 2 sts before mD, **M1R**, k2—4 sts inc.

Sizes 38, 40, 42, 44, 46, 48, 50, 52, 54, 56, 58, and 60 ONLY – Next Rnd: K to mA, smA, k1, **M1L**, k2, **M1L**, k to 3 sts before mB, **M1R**, k2, **M1R**, k1, smB, k to mC, smC, k1, **M1L**, k2, **M1L**, k to 3 sts before end, **M1R**, k2, **M1R**, k1—8 sts inc.

All Sizes Next Rnd (no inc): K to end, slipping markers as you go.

Stitch Count Check-In

Front: 66 (66, 72, 72, 72, 72, 78), 78 (78, 84, 88, 92, 96, 96, 96)

Sleeves (ea): 20 (20, 24, 34, 34, 36, 40), 40 (42, 48, 48, 50, 50, 50, 50)

Back: 66 (66, 72, 72, 72, 72, 78), 78 (78, 84, 88, 92, 96, 96, 96)

All Sizes Next Rnd (inc): K20 (20, 23, 23, 23, 23, 26), 26 (26, 29, 31, 33, 35, 35, 35), pm1, work Water Lily panel (beginning with Round 1 of chart or written instructions, worked over 26 sts), pm2, k20 (20, 23, 23, 23, 23, 26), 26 (26, 29, 31, 33, 35, 35, 35), smA, k1, **M1L**, k to 1 st before mB, **M1R**, k1, smB, k to mC, smC, k1, **M1L**, to 1 st before mD, **M1R**, k1—4 sts inc.

All Sizes Next Round (no inc): K to m1, sm, work Waterlily panel (next rnd) to m2, sm2, k to end, slipping markers as you go.

Rep the last two rnds, following the chart panel instructions between m1 and m2 and repeating chart rows 1–10 until you reach the following stitch count and have just completed a "no inc" rnd.

Stitch Count Check-In

Front: 66 (66, 72, 72, 72, 72, 78), 78 (78, 84, 88, 92, 96, 96, 96)—no change

Sleeves: 56 (54, 58, 66, 66, 66, 70), 72 (74, 76, 78, 80, 82, 84, 84)

Back: 66 (66, 72, 72, 72, 72, 78), 78 (78, 84, 88, 92, 96, 96, 96)—no change

Next Rnd (extra inc): K1, **M1L**, k2, **M1L**, k to m1, sm1, work chart (next rnd), sm2, k to 3 sts before mA, **M1R**, k2, **M1R**, k1, smA, k1, **M1L**, k to 1 st before mB, **M1R**, k1, smB, k1, **M1L**, k2, **M1L**, k to 3 sts before mC, **M1R**, k2, **M1R**, k1, smC, k1, **M1L**, k to 1 st before mD, **M1R**, k1—12 sts inc.

Next Rnd (no inc): K to m1, sm1, work chart (next rnd), sm2, k to end, slipping markers as you go.

Rep these two rnds until you reach the following stitch count and have just completed a "no inc" rnd.

Stitch Count Check-In

Front: 82 (82, 88, 88, 92, 92, 98), 98 (98, 104, 112, 116, 124, 116, 120)

Sleeves (ea): 64 (62, 66, 74, 76, 76, 80), 82 (84, 86, 90, 92, 96, 94, 96)

Back: 82 (82, 88, 88, 92, 92, 98), 98 (98, 104, 112, 116, 124, 116, 120)

Next Rnd (double extra inc): K1, [**M1L**, k2] twice, **M1L**, k to m1, sm1, work chart (next rnd), sm2, k to 5 sts before mA, [**M1R**, k2] twice, **M1R**, k1, smA, k1, **M1L**, k to 1 st before mB, **M1R**, k1, smB, k1, [**M1L**, k2] twice, **M1L**, k to 5 sts before mC, [**M1R**, k2] twice, **M1R**, k1, smC, k1, **M1L**, k to 1 st before mD, **M1R**, k1—16 sts inc.

Next Rnd (no inc): K to m1, sm1, work chart (next rnd), sm2, k to end, slipping markers as you go.

Rep these two rounds until you reach the following stitch count and have just completed a "no inc" rnd.

Stitch Count Check-In

Front: 100 (100, 106, 112, 116, 116, 122), 128 (128, 134, 142, 146, 154, 152, 150)

Sleeves (ea): 70 (68, 72, 82, 84, 84, 88), 92 (94, 96, 100, 102, 106, 106, 106)

Back: 100 (100, 106, 112, 116, 116, 122), 128 (128, 134, 142, 146, 154, 152, 150)

Next Rnd (triple extra inc): K1, [**M1L**, k2] 3 times, **M1L**, k to m1, sm1, work chart (next rnd), sm2, k to 7 sts before mA, [**M1R**, k2] 3 times, **M1R**, k1, smA, k1, **M1L**, k to 1 st before mB, **M1R**, k1, smB, k1, [**M1L**, k2] 3 times, **M1L**, k to 7 sts before mC, [**M1R**, k2] 3 times, **M1R**, k1, smC, k1, **M1L**, k to 1 st before mD, **M1R**, k1—20 st inc.

Next Rnd (no inc): K to m1, sm1, work chart (next rnd), sm2, k to end, slipping markers as you go.

Rep these two rnds until you reach the following stitch count and have just completed a "no inc" rnd.

Stitch Count Check-In
Front: 108 (116, 122, 128, 132, 140, 146), 152 (160, 166, 174, 178, 186, 192, 198)

Sleeves (ea): 72 (72, 76, 86, 88, 90, 94), 98 (102, 104, 108, 110, 114, 116, 118)

Back: 108 (116, 122, 128, 132, 140, 146), 152 (160, 166, 174, 178, 186, 192, 198)

Divide for Sleeves
Next Rnd: K to m1, sm1, work chart (next rnd), sm2, k to mA, remove mA, place next 72 (72, 76, 86, 88, 90, 94), 98 (102, 104, 108, 110, 114, 116, 118) sts onto waste yarn (loosely, so you can try it on later). Remove mB, CO 4 (6, 6, 6, 6, 6, 6), 6 (6, 6, 6, 6, 6, 6, 6) sts under arm using e-loop (backward loop) method worked tightly and join to back sts, then k to mC. Remove mC and place next 72 (72, 76, 86, 88, 90, 94), 98 (102, 104, 108, 110, 114, 116, 118) sts onto waste yarn (loosely). CO 4 (6, 6, 6, 6, 6, 6), 6 (6, 6, 6, 6, 6, 6, 6) st under arm using e-loop (backward loop) method worked tightly. Leave mD to denote BOR.

Your sleeves have now been separated from the yoke of your sweater. You will now transition to the Lower Body.

Stitch Count Check-In
224 (244, 256, 268, 276, 292, 304), 316 (332, 344, 360, 368, 384, 396, 408) sts in lower body

Lower Body
Next Rnd: K to m1, sm1, work chart (next rnd), sm2, k to end.

Continue working the lower body in the rnd, repeating the chart rnds in order, until lower body measures 12–14 in (30.5–35.5 cm) from underarm.

Transition to US Size 2 (2.75 mm) 24–32-in (60–80-cm) circular needle—or one size smaller than needed to achieve gauge—and k one rnd.

> **Note:** If you prefer more length in the lower body, continue working in pattern to your desired length before you transition to ribbing. Keep in mind that the body will grow with blocking.

Ribbing
Next Rnd: [K2, p2] rep bet brackets to end.

Rep this rnd until your ribbed edge measures approximately 2 in (5 cm) in length. BO in pattern with medium/loose tension (not too tight, not too loose—if the lower edge feels restrictive, BO more loosely).

Neckline
Before you work the neckline, use the tail left at the neckline join to weave the gap closed. With US Size 1 (2.25 mm) 16 in (40 cm) circular needle—or two sizes smaller than needed to achieve gauge—pick up and knit approximately every available st around the neckline. PM and join to work in the rnd. Work your neckline with noticeably tighter tension than the rest of your garment.

Tip: You can adjust the size and feel of your neckline by doing one of the following: For a looser neckline, pick up every available st and ensure that your bind off is not too tight. If your neckline is too open (or your edge flares out), try picking up slightly fewer sts—such as 5 of every 6 available sts—and/or binding off a little more tightly. Necklines like this one are very easy to adjust with just a few simple changes to your technique.

Garter

Next Rnd: P to end.

Next Rnd: K to end.

Next Rnd: P to end.

Rep these two rnds twice more (for a total of 3). BO on the next rnd purlwise with medium tension. (*Note: Although you will have just finished a purl rnd, binding off again purlwise creates a beautiful edge.*)

Sleeves

Beginning with US Size 3 (3.25 mm) 12 in (30 cm) circular needle or DPNs—*or size needed to achieve gauge*—transfer the sleeve sts from waste yarn to your needles and pick up the sts cast on under arm—76 (78, 82, 92, 94, 96, 100), 104 (108, 110, 114, 116, 120, 122, 124) sts. When all sts are on your needle, PM at center of underarm and join to work in the rnd.

K one rnd.

Dec Rnd: K1, k2tog, k to last 3 sts, ssk, k1—2 st dec.

Continue working your sleeve in the rnd, decreasing every 1 (1, 1, 1, 1, 1, 1), .75 (.75, .75, .75, .75, .75, .75, .75) in / 2.5 (2.5, 2.5, 2.5, 2.5, 2.5, 2.5), 2 (2, 2, 2, 2, 2, 2, 2) cm until you reach 64 (66, 70, 80, 82, 84, 88), 88 (92, 94, 98, 100, 104, 104, 104) sts and sleeve measures approximately 6 in (15.25 cm).

Transition to US Size 2 (2.75 mm) needle—*or one size smaller than needed to achieve gauge*—and work garter edge as follows:

Garter

Next Rnd: K to end.

Next Rnd: P to end.

Rep these two rnds 3 times more (for a total of 4). BO on the next rnd knitwise with medium tension.

Rep for second sleeve.

Finishing

Weave in ends and wet block for best results. Soak in lukewarm water with a splash of fiber wash for 20 minutes to gently cleanse and relax the fiber. Press out excess water and lay the garment flat, drawing out the curves around the neckline, shoulder shaping, and arms, and being careful to smooth and straighten the edges and center panel so they dry evenly. Because of the fiber content, pinning isn't recommended.

Chart Written Directions

Rnd 1: K10, p6, k10.

Rnd 2: K2, p6, [k2, p2] twice, k2, p6, k2.

Rnd 3: K10, p2, k2, p2, k10.

Rnds 4–7: Rep Rnds 2–3.

Rnd 8: Rep Rnd 2.

Rnd 9: [K2, p2] 6 times, k2.

Rnd 10: [K2, p2] twice, k10, [p2, k2] twice.

Rnd 11: [K2, p2] twice, k2, p6, [k2, p2] twice, k2.

Rnds 12–15: Rep Rnds 10–11.

Rnd 16: Rep Rnd 10.

water lily silk pullover chart

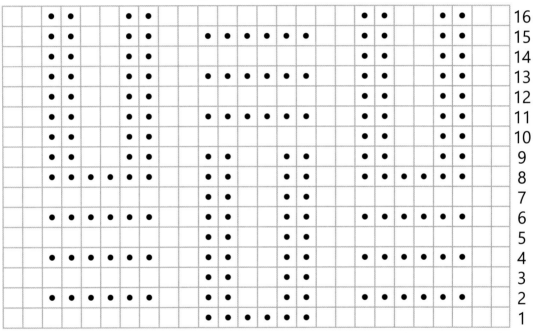

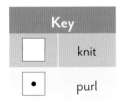

Key	
☐	knit
•	purl

minimalist designs

In my heart, I am a minimalist. I'm not sure you would agree if you looked at my yarn shelves or my cookbook collection, but when it comes to style and fashion, I prefer classic shapes and clean, modern lines. Less is more.

The patterns in this section keep the stitch details to a minimum but are, instead, elevated by key features, like the geometric shape of Alyssum (page 145) or the sassy ribbon shoulders of Dahlia (page 189). In some cases, that key feature might include the yarn choice—especially true with Lotus (page 151)—which makes the unique texture of the yarn the true star (the side ties are delightful, too). When knitting a minimalist shape, I find that yarn choice can be especially important, not only to achieve gauge and create the right fabric, but because—in some cases—it's essential to the success of the project. Certain pattern details may be less successful in other yarns, so pay careful attention to the qualities of the recommended yarns for best results.

alyssum slip-over poncho

Few of my designs start with a sketch (if you saw my drawing skills, you'd know why), but this one did—and it was all about the shape. I love geometric lines, especially in clothing; they're interesting and fun to wear, and they make a great canvas for design. Alyssum's shape offers a flattering visual for any size, and the pattern rhythm is perfect for less-focused knitting time. The recommended yarn creates a willowy fabric that's wearable as a light top layer in any weather.

sides of the neckline one at a time, then join the work again in one large piece to create a mirror image down the other side. Finishing is minimal; it requires just the slightest seaming at the sleeve edges to hold the shape in place.

Skill Level
Advanced Beginner

Construction
This geometric slip-over poncho is knit flat from side to side in one piece. Knitting begins at the sleeve edge with a seed stitch border and a stockinette stitch center with increases on either side. The work continues in one smooth piece until the middle splits for the neckline. You'll work the two

Sizes
1 (2, 3, 4, 5)

Equivalent to: 30–36 (36–42, 42–48, 48–54, 54–62) in / 76.25–91.5 (91.5–106.75, 106.75–122, 122–137.25, 137.25–157.5) cm

Fit Advice
Easy fit design intended for bust sizes 30 in (76.25 cm) to 62 in (157 cm).

Finished Measurements
A) Edge to Edge (Horizontally): 51 (53.25, 54.75, 57, 58.5) in / 129.75 (135.25, 139.25, 144.5, 148.75) cm – blocked

B) Top of Shoulder to Lowest Point: 18.25 (20.25, 22.25, 23.5, 25.25) in / 45.75 (50.25, 55.25, 59, 63) cm – blocked

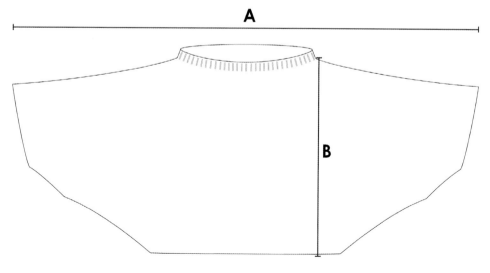

Abbreviations	
[ ]	brackets indicate a repeat
bet	between
BO	bind off
BOR	beginning of row/round
CO	cast on
dec	decrease/decreases/decreased
inc	increase/increases/increased
k	knit
k2tog	knit two stitches together (dec 1)
m	marker
M1L	make one stitch, left leaning (dec 1)
M1R	make one stitch, right leaning (dec 1)
p	purl
p2tog	purl two stitches together (inc 1)
PM	place marker
rep	repeat
RS	right side
sl	slip
sl2-k1-p2sso	slip two stitches together as if to knit, knit the next stitch, then pass the two slipped stitches over the knit stitch; this is also known as a centered double decrease (dec 2)
sm	slip marker
ssk	slip one st knitwise, slip the next st knitwise, then return the two sts back to the left needle and knit the two together through the back loop (dec 1)
st/s	stitch/stitches
WS	wrong side

Materials	
Yarn	Light DK Weight | Berroco Remix® Light | 30% Nylon, 27% Cotton, 24% Acrylic, 10% Silk, 9% Linen | 432 yards (395 meters) in 3.5 oz (100 grams) | 1425 (1550, 1675, 1810, 1955) yards / 1303 (1417, 1531, 1654, 1787) meters | **Color:** Birch **Note:** Variations in yarn choice or row/round gauge may impact yarn consumption. If in doubt, round up to the nearest skein.
Needles	**Body:** US Size 5 (3.75 mm)* 32–40-in (80–100-cm) circular needle **Neckline:** US Size 2 (2.75 mm) 24-in (60-cm) circular needle *Or size needed to achieve gauge. Adjust other needle sizes accordingly.*
Notions	Stitch markers (including locking markers) Waste yarn or spare needle for holding stitches Blocking pins and mats Darning needle to weave ends and seam sleeve edges
Gauge	22 sts and 30 rows in 4 in (10 cm) in stockinette stitch with larger needle, blocked—*row gauge is less critical but may affect yarn consumption.*

alyssum slip-over poncho pattern

With US Size 5 (3.75 mm) 32–40-in (80–100-cm) circular needle—*or size needed to achieve gauge*—CO 77 (89, 105, 113, 125) sts using cable cast-on method. Do not join in the rnd. (*Note: The cable cast-on begins your work immediately on the RS.*)

Set-Up Row 1 (RS): K1, [p1, k1] rep bet brackets to end.

Set-Up Row 2 (WS): K1, [p1, k1] rep bet brackets to end.

Row 1 (RS): K1, **M1R**, p1, [k1, p1] rep bet brackets to last st, **M1L**, k1—2 sts inc.

Row 2 (WS): P1, [k1, p1] rep bet brackets to end.

Row 3 (RS): K1, **M1R**, k1, [p1, k1] rep bet brackets to last st, **M1L**, k1—2 sts inc.

Row 4 (WS): K1, [p1, k1] rep bet brackets to end.

Rep these four rows until you reach 121 (133, 149, 157, 169) sts.

Next Row (RS): K1, [p1, k1] 10 times, PM, **M1R**, k79 (91, 107, 115, 127), **M1L**, PM, [k1, p1] 10 times, k1—2 sts inc.

Next Row (WS): K1, [p1, k1] 10 times, sm, p to m, sm, [k1, p1] 10 times, k1.

Rep these two rows (slipping markers on the RS repeats, after the initial placement) until you reach 201 (221, 243, 259, 277) sts.

Next Row (RS): K1, [p1, k1] 10 times, sm, k80 (90, 101, 109, 118), stop.

Place remaining sts onto a long separate needle or waste yarn—you will return to work them later. You will now work back and forth (flat) just on this half section of the poncho for now.

Front Half

Next Row (WS): P to m, sm, [k1, p1] 10 times, k1.

Next Row (RS): K1, [p1, k1] 10 times, sm, k to end.

Next Row (WS): P to m, sm, [k1, p1] 10 times, k1.

Rep these two rows until this section measures 18 in (46 cm) from where you separated it from the other side, ending after a WS row (ready to work a RS row).

Place these sts onto a long separate needle or waste yarn while you return to the other half section.

Back Half

Return the other half section to your needles, and rejoin yarn ready to work a RS row, with the BOR being at the center with the split.

Next Row (RS): K to m, sm, [k1, p1] 10 times, k1.

Next Row (WS): K1, [p1, k1] 10 times, sm, p to end.

Rep these two rows until this section measures 18 in (46 cm) from where you separated it from the other section and is equal in length to the other half section, ending after a WS row (ready to work a RS row).

Cut working yarn, replace held sts from first half section onto needle ready to work RS row, and rejoin at the original start of the row.

Next Row (RS): K1, [p1, k1] 10 times, sm, k to end of this first piece, then k across the second piece so that the two sections have been brought back together into one single piece. Continue knitting across second piece to the next marker, sm, [k1, p1] 10 times, k1.

Next Row (WS): K1, [p1, k1] 10 times, sm, p to m, sm, [k1, p1] 10 times, k1.

Next Row (RS): K1, [p1, k1] 10 times, sm, ssk, k to 2 st before m, k2tog, sm, [k1, p1] 10 times, k1—2 sts dec.

Next Row (WS): K1, [p1, k1] 10 times, sm, p to m, sm, [k1, p1] 10 times, k1.

Rep these two rows until you reach 121 (133, 149, 157, 169) sts. Remove markers before you continue.

Next Row (RS): K1, ssk, p1, [k1, p1] rep bet brackets to last 3 sts, k2tog, k1—2 sts dec.

Next Row (WS): P1, [k1, p1] rep bet brackets to end.

Next Row (RS): K1, p2tog, k1, [p1, k1] rep bet brackets to last 3 sts, p2tog, k1.

Next Row (WS): K1, [p1, k1] rep bet brackets to end.

Rep these four rows until you reach 77 (89, 105, 113, 125) sts.

BO all sts knitwise.

Neckline

With US Size 2 (2.75 mm) 24-in (60-cm) circular needle—*or three sizes smaller than needed to achieve gauge*—and starting at the shoulder on one side, pick up and knit approximately 4 of every 5 available sts around the neckline, ending with a multiple of 4 sts on each side (front and back). Join to work in the rnd and PM for BOR.

As you proceed, you will begin working centered double decreases at each shoulder point; these dec should be centered at the top of each shoulder and will include 2 sts before the marker and 1 st after. As you proceed, some sts of the ribbed pattern will be eliminated by dec—work the other sts as they are presented.

Ribbing

Rnd 1: [K2, p2] rep bet brackets to opposite shoulder point, PM, [k2, p2] rep bet brackets to end of rnd.

Rnd 2: Working sts as presented (you will still be working in ribbing but will adapt as the sts at the shoulder points are dec) to 2 sts before m, sl2-k1-p2sso (reposition side marker to sit after the dec), then work sts as presented to last 2 sts, sl2-k1-p2sso (reposition the BOR marker to sit after the dec). This dec consumes the first st of the next rnd—4 sts dec.

Rnd 3: Work sts as presented to end.

Rnd 4: Work sts as presented to 2 sts before m, sl2-k1-p2sso (reposition the marker to sit after the dec), work sts as presented to last 2 sts, sl2-k1-p2sso (reposition the BOR marker to sit after the dec). This dec consumes the first st of the next rnd—4 sts dec.

Rep Rnds 3 and 4 until ribbed edge measures approximately 2 in (5 cm). If you'd like a smaller neckline, continue for an additional 1–2 in (2.5–5 cm). BO in pattern with medium tension.

Finishing & Blocking

Weave in ends on the WS. Wet block for best results. Soak in lukewarm water with a splash of fiber wash for 20 minutes to gently cleanse and relax the fiber. Press out excess water, and lay flat, pinning around the perimeter and drawing the edges taut and even. Because of the single layer, it should dry quickly in a warm place and should not need to be turned during drying.

After blocking is complete, fold the poncho in half lengthwise (as shown in Figure A). If you imagine the arrow on the illustration going straight across the entire piece, that is where you will fold.

Use mattress stitch to seam a 6-in (15-cm) section of the underside of each sleeve together where the front and back pieces meet (as shown in Figure B). See seaming and grafting tutorials on my website here: oliveknits.com/grafting.

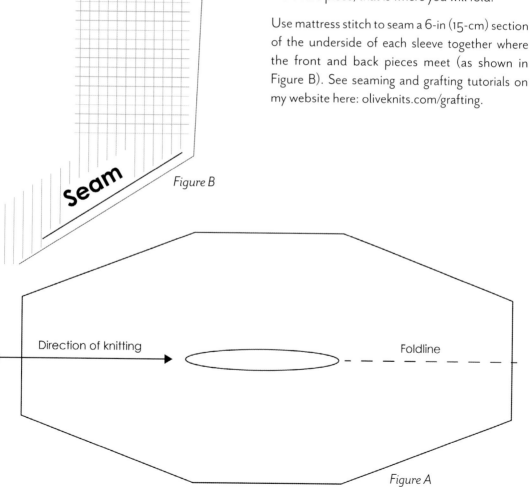

Seam

Figure B

Direction of knitting

Foldline

Figure A

lotus side-tie tee

If movement can be meditation, then surely knitting is the ideal way to unwind. The steady click of the needles, the glide of the yarn, the texture of the fiber—together they create a wonderful rhythm for finding your happy place. While I love different projects for different reasons, I try to keep a mindless pattern on my needles for times when I just need to keep my hands busy. The effortless shape and style of this top give the yarn an opportunity to take center stage; it really is the star of the show. The slightly nubby, thick-and-thin texture of the mostly cotton yarn creates an interesting, lightweight fabric that lays beautifully in place without the support of a traditional edge-like ribbing. The open sides and charming i-cord ties add extra airflow for a casual, summery vibe.

Skill
Advanced Beginner

Construction
This easy breezy top-down raglan is knit in the round (no seams!), and features mostly stockinette stitch, making it the perfect project for knitting on the go. The real stars of this design are the split side panels, which are worked flat in the lower body and tied closed with classic i-cord for a simple, charming finish. This is the perfect quick-knit top, with easy details that make it ideal for someone new to sweater knitting. (Although it's just as lovely for anyone looking for a quick project.) The body is slightly cropped, making it perfect to wear over a sundress or camisole, but you can easily add length as you go.

Size
1 (2, 3, 4, 5, 6), 7 (8, 9, 10, 11, 12)

Fit Advice
Lotus is designed to fit with about 2–3 in (5–7.5 cm) positive ease, depending on how you like to wear your tops. Choose the size with the finished bust circumference that is about 2–3 in (5–7.5 cm) larger than your actual full bust measurement. For added help, refer to Chapter 2: Planning for a Great Fit (page 13), to help determine your size. Note that the ties in the lower body are a bonus for those with ample hips—the open sides and ties provide the flexibility of several potential inches/cm of extra room around the waist and/or hip area.

Finished Measurements
A) Bust Circumference: 36 (39.25, 40.75, 43.25, 44.75, 48), 50.5 (52, 53.5, 56, 57.5, 60) in / 90 (98, 102, 108, 112, 120), 126 (130, 134, 140, 144, 150) cm – blocked

B) Yoke Depth: 9.5 (9.75, 10.25, 10.5, 10.75, 11), 11.5 (11.75, 12.25, 12.5, 13, 13) in / 23.5 (24.5, 25.75, 26.5, 27, 28), 28.75 (29.25, 30.5, 31, 32.5, 32.5) cm – blocked

C) Underarm to Hem: 11 (11, 12, 12, 13, 13), 14 (14, 14, 14, 14, 14) in / 27.5 (27.5, 30, 30, 32.5, 32.5), 35 (35, 35, 35, 35, 35) cm – prior to blocking

D) Sleeve Circumference: 11.5 (12.75, 13.5, 14, 14.5, 15.25) 15.5 (16, 16.75, 17.25, 18, 18) in / 29 (32, 34, 35, 36, 38), 39 (40, 42, 43, 45, 45) cm – blocked

(Continued)

E) Cuff Circumference: 11.25 (12.5, 13.25, 13.5, 14, 14.75), 15.25 (15.5, 16.5, 16.75, 17.5, 17.5) in / 28 (31, 33, 34, 35, 37), 38 (39, 41, 42, 44, 44) cm – blocked

F) Sleeve Length from Underarm: 3 in (7.5 cm) – prior to blocking

G) Neck Circumference: 17.25 (20, 20.5, 21.25, 21.75, 22.5), 22.5 (23.75, 24.25, 25.75, 26.5, 27) in / 42.75 (50, 51.5, 52.75, 54.75, 56), 56 (59.25, 60.75, 64.75, 66, 67.25) cm – blocked

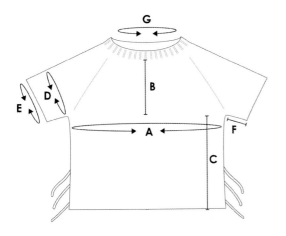

inc	increase/increases/increased
k	knit
k2tog	knit two stitches together (dec 1)
k3tog	knit three stitches together (dec 2)
kfb	knit into the front and back of next st (inc 1)
m	marker/markers
M1L	make one stitch, left leaning (inc 1)
M1R	make one stitch, right leaning (inc 1)
mX	marker "X" denotes which marker (mA, mB, mC, etc...)
p	purl
pfb	purl into the front and back of next st (inc 1)
pmX	place marker "X" denotes which marker (pmA, pmB, pmC, etc...)
rep	repeat
rnd	round/rounds
RS	right side
smX	slip marker "X" denotes which marker (smA, smB, smC, etc...)
ssk	slip one st knitwise, slip the next st knitwise, then return the two sts back to the left needle and knit the two together through the back loop (dec 1)
st	stitch/stitches
WS	wrong side
x	denotes sizes not represented in this line of instruction

Abbreviations	
[ ]	brackets indicate a repeat
Bet	between
BO	bind off
BOR	beginning of row/round
CO	cast on
dec	decrease/decreases/decreased
ea	each

Materials

Yarn	DK Weight | Berroco Meraki | 71% Cotton, 24% Hemp, 5% Polyester | 131 yards (120 meters) in 1.76 oz (50 grams) | 775 (822, 871, 923, 978, 1037), 1099 (1165, 1235, 1309, 1405, 1480) yards / 708 (751, 796, 844, 894, 948), 1005 (1065, 1129, 1197, 1284, 1353) meters | **Color:** Create **Note:** Variations in yarn choice or row/round gauge may impact yarn consumption. If in doubt, round up to the nearest skein.
Needles	**Yoke and Body:** US Size 7 (4.5 mm)* 24–32-in (60–80-cm) circular needle **Neckline:** US Size 4 (3.5 mm) 16-in (40-cm) circular needle **Sleeves:** US Size 7 (4.5 mm) 12-in (30-cm) circular needle or DPNs **I-Cord Ties:** US Size 4 (3.5 mm) DPNs or straight needles *Or size needed to achieve gauge. Adjust other needle sizes accordingly.*
Notions	Stitch markers Waste yarn or spare needles, for holding stitches Blocking pins and mats Darning needle to weave in ends **A note about markers:** Markers are labeled to make them easier to differentiate. Markers A, B, C, and D will mark the raglan "seams" or increase sections that separate the front, sleeves, and back.
Gauge	20 sts and 24 rows/rounds in 4 in (10 cm) in stockinette stitch with largest needle, blocked

lotus side-tie tee pattern

With US Size 7 (4.5 mm) 24-in (60-cm) circular needle—*or size needed to achieve gauge*—CO 74 (88, 92, 94, 104, 106), 106 (112, 116, 124, 128, 130) st using cable cast-on method. Do not join in the rnd yet. (*Note: the cable cast-on begins your work immediately on the RS.*)

Note: You will work the pattern flat for a few rows to create the shaped neckline (This is a technique I "unvented" many years ago—as Elizabeth Zimmerman would say—in order to create a beautifully shaped neckline without short rows.); the pattern will indicate when to join in the rnd to continue your work. You will shape the neckline with new sts cast on at the start of each row until the shaping is complete. You will then join your sts to work in the rnd and will reposition your working yarn as indicated when the time comes.

Set-Up Row (RS): K3, pmA, k12 (16, 18, 18, 20, 20), 20 (22, 24, 26, 28, 28), pmB, k44 (50, 50, 52, 58, 60), 60 (62, 62, 66, 66, 68), pmC, k12 (16, 18, 18, 20, 20), 20 (22, 24, 26, 28, 28), pmD, k3.

Set-Up Row (WS): P to end, slipping markers as you go.

Row 1 (RS): CO 5 sts using knitted cast-on method worked knitwise (tightly)*, k to mA, smA, k1, **M1L**, k to 1 st before mB, **M1R**, k1, smB, k1, **M1L**, k to 1 st before mC, **M1R**, k1, smC, k1, **M1L**, k to 1 st before mD, **M1R**, k1, smD, k to end—6 sts inc + 5 sts CO.

Row 2 (WS): CO 5 st using knitted cast-on worked purlwise (tightly)*, p to end, slipping markers as you go—5 sts CO.

Going forward, CO any additional sts on the RS using the knitted cast-on method worked knitwise (tightly), and any additional sts on the WS using the knitted cast-on method worked purlwise (tightly).

Row 3 (RS): CO 7 (7, 7, 7, 9, 9), 9 (5, 5, 7, 7, 7) sts, k to mA, smA, k1, **M1L**, k to 1 st before mB, **M1R**, k1, smB, k1, **M1L**, k to 1 st before mC, **M1R**, k1, smC, k1, **M1L**, k to 1 st before mD, **M1R**, k1, smD, k to end—6 sts inc + 7 (7, 7, 7, 9, 9), 9 (5, 5, 7, 7, 7) sts CO.

Row 4 (WS): CO 7 (7, 7, 9, 9), 9 (5, 5, 7, 7, 7) sts, p to end, slipping markers as you go—7 (7, 7, 7, 9, 9), 9 (5, 5, 7, 7, 7) sts CO.

Stitch Count Check-In

Fronts (ea): 15 (15, 15, 15, 17, 17), 17 (13, 13, 15, 15, 15)

Sleeves (ea): 16 (20, 22, 22, 24, 24), 24 (26, 28, 30, 32, 32)

Back: 48 (54, 54, 56, 62, 64), 64 (66, 66, 70, 70, 72)

Row 5 (RS): CO 6 (6, 6, 6, 8, 8), 8 (6, 6, 6, 6, 6) sts, k to 1 st before mA, **M1R**, k1, smA, k1, **M1L**, k to 1 st before mB, **M1R**, k1, smB, k1, **M1L**, k to 1 st before mC, **M1R**, k1, smC, k1, **M1L**, k to 1 st before mD, **M1R**, k1, smD, k1, **M1L**, k to end—8 sts inc + 6 (6, 6, 6, 8, 8), 8 (6, 6, 6, 6, 6) sts CO.

Row 6 (WS): CO 6 (6, 6, 6, 8, 8), 8 (6, 6, 6, 6, 6) sts, p to end, slipping markers as you go—6 (6, 6, 6, 8, 8), 8 (6, 6, 6, 6, 6) sts CO.

Sizes 1, 2, 3, 4, 5, 6, and 7 ONLY – Row 7 (RS): CO 6 (12, 12, 14, 12, 14), 14 (x, x, x, x, x) sts, k to 1 st before mA, **M1R**, k1, smA, k1, **M1L**, k to 1 st before mB, **M1R**, k1, smB, k1, **M1L**, k to 1 st before mC, **M1R**, k1, smC, k1, **M1L**, k to 1 st before mD, **M1R**, k1, smD, k1, **M1L**, k to end—8 sts inc + 6 (12, 12, 14, 12, 14), 14 (x, x, x, x, x) sts CO. Move ahead to **Neckline Join**.

Sizes 8, 9, 10, 11, and 12 ONLY – Row 7 (RS): CO 8 sts, k to 1 st before mA, **M1R**, k1, smA, k1, **M1L**, k to 1 st before mB, **M1R**, k1, smB, k1, **M1L**, k to 1 st before mC, **M1R**, k1, smC, k1, **M1R**, k to 1 st before mD, **M1L**, k1, smD, k1, **M1R**, k to end—8 sts inc + 8 sts CO.

Row 8 (WS): CO 8 sts, p to end, slipping markers as you go—8 sts CO.

Row 9 (RS): CO x (x, x, x, x, x), x (12, 12, 12, 12, 14) sts, k to 1 st before mA, **M1R**, k1, smA, k1, **M1L**, k to 1 st before mB, **M1R**, k1, smB, k1, **M1L**, k to 1 st before mC, **M1R**, k1, smC, k1, **M1L**, k to 1 st before mD, **M1R**, k1, smD, k1, **M1L**, k to end—8 sts inc + x (x, x, x, x, x), x (12, 12, 12, 12, 14) sts CO. Move ahead to **Neckline Join**.

Neckline Join

The neckline shaping is complete. Cut the working yarn, leaving a tail. Bring your needles together to form a circle and find mD. This will be your new BOR. Slide the sts after mD to the left needle so they are ready to be worked and join the working yarn at mD to begin your new rnd. Be sure to check that your sts are all positioned correctly and are not twisted (this is one of the few things that's impossible to fix later, so it's worth checking). You will initially have a small gap where you've joined at the front neckline; don't worry! You'll weave it closed when you finish the neckline later.

Next Rnd (no inc): Starting at your new BOR (at mD), k to end of rnd, slipping markers as you go.

Stitch Count Check-In

Front: 52 (58, 58, 60, 66, 68), 68 (72, 72, 76, 76, 78)

Sleeves (ea): 20 (24, 26, 26, 28, 28), 28 (32, 34, 36, 38, 38)

Back: 52 (58, 58, 60, 66, 68), 68 (72, 72, 76, 76, 78)

Next Rnd (inc): K1, **M1L**, k to 1 st before mA, **M1R**, k1, smA, k1, **M1L**, k to 1 st before mB, **M1R**, k1, smB, k1, **M1L**, k to 1 st before mC, **M1R**, k1, smC, k1, **M1L**, k to 1 st before mD, **M1R**, k1—8 sts inc.

Next Rnd (no inc): K to end, slipping markers as you go.

Rep these two rnds until you reach the following number and have just completed a "no inc" rnd:

Stitch Count Check-In

Front: 90 (96, 96, 98, 106, 108), 108 (108, 110, 112, 112, 112)

Sleeves (ea): 58 (62, 64, 64, 68, 68), 68 (68, 72, 72, 74, 72)

Back: 90 (96, 96, 98, 106, 108), 108 (108, 110, 112, 112, 112)

Notes: Transition to longer circular needles when necessary for sts to move comfortably.

As you proceed you will see an "x" as a placeholder for sizes that are no longer represented on that rnd.

Sizes 1 and 2 ONLY – Move ahead to **Divide for Sleeves** on page 156.

All Other Sizes Continue

Next Rnd (extra inc): K1, **M1L**, k2, **M1L**, k to 3 sts before mA, **M1R**, k2, **M1R**, k1, smA, k1, **M1L**, k to 1 st before mB, **M1R**, k1, smB, k1, **M1L**, k2, **M1L**, k to 3 sts before mC, **M1R**, k2, **M1R**, k1, smC, k1, **M1L**, k to 1 st before mD, **M1R**, k1—12 sts inc (4 sts inc on each front and back, 2 sts inc on each sleeve).

Next Rnd (no inc): K to end, slipping markers as you go.

Rep these two rnds x (x, 0, 1, 0, 1), 1 (2, 1, 2, 3, 3) time(s) more, for a total of x (x, 1, 2, 1, 2), 2 (3, 2, 3, 4, 5).

Stitch Count Check-In

Front: x (x, 100, 106, 110, 116), 116 (120, 118, 124, 128, 128)

Sleeves (ea): x (x, 66, 68, 70, 72), 72 (74, 76, 78, 82, 80)

Back: x (x, 100, 106, 110, 116), 116 (120, 118, 124, 128, 128)

Sizes 3, 4, 5, and 6 ONLY – Move ahead to **Divide for Sleeves** on page 156.

All Other Sizes Continue

Next Rnd (double extra inc): K1, **M1L**, [k2, **M1L**] twice, k to 5 sts before mA, **M1R**, [k2, **M1R**] twice, k1, smA, k1, **M1L**, k to 1 st before mB, **M1R**, k1, smB, k1, **M1L**, [k2, **M1L**] twice, k to 5 sts before mC, **M1R**, [k2, **M1R**] twice, k1, smC, k1, **M1L**, k to 1 st before mD, **M1R**, k1—16 sts inc (6 sts inc on each front and back, 2 sts inc on each sleeve).

Next Rnd (no inc): K to end, slipping markers as you go.

Rep these two rnds x (x, x, x, x, x), 0, (0, 1, 1, 1, 2) time(s) more—for a total of x (x, x, x, x, x), 1, (1, 2, 2, 2, 3).

Stitch Count Check-In
Front: x (x, x, x, x, x), 122 (126, 130, 136, 140, 146)

Sleeves (ea): x (x, x, x, x, x), 74 (76, 80, 82, 86, 86)

Back: x (x, x, x, x, x), 122 (126, 130, 136, 140, 146)

All Sizes – Move ahead to **Divide for Sleeves**.

Divide for Sleeves
Before separating the sleeves from the body, you should have the following number of sts:

Stitch Count Check-In
Front: 90 (96, 100, 106, 110, 116), 122 (126 (130, 136, 140, 146)

Sleeves (ea): 58 (62, 66, 68, 70, 72), 74 (76, 80, 82, 86, 86)

Back: 90 (96, 100, 106, 110, 116), 122 (126 (130, 136, 140, 146)

Next Rnd: K to mA, remove marker, place next 58 (62, 66, 68, 70, 72), 74 (76, 80, 82, 86, 86) sts (between mA and mB) on waste yarn (loosely, so you can try it on later). Remove mB, CO 0 (2, 2, 2, 2, 4), 4 (4, 4, 4, 4, 4) sts under arm using e-loop (backward loop) method worked tightly and join to back sts, then k to mC. Remove mC and place next 58 (62, 66, 68, 70, 72), 74 (76,

80, 82, 86, 86) sts onto waste yarn (loosely). Remove mD, CO 0 (2, 2, 2, 2, 4), 4 (4, 4, 4, 4, 4) sts under arm using e-loop (backward loop) method worked tightly. Place your new BOR marker at the center of these newly cast-on sts—this will be the start of each rnd going forward.

Your sleeves have now been separated from the yoke of your sweater. You will now transition to the Lower Body.

Stitch Count Check-In
180 (196, 204, 216, 224, 240), 252 (260, 268, 280, 288, 300) sts in lower body

Lower Body
Work the lower body in stockinette st (knitting every rnd) until body measures 5 (5, 5, 5, 6, 6), 6 (7, 7, 7, 7, 7) in / 12.75 (12.75, 12.75, 12.75, 15.25, 15.25),15.25 (17.75, 17.75, 17.75, 17.75, 17.75) cm from underarm join. On the next rnd, transition to working flat as follows:

Next Rnd: K90 (98, 102, 108, 112, 120), 126 (130, 134, 140, 144, 150) sts across the front of your top, stop. Place remaining sts onto a separate needle or waste yarn (you will return to work them later). You will work back and forth (flat) on the front section (only) for now.

Front
Next Row (WS): P1, pfb, p to last 2 sts, pfb, p1—92 (100, 104, 110, 114, 122), 128 (132, 136, 142, 146, 152) sts (2 sts inc).

Next Row (RS): K to end.

Next Row (WS): P to end.

Rep these two rows until front measures 11 (11, 12, 12, 13, 13), 14 (14, 14, 14, 14, 14) in / 27.5 (27.5, 30, 30, 32.5, 32.5), 35 (35, 35, 35, 35, 35) cm from underarm, ending after a WS row. If you prefer a longer top, feel free to knit to your preferred length. BO using i-cord bind off (see page 158). Return the 90 (98, 102, 108, 112, 120), 126 (130, 134, 140, 144, 150) sts of the back to your needles and rejoin yarn, ready to work a RS row.

Back

Next Row (RS): K1, kfb, k to last 2 sts, kfb, k1—92 (100, 104, 110, 114, 122), 128 (132, 136, 142, 146, 152) sts (2 sts inc).

Next Row (WS): P to end.

Next Row (RS): K to end.

Rep these two rows until back section measures 11 (11, 12, 12, 13, 13), 14 (14, 14, 14, 14, 14) in / 27.5 (27.5, 30, 30, 32.5, 32.5), 35 (35, 35, 35, 35, 35) cm from underarm and is equal in length to the front (not including the bind off), ending after a WS row. BO using i-cord bind off.

Neckline

With US Size 4 (3.5 mm) 16-in (40-cm) circular needle—*or three sizes smaller than needed to achieve gauge*—pick up and knit approximately 7 of every 8 available sts around the neckline for sizes 1–4. For sizes 5–12, pick up and knit approximately 5 of every 6 available sts around the neckline. All sizes should end with a multiple of 4. PM and join to work in the rnd. Your ribbing should be a tighter gauge than the body of your tee.

Ribbing

Next Rnd: [K2, p2] rep bet brackets to end.

Rep this rnd until ribbing measures 1.5 in (3.75 cm). BO in pattern with medium tension.

Tip: You can adjust the size and feel of your neckline by doing one of the following: For a looser neckline, pick up every available st and ensure that your bind off is not too tight. If your neckline is too open (or your ribbing flares out), try picking up slightly fewer sts and/or binding off a little more tightly. Necklines like this one are very easy to adjust with just a few simple changes to your technique.

Sleeves

With US Size 7 (4.5 mm) 12-in (30-cm) circular needle or DPNs—*or size needed to achieve gauge*—return held sts to the needle and pick up the sts cast on under arm. When all sts are on your needle, PM at center of underarm and join to k in the rnd—58 (64, 68, 70, 72, 76), 78 (80, 84, 86, 90, 90) sts.

Work in stockinette st (knitting every rnd) for 1.5 in (3.75 cm).

Dec Rnd: K1, k2tog, k to 3 st before m, ssk, k1—56 (62, 66, 68, 70, 74), 76 (78, 82, 84, 88, 88) sts.

Continue even in established pattern until sleeve measures 3 in (7.5 cm). BO knitwise with medium tension.

Rep for second sleeve.

Side Ties

Use locking markers to mark three evenly spaced intervals along the side edge of the split sections on your top. (See illustration on page 152.) Mark corresponding points so that the front and back sections line up where you've marked, and the marks are symmetrical on the opposite side.

With US Size 4 (3.5 mm) DPNs, and starting with the first side on the front, join working yarn and k into one leg of the st just above your first marker. Then k into one leg of the next st (this should be where you've placed your marker). Then k into the st below the marker—3 sts. Work i-cord over these 3 sts (see instructions in following section) until the cord measures about 5 in (12.5 cm). K3tog, then draw the thread through the final st and cut working yarn. Rep this process, working 3 matching i-cords (in all) along the left front side of the lower body, right front side of the lower body, and along both sides of the back to match the front. You should have 12 ties altogether. (You can adjust the number of ties to suit your preference.)

How to Knit I-Cord

Beginning with the smaller DPNs and your 3 sts on one needle, slide the 3 sts to the right side of your needle, and bring the working yarn around the back to work a new RS row. Pull it tight—do not work a WS row. [K 3 sts. Slide the 3 sts back to the right side of your needle and draw the working yarn around the back so it's repositioned to work another RS row. Pull the yarn tight.] Repeat these instructions (within brackets) until your cord is the desired length. The trick is that you are never working a WS row, and you should always pull the yarn very tight when you bring it across the WS to work the next row.

Blocking

Weave in ends on the WS and wet block for best results. Soak in lukewarm water with a splash of fiber wash for at least 30 minutes to gently cleanse and relax the fiber. Press out excess water, lay flat, and smooth into place. Pin along the neckline where the ribbing meets the stockinette, along the sleeve edges, down the flat portions of the sides, and along the lower i-cord edges to ensure that your tee dries flat and even. Be sure your side ties are not tied during blocking so they can dry completely. Turn as needed for even drying.

When dry, gently tie the side ties to close the open side panels as much or as little as you like.

poppy dotted top

If you want to make a floral statement, poppies are the way to go. The vibrant, paper-thin petals are winsome and colorful, and they're gorgeous with absolutely anything. My neighbors have a spray of poppies right at the corner of their yard, and I swoon every time they're in bloom. While poppies do come in a range of colors, I always associate them with that brilliant red orange—the same color I chose for this sample. I love vivid color any time of year, but especially for a piece like this one, where the shape itself begs to be noticed. If you've never worn a batwing shape, I think it might surprise you. I've seen this shape on a variety of body types and sizes, and it offers a flattering, modern silhouette that you can wear absolutely anywhere. I love so many of the pieces I designed for this book, but I designed this one for myself; I hope you love it as much as I do.

Skill Level
Advanced Beginner

Construction
This figure-flattering top is knit from the bottom up, with paced increases as the fabric moves to the underarm to create a generous batwing shape. The upper body features a spray of simple flower stitches on a background of stockinette stitch. The half sleeves are worked right into the fabric as you go, and the upper body is worked flat in sections (front and back). The lower body is meant to be slightly cropped—this is part of the batwing shape and important to ensure that the piece fits properly (the generous shape and fit of the fabric will naturally create more length when it's blocked and worn). It might be tempting, but I don't recommend adding extra length in the body (the design will swallow you if you do), but if you do prefer your top a little longer, you can squeeze in an extra inch or two just after the lower ribbing (before you begin the increases). Lower body length is determined by your row gauge, however, so keep this in mind when measuring your swatch, and adjust accordingly. Note that the sizing for this design is unique compared to traditional shapes; when in doubt, start with your hip measurement. (The shape of the upper body is quite forgiving of bellies and busts!)

Sizes
S/M (L, XL, 2X, 3X, 4X, 5/6X)

Fit Advice
Designed to be worn with significant positive ease in the upper body, but because of the unique shape, it will feel relaxed rather than oversized. The upper body measurements encompass not only the "bust" but also the batwing shape, so it's easier to choose a size based on your hip circumference, rather than your bust size. Choose the size that most closely matches your actual hip circumference for best fit.

Finished Measurements

A) Hip Circumference: 35.25 (39, 43, 46.75, 51.25, 55, 59) in / 88 (97.5, 107.25, 116.75, 128, 137.5, 147.25) cm – blocked

B) Wingtip to Wingtip (Including Cuff Ribbing): 35.75 (37, 38, 39.25, 40.25, 42, 44) in / 84.25 (87.5, 89.75, 93, 95.5, 100.25, 105) cm – blocked

C) Armhole Depth: 6.75 (6.75, 7, 7, 7.25, 7.5, 7.75) in / 17.25 (17.25, 17.75, 17.75, 18.5, 19, 19.75) cm – blocked

D) Underarm to Hem: 10 (10, 10.5, 11, 12.5, 13, 14) in / 25 (25, 26.25, 27.5, 31, 32.25, 35) cm – prior to blocking

E) Cuff Circumference (Hits at Elbow): 13.5 (13.5, 14, 14, 14.5, 15, 15.5) in / 34.5 (34.5, 35.5, 35.5, 37, 38, 39.5) cm – blocked

F) Neckline Width (Prior to Ribbing): 9 (9.5, 10, 10, 10, 10, 10) in / 22.75 (24.25, 25.5, 25.5, 25.5, 25.5, 25.5) cm – blocked

Abbreviations	
[ ]	brackets indicate a repeat
bet	between
BO	bind off
BOR	beginning of row/round
CO	cast on
dec	decrease/decreases/decreased
inc	increase/increases/increased
k	knit
k2tog	knit two stitches together (dec 1)
M1L	make one stitch, left leaning (inc 1)
M1R	make one stitch, right leaning (inc 1)
p	purl
p2tog	purl two stitches together (dec 1)
p3tog	purl three sts together (dec 2)
PM	place marker
rep	repeat
rnd/s	round/rounds
RS	right side
sm	slip marker
ssk	slip one st knitwise, slip the next st knitwise, then return the two sts back to the left needle and knit the two together through the back loop (dec 1)
st/s	stitch/stitches
WS	wrong side
yo	yarn over (inc 1)

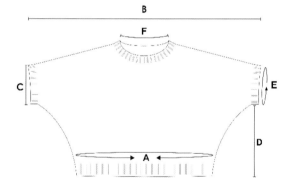

Materials	
Yarn	Fingering Weight | Purl Soho Linen Quill | 50% Fine Highland Wool, 35% Alpaca, 15% Linen | 439 yards (410 meters) in 3.5 oz (100 grams) | 1100 (1166, 1236, 1310, 1389, 1472, 1560) yards / 1005 (1066, 1130, 1197, 1270, 1346, 1426) meters | **Color:** Red Poppy **Note:** Variations in yarn choice or row/round gauge may impact yarn consumption. If in doubt, round up to the nearest skein.
Needles	**Body:** US Size 5 (3.75 mm)* 24–40-in (60–100-cm) circular needle **Lower Ribbing:** US Size 3 (3.25 mm) 24–40-in (60–100-cm) circular needle **Neckline:** US Size 3 (3.25 mm) 16-in (40-cm) circular needle **Sleeve Cuffs:** US Size 3 (3.25 mm) 12-in (30-cm) circular needle or DPNs *Or size needed to achieve gauge. Adjust other needle sizes accordingly.*
Notions	Stitch markers (including locking markers) Waste yarn or spare needles, for holding stitches Blocking pins and mats Darning needle to weave ends and seam shoulders
Gauge	25 sts and 34 rows/rounds in 4 in (10 cm) in stockinette stitch with largest needle, blocked

how to make poppies

P3tog-yo-p3tog. This is worked as follows: P3tog, but do not slip them off the needle. Work a yo with the same stitch cluster, then p3tog again. Slip off the needle—no sts inc or dec.

poppy dotted top pattern

With US Size 3 (3.25 mm) 24–40-in (60–100-cm) circular needle—or *two sizes smaller than needed to achieve gauge*—CO 220 (244, 268, 292, 320, 344, 368) sts using cable cast-on method. Do not join in the rnd yet. (*Note: The cable cast-on begins your work immediately on the RS.*)

Set-Up Row (RS): [K2, p2] rep bet brackets to end. PM and join to work in the rnd, being careful not to twist your sts.

Ribbing: [K2, p2] rep bet brackets to end. Rep this rnd until work measures 2 in (5 cm) from cast-on edge.

Next Rnd: Transition to US Size 5 (3.75 mm) needle—or *size needed to achieve gauge*—and knit 13 (13, 13, 17, 25, 29, 38) rnds.

Next Rnd: K110 (122, 134, 146, 160, 172, 184), PM, k to end.

Next Rnd (inc): K2, **M1L**, k to 2 sts before next marker, **M1R**, k2, sm, k2, **M1L**, k to last 2 sts, **M1R**, k2—4 sts inc.

Next Rnd (no inc): K to end.

Rep these two rnds 11 (13, 20, 22, 30, 30, 30) times more for a total of 12 (14, 21, 23, 31, 31, 31)—268 (300, 352, 384, 444, 468, 492) sts.

Next Rnd (extra inc): K2, **M1L**, k2, **M1L**, k to 4 sts before next marker, **M1R**, k2, **M1R**, k2, sm, k2, **M1L**, k2, **M1L**, k to last 4 sts, **M1R**, k2, **M1R**, k2—8 sts inc.

Next Rnd (no inc): K to end.

Rep these two rnds 15 (13, 8, 6, 0, 0, 0) times more for a total of 16 (14, 9, 7, 1, 1, 1)—396 (412, 424, 440, 452, 476, 500) sts.

Remove side marker (keep BOR marker).

Separate the Upper Body
Next Row: K198 (206, 212, 220, 226, 238, 250), stop. Slide remaining 198 (206, 212, 220, 226, 238, 250) sts onto a long separate needle or waste yarn. You will work back and forth (flat) on the front section (only) for now.

Front
Next Row (WS): P to end.

Row 1 (RS): K2 (1, 4, 3, 1, 2, 3), make poppy, [k7, make poppy] rep bet brackets to last 3 (2, 5, 4, 2, 3, 4) sts, k to end.

Row 2 (WS): P to end.

Row 3 (RS): K to end.

Row 4 (WS): P to end.

Row 5 (RS): K7 (6, 9, 8, 6, 7, 8), [make poppy, k7] rep bet brackets to last 11 (10, 13, 12, 10, 11, 12) sts, make poppy, k to end.

Row 6 (WS): P to end.

Row 7 (RS): K to end.

Row 8 (WS): P to end.

Rep these 8 rows until your upper body measures 6.75 (6.75, 7, 7, 7.25, 7.5, 7.75) in / 17.25 (17.25, 17.75, 17.75, 18.5, 19, 19.75) cm, ending in a stockinette section and after a WS row (ready to work a RS row).

Front Shoulder and Neckline Shaping
You will maintain the dotted poppy texture as you proceed with the shoulder shaping, but do not work the poppies in sections that will be bound off on the next row. If in doubt, eliminate the poppies.

Next Row (RS): BO7 (6, 6, 6, 6, 7, 7) sts knitwise, work in established pattern for 72 (77, 80, 84, 87, 92, 98) sts—this is left front shoulder. BO next 40 (40, 40, 40, 40, 40, 40) sts knitwise for center front neckline. Work remaining 79 (83, 86, 90, 93, 99, 105) sts in established pattern to end— this is the right front shoulder.

Place the 72 (77, 80, 84, 87, 92, 98) sts of left front shoulder onto a holder; you will return to work them later. You will now work only on the right front shoulder and neckline dec as you proceed in this section.

> **Tip:** As you proceed with the shoulder bind-off sections, transition away from working the poppies near the shoulder sides and neckline as you get closer to where you'll BO or dec. This will make it easier to seam the shoulders later (and will look more balanced). When you are within 10 sts of the edge, skip the poppies and work those sts in stockinette.

Right Front Shoulder

Next Row (WS): BO 7 (6, 6, 6, 6, 7, 7) sts purlwise, work in established pattern to end.

Next Row (RS): K1, ssk, work in pattern to end—1 st dec.

Rep these two rows 7 (9, 10, 10, 10, 10, 10) times more for a total of 8 (10, 11, 11, 11, 11, 11). (*Note: Do not work a poppy row on the final RS row. If it would normally be a poppy row, simply work it in stockinette st, instead.*)

Next Row (WS): BO remaining 15 (13, 9, 13, 16, 11, 17) sts purlwise.

Left Front Shoulder

Return to left shoulder sts and place them back on your working needles. Position your yarn to begin a WS row.

Next Row (WS): P1, p2tog, p to end—1 st dec.

Next Row (RS): BO 7 (6, 6, 6, 6, 7, 7) sts knitwise, work in pattern, as established, to end.

Rep these two rows 6 (8, 9, 9, 9, 9, 9) times more for a total of 7 (9, 10, 10, 10, 10, 10). (*Note: Do not work a poppy row on the final RS row. If it would normally be a poppy row, simply work it in stockinette st, instead.*)—15 (13, 9, 13, 16, 11, 17) sts.

Next Row (WS): P1, p2tog, BO remaining sts purlwise (including the first two).

Back

Return back sts to needles and join working yarn, ready to work a RS row—198 (206, 212, 220, 226, 238, 250) sts.

Next Row (RS): K to end.

Next Row (WS): P to end.

Row 1 (RS): K2 (1, 4, 3, 1, 2, 3), make poppy, [k7, make poppy] rep bet brackets to last 3 (2, 5, 4, 2, 3, 4) sts, k to end.

Row 2 (WS): P to end.

Row 3 (RS): K to end.

Row 4 (WS): P to end.

Row 5 (RS): K7 (6, 9, 8, 6, 7, 8), [make poppy, k7] rep bet brackets to last 11 (10, 13, 12, 10, 11, 12) sts, make poppy, k to end.

Row 6 (WS): P to end.

Row 7 (RS): K to end.

Row 8 (WS): P to end.

Rep these 8 rows until your upper body measures 6.75 (6.75, 7, 7, 7.25, 7.5, 7.75) in / 17.25 (17.25, 17.75, 17.75, 18.5, 19, 19.75) cm and matches the front section before your BO shaping began, ending with a stockinette section and ending after a WS row (ready to work a RS row).

Back Shoulder Shaping

Note: As you proceed, if you are within 10 sts of the bind-off edge, omit the poppies and work those sts in stockinette.

Next Row (RS): BO 7 (6, 6, 6, 6, 7, 7) sts knitwise, work in established pattern to end.

Next Row (WS): BO 7 (6, 6, 6, 6, 7, 7) sts purlwise, p to end.

Rep these two rows 4 (5, 6, 6, 6, 7, 7) times more for a total of 5 (6, 7, 7, 7, 8, 8)—128 (134, 128, 136, 142, 126, 138) sts.

Next Row (RS): BO 7 (6, 6, 6, 6, 7, 7) sts knitwise, work in established pattern for 32 (35, 32, 35, 38, 28, 34) sts—this is the right back shoulder. BO next 50 (52, 52, 54, 54, 56, 56) sts knitwise for center back neckline. Work 39 (41, 38, 41, 44, 35, 41) sts in pattern to end—this is the left back shoulder.

Place 32 (35, 32, 35, 38, 28, 34) sts for right back shoulder onto a separate needle or holder—you will return to work these sts later. You will now work only on the left back shoulder and neckline dec as you proceed in this section.

Left Back Shoulder

Next Row (WS): BO 7 (6, 6, 6, 6, 7, 7) sts purlwise, p to end.

Next Row (RS): K1, ssk, k to end—1 st dec.

Rep these two rows 3 times more (for a total of 4). (*Note: Do not work a poppy row on the final RS row. If it would normally be a poppy row, simply work it in stockinette st, instead.*)

Next Row (WS): BO remaining 7 (13, 10, 13, 16, 3, 9) sts purlwise.

Right Back Shoulder

Return the Right Back Shoulder sts to your needle and rejoin working yarn, ready to work a WS row.

Next Row (WS): P1, p2tog, p to end—1 st dec.

Next Row (RS): BO 7 (6, 6, 6, 6, 7, 7) sts knitwise, k to end.

Rep these two rows twice more (for a total of 3). (*Note: Do not work a poppy row on the final RS row. If it would normally be a poppy row, simply work it in stockinette st instead.*)

Next Row (WS): P1, p2tog, BO remaining sts purlwise (including the first two sts of the row).

Shoulder Finishing

Seam the shoulder sts together on each side to the neckline, ensuring that the front, back, and shoulder bind-off sections line up perfectly. See seaming and grafting tutorials on my website here: oliveknits.com/grafting.

Neckline

With US Size 3 (3.25 mm) 16-in (40-cm) circular needle—or *two sizes smaller than needed to achieve gauge*—pick up and knit approximately every available st around the neckline, ending with a multiple of 4 sts to work ribbing. PM and join to work in the rnd. (For best results, I recommend beginning your neckline at the shoulder on either side.)

Ribbing

Next Rnd: [K2, p2] rep bet brackets to end.

Rep this rnd until ribbed edge measures approximately 1.5 in (3.75 cm). BO in pattern with medium tension.

Tip: You can adjust the size and feel of your neckline by doing one of the following: For a looser neckline, pick up every available st and ensure that your bind off is not too tight. If your neckline is too open (or your ribbing flares out), try picking up slightly fewer sts and/or binding off a little more tightly. Necklines like this one are very easy to adjust with just a few simple changes to your technique.

Sleeve Ribbing

Beginning with either armhole, and with US Size 3 (3.25 mm) 12-in (30-cm) circular needle or DPNs—or *two sizes smaller than needed to achieve gauge*—pick up and knit approximately 6 of every 7 available sts around the sleeve opening, ending with a multiple of 4 sts to work ribbing. Jot down the number of sts you've picked up so you can match the same number on the other sleeve. Starting at the center of the underarm, PM and join to work in the rnd.

Ribbing

Next Rnd: [K2, p2] rep bet brackets to end.

Rep this rnd until ribbed edge measures approximately 2 in (5 cm). BO in pattern with medium tension. (*Note: If your cuff edge feels restrictive, bind off more loosely.*)

Rep for second armhole.

Finishing

Weave in ends on the WS. Wet block for best results, soaking in lukewarm water with a splash of fiber wash for 20 minutes to gently cleanse and relax the fiber. Press out excess water, and lay flat, patting into shape to ensure it dries evenly. Pin around the neckline where the ribbing meets the stockinette, and along the cuffs and lower edge where the ribbing meets the stockinette. No other pinning should be needed if you smooth your tee out flat and even. Adjust if necessary for best results. Turn as needed for even drying.

laurel sleeveless duster

I think layers might be the reason we're so fond of our fall and winter wardrobes, but I hope the designs in this book might change a few minds about what's possible for the sunnier seasons. Surely layers can be worn year-round if we're mindful about our approach. This long sleeveless duster is the perfect finishing piece for your on-the-go look. It has an easy fit that covers all the right places, and if you knit yours in a neutral color, you can wear it with just about anything. Slipped stitches sit on a bed of reverse stockinette, creating a relaxed and flattering silhouette. The open-front style and contemporary details remind me of some of my favorite clothing brands; this is the kind of piece I'd buy right off the shelf. Let's just knit one, instead!

Skill Level
Advanced Beginner

Construction
Slipped stitches sit on a bed of reverse stockinette stitch to create eye-catching texture from start to finish. It's knit from the bottom up, starting with ribbing, then moves into the pattern texture. It's worked in one flat piece to the underarms, then the bodice is worked in three sections (first the back and then two fronts) with shaped shoulders. The long rectangular shape and vertical slipped stitch columns work together to create a sleek silhouette that's perfect for everyday wear.

Sizes
1 (2, 3)
Equivalent to S–L (XL–3X, 4X–6X)

Fit Advice
Designed to fit 32–42 (42–52, 52–62) in / 81.25–106.75 (106.75–132, 132–157.5) cm bust circumference.

Finished Measurements
A) **Width Across Back:** 22 (28.5, 34) in / 54.75 (71, 85.25) cm – blocked

B) **Armhole Depth:** 9 (10, 11) in / 22.7 (25.5, 28) cm – prior to blocking

C) **Underarm to Hem:** 19 (20, 21) in / 48.25 (50.75, 53.25) cm – prior to blocking

D) **Back Neckline Width (Prior to Ribbing):** 8.5 (11.25, 11.25) in / 21.5 (28, 28) cm – blocked

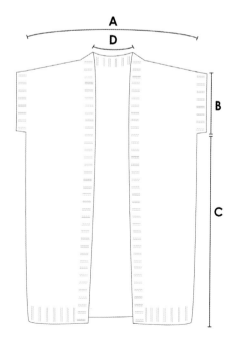

Abbreviations	
[ ]	brackets indicate a repeat
bet	between
BO	bind off
BOR	beginning of row/round
CO	cast on
dec	decrease/decreases/decreased
inc	increase/increases/increased
k	knit
k2tog	knit two stitches together (dec 1)
kfb	knit into the front and back of the same stitch (inc 1)
p	purl
PM	place marker
rnd/s	round/rounds
RS	right side
st/s	stitch/stitches
sl1wyif	slip one st with yarn held in front
sl1wyib	slip one st with yarn held in back
WS	wrong side
x	x represents sizes not represented in this line of instruction

Materials	
Yarn	DK Weight	Madelinetosh Wool + Cotton	50% Superwash Merino Wool, 50% Pima Cotton	219 yards (200 meters) in 3.5 oz (100 grams)	1500 (1680, 1882) yards / 1371 (1536, 1720) meters	**Color:** Moonglow **Note:** Variations in yarn choice or row/round gauge may impact yarn consumption. If in doubt, round up to the nearest skein.
Needles	**Body:** US Size 5 (3.75 mm)* 40–60-in (100–150-cm) circular needle **Ribbing:** US Size 4 (3.5 mm) 40–60-in (100–150-cm) circular needle **Sleeve Ribbing:** US Size 4 (3.5 mm) 12-in (30-cm) circular needle or DPNs *Or size needed to achieve gauge. Adjust other needle sizes accordingly.*
Notions	Stitch markers (including locking markers) Waste yarn or spare needles, for holding stitches Blocking pins and mats Darning needle to weave in ends and seam shoulders
Gauge	21 sts and 32 rows in 4 in (10 cm) in slipped st pattern (see next page) with largest needle, blocked—*row gauge is less critical but may affect yarn consumption.*

pattern for swatching

CO 29 sts using the cable cast-on method. Note that the cable cast-on begins your work immediately on the RS. If you use another CO method, adjust accordingly.

Set-up Row 1 (RS): [P5, k1] rep bet brackets to last 5 sts, p5.

Set-up Row 2 (WS): [K5, p1] rep bet brackets to last 5 sts, k5.

Row 1 (RS): [P5, sl1wyib] rep bet brackets to last 5 sts, p5.

Row 2 (WS): [K5, sl1wyif] rep bet brackets to last 5 sts, k5.

Row 3 (RS): Rep Row 1.

Row 4 (WS): [K5, p1] rep bet brackets to last 5 sts, k5.

Rep rows 1–4 for pattern.

laurel sleeveless duster pattern

With US Size 4 (3.5 mm) 24–40-in (60–100-cm) circular needle—*or one size smaller than needed to achieve gauge*—CO 182 (238, 298) sts using cable cast-on method. Do not join. (*Note: The cable cast-on begins your work immediately on the RS.*)

Next Row (RS): [K2, p2] rep bet brackets to last 2 sts, k2.

Next Row (WS): P2, [k2, p2] rep bet brackets to end.

Rep these two rows until work measures approximately 2 in (5 cm).

Tip: Since this entire garment is worked flat, you'll want to make sure to keep your edges tidy. To do this, work the first st tighter than usual, then insert the tip of your needle into the second st, and pull the working yarn tight again to draw the first st a little tighter. Then proceed with the remainder of the row with normal tension. Do this at the start of every row (RS and WS) for nicer edges.

Size 1 ONLY – Set-Up Row 1 (RS): Transition to US Size 5 (3.75 mm) needle—*or size needed to achieve gauge*—as you work the next row. P5, (kfb, p4) twice, [k1, p5], rep bet brackets to last 5 sts, kfb, p4 (3 sts inc)—185 (x, x) sts.

Sizes 2 and 3 ONLY – Set-Up Row 1 (RS): Transition to US Size 5 (3.75 mm) needle—*or size needed to achieve gauge*—as you work the next row. P5, [k1, p5] rep bet brackets to last 5 sts, kfb, p4 (1 st inc)—x (239, 299) sts.

All Sizes Continue

Set-up Row 2 (WS): [K5, p1] rep bet brackets to last 5 sts, k5.

Row 1 (RS): [P5, sl1wyib] rep bet brackets to last 5 sts, p5.

Row 2 (WS): [K5, sl1wyif] rep bet brackets to last 5 sts, k5.

Row 3 (RS): Rep Row 1.

Row 4 (WS): [K5, p1] rep bet brackets to last 5 sts, k5.

Rep Rows 1–4 to establish pattern until the body of your tunic measures 19 (20, 21) in / 48.25 (50.75, 53.25) cm from cast-on edge, and you have just completed a Pattern Row 4 (ready to start Row 1).

Upper Bodice

Going forward, you will separate the two front and one back bodice sections and work back and forth on each section, flat, beginning with the back. You will return to work the left front and then the right front sections afterward.

Next Row (RS): Work the first 35 (45, 60) sts in established pattern, stop—this will be the right front. Slide these sts onto a long separate needle or waste yarn; you'll come back to work them later. Work across the next 115 (149, 179) sts in established pattern, stop—this is the back section.

Slide remaining 35 (45, 60) sts onto a long separate needle or waste yarn—this is the left front. You will work back and forth (flat) on the back section (only) for now.

> **Note:** If a slipped st lands in the first or last 2 sts of your section, eliminate these slipped sts from the pattern going forward by working them in stockinette as the rest of the selvedge stitches.

Back

Next Row (WS): P2, work in established pattern to last 2 sts, p2.

Next Row (RS): K2, work in established pattern to last 2 sts, k2.

Rep these two rows until your flat section measures approximately 9 (10, 11) in / 22.75 (25.5, 28) cm from where you separated it from the other sections, ending after a WS row (ready to work a RS).

Back Shoulder and Neckline Shaping

As you proceed, continue in pattern as you are able. Switch to reverse stockinette stitch when you are within 12 sts of the shoulder edge for easier seaming later.

Next Row (RS): BO 7 (9, 12) sts knitwise, work in established pattern to end.

Next Row (WS): BO 7 (9, 12) sts purlwise, work in established pattern to end.

Rep these two rows 4 times more (for a total of 5).

BO remaining 45 (59, 59) sts knitwise for center back neckline.

Left Shoulder Shaping

Next Row (RS): BO 7 (9, 12) knitwise, then work in established pattern to end.

Next Row (WS): Work in established pattern to end.

Rep these two rows 3 times more (for a total of 4).

Next Row (RS): BO remaining 7 (9, 12) sts knitwise.

Right Front

Return right front sts to your needles and rejoin working yarn, ready to work a WS row.

Next Row (WS): P2, work in established pattern to end.

Next Row (RS): Work in established pattern to last 2 sts, k2.

Rep these two rows until your flat section measures approximately 9 (10, 11) in / 22.75 (25.5, 28) cm from where you separated it from the other sections and is the same length as the other two pieces, ending after a RS row (ready to work a WS).

Right Shoulder Shaping

Next Row (WS): BO 7 (9, 12) purlwise, then work in established pattern to end.

Next Row (RS): Work in established pattern to end.

Rep these two rows 3 times more (for a total of 4).

Next Row (WS): BO remaining 7 (9, 12) sts purlwise.

Left Front

Return left front to your needles and rejoin working yarn ready to work a RS row.

Next Row (RS): K2, work in pattern to end.

Next Row (WS): Work in established pattern to last 2 sts, p2.

Rep these two rows until your flat section measures approximately 9 (10, 11) in / 22.75 (25.5, 28) cm from where you separated it from the other sections and is the same length as the back piece, ending after a WS row (ready to work a RS).

Shoulder Finishing

Seam the shoulder sts together on each side to the neckline, ensuring that the front, back, and shoulder bind-off sections line up perfectly. See seaming and grafting tutorials on my website here: oliveknits.com/grafting.

Trim

With US Size 4 (3.5 mm) 60-in (150-cm) circular needle—*or one size smaller than needed to achieve gauge*—start at the bottom edge of the right front and pick up and knit approximately 5 of every 6 available sts (counting from rows along the front edges and sts across back neck) around the front. You will pick up along the right side of the right front, from the lower edge up to the neckline, around the back neck, and back down the left front, ending with a multiple of 4+2. *(If you end up with one st too many, k2tog. If you need an extra st, pick up one extra.)*

Ribbing

Next Row (WS): [P2, k2] rep bet brackets to last 2 sts, p2.

Next Row (RS): K2, [p2, k2] rep bet brackets to end.

Rep these two rows until your ribbed edge measures approximately 1.5 in (3.75 cm).

BO in pattern with medium tension.

Armhole Ribbing

Beginning with either armhole and with US Size 4 (3.5 mm) circular needle or DPNs—*or one size smaller than needed to achieve gauge*—pick up and knit 4 of every 5 available sts (counting by rows) around the first sleeve edge, starting at the underarm and ending with a multiple of 4. Starting at the center of the underarm, PM and join to work in the rnd.

Ribbing

Next Rnd: [K2, p2] rep bet brackets to end.

Rep this rnd until ribbed edge measures approximately 1.25 in (3.25 cm).

BO in pattern with medium tension.

Rep for second armhole.

> **Tip:** If your armhole ribbing flares out, it means you've either picked up slightly too many sts or have worked your ribbing or bind off too loosely. If this happens, try again with slightly fewer sts and/or go down another needle size to work your ribbing more tightly.

Finishing

Weave in ends on the WS and wet block for best results. Soak in lukewarm water with a splash of fiber wash for 20 minutes to gently cleanse and relax the fiber. Press out excess water and lay flat, drawing the sides and length out taut and pinning into shape along the ribbing and front panels. (For stellar results with your ribbed edges, use comb-style pins along the ribbing where it meets the body of your work, rather than along the outer edge. This will create smooth ribbing transitions that lay beautifully flat when you wear your garment.)

jasmine v-neck tee

My home and garden are filled with greenery and flowers, but I can always find a spot for *just one more thing*. One of the latest additions is a climbing jasmine—a gift from my oldest son—which arrived at a busy time, so I quickly potted it and hung it in my kitchen without a spot of research. Months later, its thin, dark green tendrils had grown long enough to coil themselves around the window blinds. Oops! My jasmine has since found a new home outside where she can grow, unfettered. I borrowed just a touch of those narrow jasmine tendrils for the contrasting edges on this ultra comfy, modern twist on a V-neck tee. The deep V at the neckline creates a contemporary look for this generously sized, drop-shoulder style. Jasmine will have the easy care of your favorite T-shirt, and it's perfect for a relaxing day or lounging on the patio.

Skill Level
Advanced Beginner

Construction
This bottom-up, oversized tee is worked in stockinette stitch in the round to the underarms. The upper bodice is worked flat to the shoulders, with a deep V-neck shape and drop-shoulder sleeves. The shoulders are seamed with horizontal mattress stitch, and the neckline and sleeve edges are finished with a thin, rolled edge in a contrasting color. Don't let the generous size worry you; it might look astonishing on your needles, but it's a surprisingly comfortable style for loungewear.

Sizes
S (M, L, XL, 2X, 3X, 4X, 5X, 6X)

Fit Advice
Designed to be worn with approximately 15 in (37.5 cm) positive ease for an oversized fit.

Finished Measurements
A) Bust Circumference: 45.75 (50.25, 54.5, 59, 64, 68.25, 72.75, 77, 82.25) in / 114.5 (125.5, 136.25, 147.25, 160, 171, 181.75, 192.75, 205.5) cm – blocked

B) Armhole Depth: 7 (7.5, 7.75, 7.75, 8.25, 8.25, 8.5, 8.5, 9) in / 17.25 (18.5, 19.25, 19.25, 20.5, 20.5, 21.25, 21.25, 22.5) cm – blocked (because of the generous sizing and construction, this will sit further down the arm toward the elbow)

C) Underarm to Hem: 13 (13, 13, 14, 14, 15, 15, 15, 15) in / 33 (33, 33, 35.5, 35.5, 38, 38, 38, 38) cm – prior to blocking

D) Back Neckline Width: 8.75 (8.75, 9.5, 9.5, 9.75, 10.25, 10.75, 10.75, 10.75) in / 21.75 (21.75, 23.75, 23.75, 24.5, 26, 26.75, 26.75, 26.75) cm – blocked

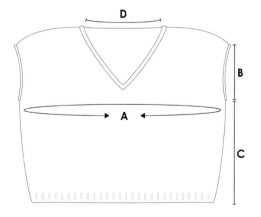

Abbreviations	
[ ]	brackets indicate a repeat
bet	between
BO	bind off
BOR	beginning of row/round
CC	contrast color
CO	cast on
dec	decrease/decreases/decreased
k	knit
MC	main color
p	purl
p2tog	purl two stitches together (dec 1)
PM	place marker
rep	repeat
rnd/s	round/rounds
RS	right side
ssk	slip one st knitwise, slip the next st knitwise, then return the two sts back to the left needle and knit the two together through the back loop (dec 1)
st/s	stitch/stitches
WS	wrong side

Materials	
Yarn	Sport Weight | Scheepjes Stone Wash | 78% Cotton, 22% Acrylic | 142 yards (130 meters) in 1.76 oz (50 grams) | **Colors:** Smoky Quartz & Black Onyx **Note:** Variations in yarn choice or row/round gauge may impact yarn consumption. If in doubt, round up to the nearest skein. **MC (Smoky Quartz):** 1029 (1111, 1199, 1295, 1399, 1511, 1632, 1763, 1904) yards / 941 (1016, 1096, 1184, 1279, 1381, 1492, 1612, 1740) meters **CC (Black Onyx):** scant amounts for contrast (no more than 50 yards [45 meters])
Needles	**Body:** US Size 5 (3.75 mm)* 24–40-in (60–100-cm) circular needle **Lower Ribbing:** US Size 4 (3.5 mm) 24–40-in (60–100-cm) circular needle **Neckline:** US Size 3 (3.25 mm) 16-in (40-cm) circular needle **Sleeve Edge:** US Size 3 (3.25 mm) 12-in (30-cm) or DPNs *Or size needed to achieve gauge. Adjust other needle sizes accordingly.
Notions	Stitch markers (including locking markers) Waste yarn or spare needles, for holding stitches Blocking pins and mats Darning needle to weave ends and seam shoulders
Gauge	22 sts and 30 rows/rounds in 4 in (10 cm) in stockinette stitch with largest needle, blocked—because this is knit bottom-up, row gauge is less critical but may affect yarn consumption.

jasmine v-neck tee pattern

With US Size 4 (3.5 mm) 24–40-in (60–100-cm) circular needle—or one size smaller than needed to achieve gauge—and MC, CO 252 (276, 300, 324, 352, 376, 400, 424, 452) sts using cable cast-on method. Do not join in the rnd yet. (Note: The cable cast-on begins your work immediately on the RS.)

Set-Up Row (RS): [K2, p2] rep bet brackets to end, then PM and join to work in the rnd, being careful not to twist your sts.

Ribbing

Next Rnd: [K2, p2] rep bet brackets to end.

Next Rnd: With MC, [k2, p2] rep bet brackets to end.

Rep this rnd until work measures approximately 1–2 in (2.5–5 cm).

Transition to US Size 5 (3.75 mm) 24–40-in (60–100-cm) circular needle—or size needed to achieve gauge—and k one rnd.

Continue working in the rnd, as established, until lower body measures approximately 13 (13, 13, 14, 14, 15, 15, 15, 15) in / 33 (33, 33, 35.5, 35.5, 38, 38, 38, 38) cm from cast-on edge.

Upper Bodice

Going forward, you will separate the front and back bodice sections and work back and forth on each section, flat, beginning with the front. You will return to work the back afterward.

Tip: As you begin working flat, be sure to keep your edges tidy. To do this, work the first st tighter than usual, then insert the tip of your needle into the second st and pull the working yarn tight again to draw the first st a little tighter. Then proceed with the remainder of the row with normal tension. Do this at the start of every row (RS and WS) for nicer edges that will be easier to finish later.

Next Rnd: K126 (138, 150, 162, 176, 188, 200, 212, 226) sts, stop. Slide remaining 126 (138, 150, 162, 176, 188, 200, 212, 226) sts onto a long separate needle or waste yarn. You will work back and forth (flat) on the front section (only) for now.

Front

Next Row (WS): P to end.

Next Row (RS): K to end.

Rep these two rows until your flat section measures approximately 0.75 (1.25, 1, 1, 1.25, 0.75, 0.75, 0.75, 1.25) in / 2 (3, 2.5, 2.5, 3, 2, 2, 2, 3) cm from where you began working flat, ending after a WS row (ready to work the RS).

Front Shoulder and Neckline Shaping

Next Row (RS): K63 (69, 75, 81, 88, 94, 100, 106, 113) sts to center of front, stop. Place remaining 63 (69, 75, 81, 88, 94, 100, 106, 113) sts onto a separate needle or holder—this is the right front shoulder. You will work back and forth on the left front section for now, decreasing at the center of the front to begin the V-neck shaping.

Right Front Shoulder

Next Row (RS): K1, ssk, k to end—1 st dec.

Next Row (WS): P to end of row.

Rep these two rows until you reach 40 (46, 50, 56, 62, 66, 71, 77, 84) sts and have just completed a WS row, ready to work the RS.

Right Front Neckline and Shoulder Shaping

Next Row (RS): K1, ssk, k to end—1 st dec.

Next Row (WS): BO 5 (6, 7, 8, 9, 10, 11, 12, 13) sts purlwise, p to end.

Rep these two rows 4 times more (for a total of 5).

Next Row (RS): BO remaining 10 (11, 10, 11, 12, 11, 11, 12, 14) sts knitwise.

Back

Return back sts to needles and join MC, ready to work a RS row—126 (138, 150, 162, 176, 188, 200, 212, 226) sts.

Next Row (RS): K to end.

Next Row (WS): P to end.

Rep these two rows until your flat section is approximately the same length as the front section prior to the first bind-off row on the shoulders from where you began working flat. End after a WS row (ready to work a RS).

Back Shoulder Shaping

Next Row (RS): BO 5 (6, 7, 8, 9, 10, 11, 12, 13) sts knitwise, k to end.

Next Row (WS): BO 5 (6, 7, 8, 9, 10, 11, 12, 13) sts purlwise, k to end.

Rep these two rows 4 times more (for a total of 5).

Left Front Shoulder

Next Row (WS): P1, p2tog, p to end—1 st dec.

Next Row (RS): K to end.

Rep these two rows until you reach 40 (46, 50, 56, 62, 66, 71, 77, 84) sts and have just completed a WS row, ready to work the RS.

Left Front Neckline and Shoulder Shaping

Next Row (RS): BO 5 (6, 7, 8, 9, 10, 11, 12, 13) sts knitwise, k to end.

Next Row (WS): P1, p2tog, p to end—1 st dec.

Rep these two rows 4 times more (for a total of 5).

Next Row (RS): BO remaining 10 (11, 10, 11, 12, 11, 11, 12, 14) sts knitwise.

Return right front shoulder sts to your needles and rejoin working yarn in MC, ready to work a RS row.

Next Row (RS): BO 10 (11, 10, 11, 12, 11, 11, 12, 14) sts knitwise, k to end.

Next Row (WS): BO 10 (11, 10, 11, 12, 11, 11, 12, 14) sts purlwise, p to end.

BO remaining 56 (56, 60, 60, 62, 66, 68, 68, 68) sts knitwise for center back neckline.

Shoulder Finishing

Seam the shoulder sts together on each side to the neckline, ensuring that the front, back, and shoulder dec shaping lines up perfectly. See seaming and grafting tutorials on my website here: oliveknits.com/grafting.

Neckline

With US Size 3 (3.25 mm) 16-in (40-cm) circular needle—*or two sizes smaller than needed to achieve gauge*—and using CC, pick up and k approximately 6 of every 7 available sts around the neckline edge. I recommend starting at the shoulder seam on one side, then picking up and knitting all the way around, including at the point of the V, to create a closed loop with your needles. K three rnds and BO. The edge should roll slightly.

Tip: You can adjust the size and feel of your neckline by doing one of the following: For a looser neckline, pick up every available st and ensure that your bind off is not too tight. If your neckline is too open (or your edge flares or looks too wavy), try picking up slightly fewer sts and/or binding off a little more tightly. Necklines like this one are very easy to adjust with just a few simple changes to your technique.

Armhole

Beginning with either armhole, and with US Size 3 (3.25 mm) 12-in (30-cm) circular needle or DPNs—*or two sizes smaller than needed to achieve gauge*—and CC, pick up and knit approximately 5 of every 6 available sts (5 sts for every 6 rows accounted for) around the first armhole opening, starting at the underarm and ending with a multiple of 4. Jot down the number of sts you've picked up so you can match the same number on the other arm. Starting at the center of the underarm, PM, join working yarn, and join to work in the rnd.

With CC, K three rnds. Then BO in pattern with medium tension. If desired, you can adjust the fit of the armhole using the same tip mentioned in the neckline instructions.

Rep for second armhole.

Finishing

Weave in ends on the WS, taking care to weave ends in areas of their own color. Wet block for best results, soaking in lukewarm water with a splash of fiber wash for 20 minutes to gently cleanse and relax the fiber. Press out excess water and lay flat, smoothing and pinning into shape. Pin around the neckline especially, as well as where the rolled edge meets the body of the sweater and along the sleeve edges (where the rolled edge meets the stockinette). Pin along the lower body edge and sides as well. Turn as needed for even drying.

marigold wave top

I've always been fond of marigolds; they're easy to grow, they come back every year without fail, and they add a happy burst of color to my garden. And what they lack in scent, they make up for in usefulness. For this design, I envisioned a bright spring top with just a hint of waves to mimic marigold petals. The delicate feather-and-fan lace variation draws the eye upward, adding a little dash of charm. It fits with a little extra room in the body and closer-fitting sleeves for a flattering silhouette with a little swing to it. If you like a little more room in the body (especially around the belly or hips), you'll love the fit of this design.

Skill Level
Advanced Beginner

Construction
This half-sleeve tee is knit top down in the round (in one seamless piece) with round yoke construction and evenly spaced increases to create the shape. The top and sleeves are worked all in one down to the underarm, then the sleeves are separated onto waste yarn while you complete the rest of the body. The lower body is worked straight with a ribbed finish. The ribbed neckline is picked up and knit afterward, providing added structure and giving you more control over the finished fit of the neckline.

Sizes
S (M, L, XL, 2X, 3X, 4X, 5X, 6X)

Fit Advice
Designed for a casual fit with approximately 5–6 in (12.5–15 cm) positive ease.

Finished Measurements

A) Bust Circumference: 38.25 (41.75, 45.5, 50.5, 54.75, 57.75, 60, 65.25, 68.25) in / 95.75 (104.25, 114, 126, 137, 144.25, 150, 163, 170.5) cm – blocked

B) Yoke Depth (from Center Front Neckline Below Ribbing): 8.25 (9.5, 9.5, 10, 10, 10.5, 11.25, 12.25, 12.75 / 20.25 (23.75, 23.75, 25.25, 25.25, 26.5, 28, 30.75, 32) cm – blocked

C) Underarm to Hem: 11 (11.5, 11.5, 11.5, 12, 12.5, 12.5, 13.5, 13.5) in / 28 (29.25, 29.25, 29.25, 30.5, 31.75, 31.75, 34.25, 34.25) cm – prior to blocking

D) Sleeve Circumference: 11.25 (12.75, 14, 15.75, 16, 16.25, 17, 18, 18.5) in / 27.75 (32.25, 34.75, 39.25, 40, 40.75, 42.5, 45.25, 46) cm - blocked

E) Sleeve Length: 5.5 in (14 cm) – prior to blocking

F) Neck Circumference: 20.75 (20.75, 20.75, 20.75, 22.25, 22.25, 22.25, 22.25, 22.25) in / 52.25 (52.25, 52.25, 52.25, 55.75, 55.75, 55.75, 55.75, 55.75) cm – blocked

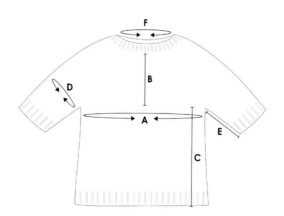

Abbreviations	
[ ]	brackets indicate a repeat
bet	between
BO	bind off
BOR	beginning of row/round
CO	cast on
dec	decrease/decreases/decreased
inc	increase/increases/increased
k	knit
k2tog	knit two stitches together (dec 1)
M1L	make one stitch, left leaning (inc 1)
p	purl
p2tog	purl two stitches together (dec 1)
PM	place marker
rep	repeat
rnd/s	round/rounds
RS	right side
sm	slip marker
ssk	slip one st knitwise, slip the next st knitwise, then return the two sts back to the left needle and knit the two together through the back loop (dec 1)
st/s	stitch/stitches
WS	wrong side
x	x represents sizes not represented on this line of instruction
yo	yarn over (inc 1)

Materials	
Yarn	DK Weight	Juniper Moon Zooey	60% Cotton, 40% Linen	284 yards (260 meters) in 3.5 oz (100 grams)	1029 (1111, 1199, 1295, 1399, 1511, 1632, 1763, 1904) yards / 941 (1016, 1096, 1184, 1279, 1381, 1492, 1612, 1740) meters	**Color:** Goldenrod **Note:** Variations in yarn choice or row/round gauge may impact yarn consumption. If in doubt, round up to the nearest skein.
Needles	**Body:** US 5 (3.75 mm)* 16–40-in (40–100-cm) circular needle **Lower Ribbing:** US 4 (3.5 mm) 24–40-in (60–100-cm) circular needle **Neckline:** US 3 (3.25 mm) 16-in (40-cm) circular needle **Sleeves:** US 5 (3.75 mm) 12-in (30-cm) circular needle or DPNs **Sleeve Cuffs:** US 3 (3.25 mm) 12-in (30-cm) circular needle or DPNs *Or size needed to achieve gauge. Adjust other needle sizes accordingly.*
Notions	Stitch markers (including locking markers and several unique markers) Waste yarn or spare needles, for holding stitches Blocking pins and mats Darning needle to weave ends
Gauge	23 sts and 29 rows/rounds in 4 in (10 cm) in stockinette st with largest needle, blocked

marigold wave top pattern

With US Size 3 (3.25 mm) 16-in (40-cm) circular needle—or two sizes smaller than used to achieve gauge—CO 120 (120, 120, 120, 128, 128, 128, 128, 128) sts using cable cast-on method. Do not join in the rnd yet. (Note: The cable cast-on begins your work immediately on the RS.)

Set-Up Row (RS): [K2, p2] rep bet brackets to end. PM and join to work in the rnd, being careful not to twist your sts.

Ribbing Rnd: [K2, p2] rep bet brackets to end. Rep this rnd until neckline ribbing measures 1.25 in (3.25 cm)—or slightly longer, if desired.

Next Rnd: With US Size 5 (3.75 mm) circular needle—or size needed to obtain gauge—k one rnd to begin the upper yoke.

Next Rnd: K60 (60, 60, 60, 64, 64, 64, 64, 64) sts, place a side marker, k60 (60, 60, 60, 64, 64, 64, 64, 64) sts to end. Stop.

Turn your work to the wrong side to begin 8 short rows using the Japanese short row method. You will need two locking markers for this technique.

Short Rows

> **Tip:** If you prefer a different short row method, simply work 8 short rows in your preferred method, using these details as a guide for the turning point. Be sure to keep your BOR and side markers in place as you create the short rows.

Short Row 1 (WS): Slip first st to right needle (purlwise) without working it and place a locking marker on your working yarn (holding the marker to the WS of your work). P to the side marker. Stop and turn to RS.

Short Row 2 (RS): Slip first st to right needle (purlwise) without working it and place a locking marker on your working yarn (holding the marker to the WS of your work). K to the gap that is marked with locking marker. Using the marker to pull, draw up the marked yarn from the WS of your work and place it on the left needle as if a new st (adjusting the BOR marker, as needed, to work the short row, and then replacing it to its original location), then knit it together (k2tog) with the next st on the left needle (closing the gap) and remove locking marker. K1, stop, and turn to WS.

Short Row 3 (WS): Slip first st to right needle (purlwise) without working it and place a locking marker on the working yarn (holding the marker to the WS of your work). P to gap that is marked with a locking marker. Slip the next st to the right needle purlwise without working it (adjusting the side marker, as needed, to work the short row, and then replacing it to its original location). Using the locking marker to pull, draw up the marked yarn from the WS of your work and place it on the left needle as if a new st. Place the st that you previously slipped back to the left needle and purl it together (p2tog) with the "new" st (closing the gap) and remove locking marker. P1, stop, and turn to RS.

Short Row 4 (RS): Slip the first st to right needle (purlwise) without working it, place a locking marker on the working yarn (held at the WS of your work). K to gap that is marked with locking marker. Using the marker to pull, draw up the marked yarn from the WS of your work and place it on the left needle as if a new st, then knit it together (k2tog) with the next st on the left needle (closing the gap) and remove locking marker. K1, stop, and turn to WS.

Short Rows 5–8: Rep Short Rows 3 and 4 twice more. Do not turn work to WS after final repeat of Short Row 4.

Continue on RS and work in pattern to end of rnd until you are one stitch before the final gap. Slip this st to your right needle purlwise without working it, then, using the marker to pull, draw up the marked yarn from the WS of your work and place it on the left needle as if a new st. Place the st that you previously slipped back to the left needle and knit it together (k2tog) with the "new" st (closing the gap) and remove the locking marker. Knit to end of rnd. Your short rows have been completed and your gaps should be closed.

K one rnd.

Inc # 1 – Next Rnd: [K6 (6, 5, 5, 6, 6, 6, 6, 6), M1L] rep bet brackets to last 0 (0, 5, 5, 2, 2, 2, 2, 2) sts, k to end—20 (20, 23, 23, 21, 21, 21, 21) sts inc.

Work 4 (4, 3, 3, 3, 3, 3, 3, 3) rnds even in stockinette st.

Inc # 2 – Next Rnd: [K7 (7, 6, 6, 7, 7, 7, 7, 7), M1L] rep bet brackets to last 0 (0, 5, 5, 2, 2, 2, 2, 2) sts, k to end—20 (20, 23, 23, 21, 21, 21, 21) sts inc.

Work 4 (4, 3, 3, 3, 3, 3, 3, 3) rnds even in stockinette st.

Stitch Count Check-In

160 (160, 166, 166, 170, 170, 170, 170, 170)

> **Note:** Transition to a longer circular needle when necessary for stitches to move comfortably.

Inc #3 – Next Rnd: [K8 (8, 7, 7, 8, 8, 8, 8, 8), M1L] rep bet brackets to last 0 (0, 5, 5, 2, 2, 2, 2, 2) sts, k to end—20 (20, 23, 23, 21, 21, 21, 21) sts inc.

Work 4 (4, 3, 3, 3, 3, 3, 3, 3) rnds even in stockinette st.

Inc #4 – Next Rnd: [K9 (9, 8, 8, 9, 9, 9, 9, 9), M1L] rep bet brackets to last 0 (0, 5, 5, 2, 2, 2, 2, 2) sts, k to end—20 (20, 23, 23, 21, 21, 21, 21) sts inc.

Work 4 (4, 3, 3, 3, 3, 3, 3, 3) rnds even in stockinette st.

Stitch Count Check-In

200 (200, 212, 212, 212, 212, 212, 212, 212)

Inc #5 – Next Rnd: [K10 (10, 9, 9, 10, 10, 10, 10, 10), M1L] rep bet brackets to last 0 (0, 5, 5, 2, 2, 2, 2, 2) sts, k to end—20 (20, 23, 23, 21, 21, 21, 21) sts inc.

Work 4 (4, 3, 3, 3, 3, 3, 3, 3) rnds even in stockinette st.

Inc #6 – Next Rnd: [K11 (11, 13, 13, 12, 12, 12, 12, 12), M1L] rep bet brackets to last 0 (0, 14, 14, 5, 5, 5, 5, 5) sts, k to end—20 (20, 17, 17, 19, 19, 19, 19, 19) sts inc.

Stitch Count Check-In
240 (240, 252, 252, 252, 252, 252, 252, 252)

Waves Begin
Work the Marigold Lace Chart (beginning with Rnd 1 of chart or written instructions, worked over 12 sts per repeat) to end. After Rnd 7, you will return to stockinette stitch.

Inc #7 – Next Rnd: [K12 (12, 14, 14, 12, 12, 12, 12, 12), M1L] rep bet brackets to end—20 (20, 18, 18, 21, 21, 21, 21, 21) sts inc.

Work 4 (4, 3, 3, 3, 3, 3, 3, 3) rnds even in stockinette st.

Inc #8 – Next Rnd: [K13 (13, 15, 15, 13, 13, 13, 13, 13), M1L] rep bet brackets to end—20 (20, 18, 18, 21, 21, 21, 21, 21) sts inc.

Work 4 (4, 3, 3, 3, 3, 3, 3, 3) rnds even in stockinette st.

Stitch Count Check-In
280 (280, 288, 288, 294, 294, 294, 294, 294)

Inc #9 – Next Rnd: [K14 (14, 16, 16, 14, 14, 14, 14, 14), M1L] rep bet brackets to end—20 (20, 18, 18, 21, 21, 21, 21, 21) sts inc.

Work 4 (4, 3, 3, 3, 3, 3, 3, 3) rnds even in stockinette st

Inc #10 – Next Rnd: [K15 (15, 17, 17, 15, 15, 15, 15, 15), M1L] rep bet brackets to end—20 (20, 18, 18, 21, 21, 21, 21, 21) sts inc.

Work 4 (4, 3, 3, 3, 3, 3, 3, 3) rnds even in stockinette st.

Stitch Count Check-In
320 (320, 324, 324, 336, 336, 336, 336, 336)

Inc #11 – Next Rnd: [K16 (16, 18, 18, 16, 16, 16, 16, 16), M1L] rep bet brackets to end—20 (20, 18, 18, 21, 21, 21, 21, 21) sts inc.

Work 2 (4, 3, 3, 3, 3, 3, 3, 3) rnds even in stockinette st.

Note: As you proceed you will see an "x" as a placeholder for sizes that are no longer represented on that rnd.

Size S ONLY – Move ahead to **Divide for Sleeves** on page 187.

All Other Sizes Continue

Inc #12 – Next Rnd: [Kx (17, 19, 19, 17, 17, 17, 17, 17), M1L] rep bet brackets to end—x (20, 18, 18, 21, 21, 21, 21, 21) sts inc.

Work x (4, 3, 3, 3, 3, 3, 3, 3) rnds even in stockinette st.

Inc #13 – Next Rnd: [Kx (18, 20, 20, 18, 18, 18, 18, 18), M1L] rep bet brackets to end—x (20, 18, 18, 21, 21, 21, 21, 21) sts inc.

Work x (4, 3, 3, 3, 3, 3, 3, 3) rnds even in stockinette st.

Stitch Count Check-In

x (380, 378, 378, 399, 399, 399, 399, 399)

Size M ONLY – Move ahead to **Divide for Sleeves** on page 187.

All Other Sizes Continue

Inc #14 – Next Rnd: [Kx (x, 21, 21, 19, 19, 19, 19, 19), M1L] rep bet brackets to end—x (x, 18, 18, 21, 21, 21, 21, 21) sts inc.

Work x (x, 3, 3, 3, 3, 3, 3, 3) rnds even in stockinette st.

Inc #15 – Next Rnd: [Kx (x, 22, 22, 20, 20, 20, 20, 20), M1L] rep bet brackets to end—x (x, 18, 18, 21, 21, 21, 21, 21) sts inc.

Work x (x, 9, 3, 3, 3, 3, 3, 3) rnds even in stockinette st.

Size L ONLY – Move ahead to **Divide for Sleeves** on page 187.

Inc #16 – Next Rnd: [Kx (x, x, 23, 21, 21, 21, 21, 21), M1L] rep bet brackets to end—x (x, x, 18, 21, 21, 21, 21, 21) sts inc.

Work 3 rnds even in stockinette st.

Stitch Count Check-In

x (x, x, 432, 462, 462, 462, 462, 462)

Inc #17 – Next Rnd: [Kx (x, x, 14, 22, 22, 22, 22, 22), M1L] rep bet brackets to to last x (x, x, 12, 0, 0, 0, 0, 0) sts, k to end—x (x, x, 30, 21, 21, 21, 21) sts inc.

Work 3 rnds even in stockinette st.

Sizes XL and 2X ONLY – Move ahead to **Divide for Sleeves** on page 187.

Inc #18 – Next Rnd: [Kx (x, x, x, x, 23, 23, 23, 23), M1L] rep bet brackets to end—x (x, x, x, x, 21, 21, 21, 21) sts inc.

Work 3 rnds even in stockinette st.

Size 3X ONLY – Move ahead to **Divide for Sleeves** on page 187.

Inc #19 – Next Rnd: [Kx (x, x, x, x, x, 24, 24, 24), M1L] rep bet brackets to end—x (x, x, x, x, x, 21, 21, 21) sts inc.

Work 3 rnds even in stockinette st.

Size 4X ONLY – Move ahead to **Divide for Sleeves** on page 187.

Inc #20 – Next Rnd: [Kx (x, x, x, x, x, x, 25, 25), M1L] rep bet brackets to end—x (x, x, x, x, x, x, 21, 21) sts inc.

Work 3 rnds even in stockinette st.

Inc #21 – Next Rnd: [Kx (x, x, x, x, x, x, 26, 26), M1L] rep bet brackets to end—x (x, x, x, x, x, x, 21, 21) sts inc.

Work 3 rnds even in stockinette st.

Size 5X ONLY – Move ahead to **Divide for Sleeves.**

Inc #22 – Next Rnd: [Kx (x, x, x, x, x, x, x, 27), M1L] rep bet brackets to end—x (x, x, x, x, x, x, x, 21) sts inc.

Work 3 rnds even in stockinette st.

Divide for Sleeves

Before separating the sleeves from the body, you should have the following number of sts: 340 (380, 414, 462, 483, 504, 525, 567, 588).

Next Rnd: K31(36, 39, 44, 44, 45, 47, 50, 51), PM (*Note: This marker is to save your spot for the edge of your right sleeve, which you will come back to as you finish this round.*), k108 (118, 129, 143, 154, 162, 169, 184, 192)—this is the front of the body. Place next 62 (72, 78, 88, 88, 90, 94, 100, 102) sts onto waste yarn (loosely, so you can try it on later)—this is the left sleeve. CO 2 (2, 2, 2, 4, 4, 4, 4, 4) sts under arm using e-loop (or backward loop) method worked tightly and join to back sts. K108 (118, 129, 143, 153, 162, 168, 183, 192) sts—this is the back. Place next 62 (72, 78, 88, 88, 90, 94, 100, 102) sts onto waste yarn (loosely)—this is the right sleeve. CO 2 (2, 2, 2, 4, 4, 4, 4, 4) under arm using e-loop (or backward loop) method worked tightly—end of rnd. Place your new BOR marker at the center of these newly cast-on sts—this will be the start of each rnd going forward.

Your sleeves have now been separated from the yoke of your sweater. You will now transition to the Lower Body.

Stitch Count Check-In

220 (240, 262, 290, 315, 332, 345, 375, 392) sts in lower body

Lower Body

Work the lower body in stockinette st (knitting every rnd) until body measures approximately 9.5 (10, 10, 10, 10.5, 11, 11, 12, 12) in / 23.75 (25, 25, 25, 26.25, 27.5, 27.5, 30, 30) cm from underarm.

Sizes S, M, 3X, and 6X ONLY – Next Rnd: Transition to US 4 (3.5 mm) needle—*or one size smaller than used to achieve gauge on the body*—and k one rnd.

Sizes L, XL, 2X, 4X, and 5X ONLY – Next Rnd: Transition to US 4 (3.5 mm) needle—*or one size smaller than used to achieve gauge on the body*—and k one rnd, decreasing x (x, 2, 2, 3, x, 1, 3, x) sts as evenly as possible using k2tog.

Ribbing

Next Rnd: [K2, p2] rep bet brackets to end.

Rep this rnd until ribbed edge measures approximately 1.5 in (3.75 cm) in length. BO in pattern with medium tension (not too tight, but not too loose—if the lower edge feels restrictive, BO more loosely).

Sleeves

Beginning with either sleeve, and with US Size 5 (3.75 mm) needle—*or size needed to achieve gauge*—transfer the sleeve sts from waste yarn to your needles and pick up the sts cast on under arm—64 (74, 80, 90, 92, 94, 98, 104, 106) sts. When all sts are on your needle, PM at center of underarm and join to knit in the rnd.

Work 2 rnds even in established stockinette stitch.

Dec Rnd: K2, k2tog, k to last 4 sts, ssk, k2—2 st dec.

Continue working your sleeve in the rnd, decreasing every 1.25 (1.75, 1.25, 1.75, 1.25, 1.75, 1.75, 1.25, 1.75) in / 3.25 (4.25, 3.25, 4.25, 3.25, 4.25, 4.25, 3.25, 4.25) cm until you reach 56 (68, 72, 84, 84, 88, 92, 96, 100) sts and sleeve measures approximately 3.75 in (9.5 cm).

Transition to US 3 (3.25 mm) circular needle or DPNs—*or two sizes smaller than needed to achieve gauge*—and k one rnd.

Ribbing

Next Rnd: [K2, p2] rep bet brackets to end.

Rep this rnd until ribbed edge measures 1.75 in (4.25 cm). BO in pattern with medium tension. (If your edge is too restrictive, BO again more loosely.)

Rep for second sleeve.

Finishing

Weave in ends on the WS and wet block for best results. Soak in lukewarm water with a splash of fiber wash for about 20 minutes to gently cleanse and relax the fiber. Press out excess water, lay flat, and smooth into place, pinning along the neckline, the lace panel waves, the sleeve cuffs, and down the sides. Turn as needed for even drying.

Chart Written Directions

Chart Rnd 1: [(Ssk) twice, (yo, k1) 4 times, (k2tog) twice] rep bet brackets to end of rnd.

Chart Rnd 2: P to end.

Chart Rnds 3–7: Rep Rnds 1 and 2 2 times more (for a total of three), then repeat Chart Rnd 1 once more.

marigold wave top chart

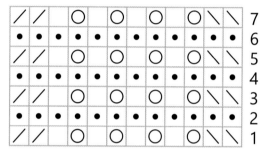

12 11 10 9 8 7 6 5 4 3 2 1

Key	
☐	knit
\	ssk
/	k2tog
O	yo
•	purl

dahlia gathered top

Summer is the season for fabrics that flow, and this sweet, gathered top is everything that's good about dressing for a sunny day. The fabric is light and breezy. The texture is steady and easy, both to knit and to wear. But it's the shoulder details that really dress up this design, adding a little extra something to elevate the minimal shape. The lowkey texture is easy to follow and provides satisfying milestones as you knit through the body. (It's the perfect project for knitting on the go—very little focus is required.) Your choice of yarn will make all the difference; I gravitate toward solid and tonal colors for a classic look, but you could easily spice this up with multicolor yarn (or even use contrast colors for your garter ridges).

Skill Level
Intermediate (due to the shoulder details, otherwise Advanced Beginner)

Construction
This airy top is knit from the bottom up with a background of stockinette stitch and spaced garter ridge stripes. The body is worked in the round to the underarms, then flat to the shoulders. The shoulders aren't attached like you'd normally see in a bottom-up top; instead, the front and back shoulder flaps are folded over, and each is sewn with a tapestry needle to create narrow pockets (or tubes) to be joined (and gathered) with ribbon. If you're a sewist, you could use a wide running stitch on your machine (in coordinating thread) to accomplish the same thing—a straight line is all that's needed. The shoulder details offer versatility to adjust to your preference, creating a slight A-line effect from the top of the shoulder to the lower body edge.

Sizes
S (M, L, XL, 2X, 3X, 4X, 5X, 6X)

Fit Advice
Designed to be worn with approximately 6–8 in (15–20 cm) positive ease, which will be gathered closer to the body at the shoulders for a swingy fit.

Finished Measurements

A) Bust Circumference: 38 (42, 46, 50, 54, 58, 62, 66, 70) in / 95 (105, 115, 125, 135, 145, 155, 165, 175) cm – blocked

B) Drop Shoulder Depth: 9.5 (10, 10.5, 11, 11, 11.5, 12, 12, 12.5) in / 24.25 (25.5, 26.75, 28, 28, 29.25, 30.5, 30.5, 31.75) cm – blocked

C) Underarm to Hem: 13 (13, 13, 14, 14, 15, 15, 15, 15) in / 33 (33, 33, 35.5, 35.5, 38, 38, 38, 38) cm – prior to blocking

D) Back Neckline Width: 9.25 (9.25, 9.25, 10, 10, 10, 10.25, 10.25, 10.25) in / 23.25 (23.25, 23.25, 25, 25, 25, 25.75, 25.75, 25.75) cm – blocked

Abbreviations	
BO	bind off
CO	cast on
dec	decrease/decreases/decreased
k	knit
p	purl
p2tog	purl two stitches together (dec 2)
PM	place marker
rep	repeat
rnd/s	round/rounds
RS	right side
ssk	slip one st knitwise, slip the next st knitwise, then return the two sts back to the left needle and knit the two together through the back loop (dec 1)
st/s	stitch/stitches
WS	wrong side

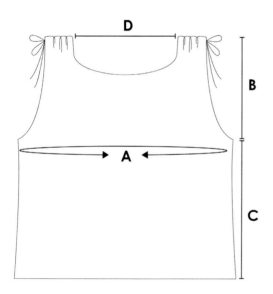

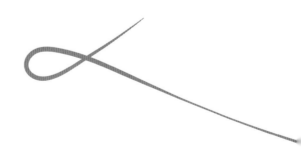

Materials

Yarn	Fingering Weight	Miss Babs Damask| 65% Cultivated Silk, 35% Bleached Linen	420 yards (380 meters) in 3.5 oz (100 grams)	795 (853, 915, 982, 1055, 1133, 1218, 1320, 1432) yards / 727 (780, 836, 898, 964, 1036, 1113, 1207, 1309) meters	**Color:** Mahi Mahi **Note:** Variations in yarn choice or row/round gauge may impact yarn consumption. If in doubt, round up to the nearest skein.
Needles	**Body:** US Size 4 (3.5 mm)* 24–40-in (60–100-cm) circular needle *Or size needed to achieve gauge. Adjust other needle sizes accordingly.*
Notions	Stitch markers Waste yarn or spare needles, for holding stitches Blocking pins and mats Darning needle to weave ends and close shoulder flaps ⅜-in (about 1-cm) width double-faced satin ribbon—approximately 48 in (122 cm) total, cut into 2 equal lengths, about 24 in (61 cm) each. Choose ribbon that complements the color of your yarn for best results.
Gauge	24 sts and 32 rows/rounds in 4 in (10 cm) in stockinette stitch with largest needle, blocked—*because this is knit bottom-up, row gauge is less critical but may affect yarn consumption.*

dahlia gathered top pattern

With US Size 4 (3.5 mm) 24–40-in (60–100-cm) circular needle—*or size needed to achieve gauge*—CO 228 (252, 276, 300, 324, 348, 372, 396, 420) sts using cable cast-on method. Do not join in the rnd yet. (*Note: The cable cast-on begins your work immediately on the RS.*)

Set-Up Row (RS): K to end. PM and join to work in the rnd, being careful not to twist your sts.

Rnd 1: K to end.

Rnd 2: P to end.

Rep these rnds twice more (for a total of 3).

Rnds 7-18: K to end.

Rep Rnds 1–18 until your work measures 13 (13, 13, 14, 14, 15, 15, 15, 15) in / 33 (33, 33, 35.5, 35.5, 38, 38, 38, 38) cm from cast-on edge, **ending after Rnds 8, 9, 10, 11, or 12** so that you'll be working on a stockinette section when you split the upper bodice.

Upper Bodice

Going forward, you will separate the front and back bodice sections and work back and forth on each section, flat, beginning with the front. You will return to work the back afterward.

Tip: As you begin working flat, be sure to keep your edges tidy. To do this, work the first st tighter than usual, then insert the tip of your needle into the second st and pull the working yarn tight again to draw the first st a little tighter. Then proceed with the remainder of the row with normal tension. Do this at the start of every row (RS and WS) for nicer edges that will be easier to finish later.

Next Rnd: Work across 114 (126, 138, 150, 162, 174, 186, 198, 210) sts in established pattern, stop.

Slide remaining 114 (126, 138, 150, 162, 174, 186, 198, 210) sts onto a long separate needle or waste yarn. You will work back and forth (flat) on the front section (only) for now.

Front

Next Row (WS): P2, work in established pattern to last 2 sts, p2.

Next Row (RS): K2, work in established pattern to last 2 sts, k2.

Rep these two rows, continuing the established garter/stockinette pattern and maintaining 2 sts in stockinette on each side for your edges, until your flat section measures approximately 8 (8.5, 9, 9.5, 9.5, 10, 10.5, 10.5, 11) in / 20.25 (21.5, 22.75, 24.25, 24.25, 25.5, 26.75, 26.75, 28) cm from where you began working flat, ending after a WS row (ready to work a RS).

Front Shoulder and Neckline Shaping

As you proceed, you will transition to stockinette st only (no additional garter rows).

Next Row (RS): K33 (39, 45, 49, 55, 61, 66, 72, 78) sts—this is left front shoulder. BO* next 48 (48, 48, 52, 52, 52, 54, 54, 54) sts knitwise for the center front neckline. K33 (39, 45, 49, 55, 61, 66, 72, 78) to end of row—this is the right front shoulder.

***Note** that this BO is the finished neckline edge, so keep your sts tidy as you work.

Place the 33 (39, 45, 49, 55, 61, 66, 72, 78) sts of left front shoulder onto a holder; you will return to work them later. You will now work only on the right front shoulder and neckline dec as you proceed in this section.

Right Front Shoulder

Next Row (WS): P to end.

Next Row (RS): K1, ssk, k to end—1 st dec.

Next Row (WS): P to end.

Rep these two rows 3 times more (for a total of 4)—29 (35, 41, 45, 51, 57, 62, 68, 74) sts.

Next Row (RS): K to end.

Next Row (WS): P to end.

Rep these two rows 3 times more (for a total of 4).

Next Row (RS): BO remaining sts knitwise.

Left Front Shoulder

Return to the left front shoulder sts and place them back on your working needles. Position your yarn to begin a WS row.

Next Row (WS): P1, p2tog, p to end—1 st dec.

Next Row (RS): K to end.

Rep these two rows 3 times more (for a total of 4)—29 (35, 41, 45, 51, 57, 62, 68, 74) sts.

Next Row (WS): P to end.

Next Row (RS): K to end.

Rep these two rows 3 times more (for a total of 4).

Next Row (WS): BO remaining sts purlwise.

Back

Return back sts to needles and join working yarn, ready to work a RS row.

Next Row (RS): K2, work in established pattern to last 2 sts, k2.

Next Row (WS): P2, work in established pattern to last 2 sts, p2.

Rep these two rows, continuing the established garter/stockinette pattern and maintaining 2 sts in stockinette on each side for your edges, until your flat section measures approximately 8 (8.5, 9, 9.5, 9.5, 10, 10.5, 10.5, 11) in / 20.25 (21.5, 22.75, 24.25, 24.25, 25.5, 26.75, 26.75, 28) cm and is the same length as the front section from where you began working flat, then work 6 additional rows.

Back Shoulder Shaping

Next Row (RS): K30 (36, 42, 46, 52, 58, 63, 69, 75) sts—this is the right back shoulder. BO the next 54 (54, 54, 58, 58, 58, 60, 60, 60) sts knitwise for center back neckline. K30 (36, 42, 46, 52, 58, 63, 69, 75) to end—this is the back left shoulder.

Place first 30 (36, 42, 46, 52, 58, 63, 69, 75) sts for right back shoulder section onto separate needle or holder—you will return to work these sts later. You will now work only on the back left shoulder and neckline dec as you proceed in this section.

Left Back Shoulder

Next Row (WS): P to end.

Next Row (RS): K1, ssk, k to end—29 (35, 41, 45, 51, 57, 62, 68, 74) sts.

Next Row (WS): P to end.

Next Row (RS): K to end.

Next Row (WS): P to end,

Rep these two rows 3 times more (for a total of 4).

Next Row (RS): BO remaining sts knitwise.

Right Back Shoulder

Return the right back shoulder sts to your needle and rejoin working yarn, ready to work a WS row.

Next Row (WS): P1, p2tog, p to end—29 (35, 41, 45, 51, 57, 62, 68, 74) sts.

Next Row (RS): K to end.

Next Row (WS): P to end.

Next Row (RS): K to end.

Next Row (WS): P to end.

Rep these two rows 3 times more (for a total of 4).

Next Row (RS): BO remaining sts knitwise.

Shoulder Finishing

Starting with either shoulder, fold the top edge to the WS of the work—about ½ in (1.25 cm) over (see Figure A)—and use a darning or tapestry needle with matching yarn to stitch the bottom edge of the fold down to create a narrow pocket. Rep for the three remaining shoulder sections. (See Figure B.)

You will complete the remainder of the gathered shoulders after you've finished blocking.

Neckline

There is no neckline finishing.

Finishing

Weave in ends on the WS and wet block for best results. Soak in lukewarm water with a splash of fiber wash for about 20 minutes to gently cleanse and relax the fiber. Press out excess water and lay flat, smoothing into shape so that the edges are even. Pin the shoulder flaps flat so they're easy to work with when they're dry. Pinning is optional on the other portions of the top. Turn as needed for even drying and adjust as necessary for best results.

Post-Blocking: You will now draw the first pre-cut ribbon length through the tubes on the first shoulder in a U shape as follows: Insert the darning needle with threaded ribbon into the first tube starting at the shoulder edge toward the neckline and draw it out the other side of the tube. Make a U-turn and draw it back into the second tube starting at the neckline edge and working back toward the shoulder. You should now have two ribbon tails poking out of the shoulder side of the tubes on one side of your top. Repeat this on the other shoulder. (See Figure C.) (*Note: There should not be ribbon sticking out at the neckline edge.*)

Gently gather the shoulder fabric on one side, using the ribbon as leverage, until you've gathered it to your preferred width. Then tie the ribbons into a bow that sits on the exterior of the shoulder edge to secure your gather. To adjust the gathered edge, simply untie the ribbon and adjust. Trim excess ribbon. (If your ribbon edges fray, you can use a product called Fray Check®, or something similar, to seal the ends.)

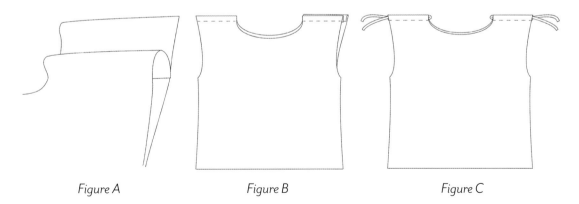

Figure A   *Figure B*   *Figure C*

blocking & care

You've heard me say that I steer clear of words like "always" or "never" when it comes to knitting; many of us were taught that there's only one right way to do a thing, but not all advice is good advice, my friend. Many a well-meaning knitter will preach the gospel of the "right way" only to find out for ourselves (sometimes years later) that we'd been accidentally led astray. No one passes along bad advice on purpose—we teach others what we know to be true. But I've worked with thousands of knitters over the years, and I've watched some incredibly brilliant people share absolutely terrible knitting advice as if it's fact.

And while I hope you'll take my advice here, the best thing you can do is learn for yourself. If you don't think blocking matters, try it and see.

I've been knitting for nearly 40 years and have both knit and designed hundreds of sweaters. But there are two things I do staunchly believe are critical to the success of any garment knitter: swatching and blocking. Those are my two non-negotiables; they're the hill I'll die on.

Swatching is how you'll find out if you've chosen the right yarn and needles for your project and ensures that your finished measurements will align with the pattern—but only if you wet blocked your swatch before you measured. And only if you wet block your sweater when it's finished.

There are other kinds of blocking, I know. Steam blocking, for example, is helpful in a pinch. (I like steam blocking for removing creases from a sweater that's been folded for too long.) But there's no substitute for the real thing.

blocking & finishing

When you finally reach the bind-off part of your project, you might feel like you've reached the finish line, but *au contraire!* There's a last step (or two) to bring it all together so your handiwork can put its best foot forward. I'd been knitting for at least a decade before I discovered blocking and was absolutely stunned at the difference it makes; so much so, that it's now one of my favorite parts of the process. Here are some tips for weaving ends and wet blocking your plant-forward tops and tees so they'll be fabulous and ready to wear.

Weaving Ends

Before you block your project, it's wise to weave your ends. But weaving the ends of plant-based yarn can be a little trickier than weaving the ends of other kinds of fiber. For one thing, plant-based yarn shows every lump, bump, and inconsistency, so even the most carefully woven ends might disrupt the look of your fabric on the right side. Worse still, you'll notice quickly that the ends of your plant-based project can slide out of their place more easily than they might with wool and other similar protein fibers.

To make the process easier (and to ensure better results), try not to join new yarn in an obvious area of your project. Rather than joining right in the front, join the next skein near the side, where it will be less noticeable.

Leave yourself a longer tail than you might think you need. Plant-based yarn can be slippery, and it can help to weave it through a longer section of stitches than you might ordinarily have to do with wool. Giving yourself a little extra length can give you the room you need to weave your ends securely. I recommend weaving it over a space of about 2 in (5 cm) using the process outlined below.

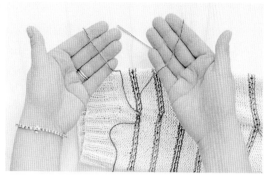

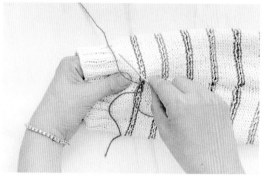

1. Divide the strand. Plant-based yarn can feel pretty bulky, especially when you double it to weave in your ends. So, when it comes time to weave in those tails, split the strands of each tail in half, to create two strands from one.

2. Thread one of the half strands onto a darning needle and weave it securely by moving horizontally from the origin of the strand, and following the path of stitches as if you were working duplicate stitch on the wrong side. I call it "following the revolution of the stitches," and it's one of the most secure ways I know to weave in ends. If you'd like to see the process in motion, check out a video tutorial on my website here: oliveknits.com/weaving-ends.

3. When the first half of the strand is secure, return to the second half of your tail. Repeat the process, this time working in the opposite direction. Doing this will ease the thickness of the tail to create a nearly invisible finish that won't add bulk or disturb the fabric on the right side. I developed this trick specifically for plant-based fiber, and it works like a charm.

The downside of this technique is that you'll be weaving twice as many ends (two strands for every one tail), but the results are super secure (keeping those slippery strands in place, no matter how much wear and tear they get), and it looks great, too.

Wet Blocking

In its simplest form, wet blocking can be done with a basin of clean water, a towel, and a flat surface to let your sweater dry; fancy equipment isn't necessary. But if you can spring for a gentle wool wash, interlocking rubber mats, and blocking pins (see the Resources on page 204 for details), you'll have everything you need for perfect blocking results.

The purpose of blocking is two-fold:

1. Blocking cleanses and relaxes the fiber, removing oils, residue, and excess dye. If you use a softening fiber wash, you'll also have a softer (and usually sweet-smelling) sweater at the end. This process happens in the blocking water as you give your garment a good long soak (20 to 30 minutes is usually plenty).

2. Blocking enhances the stitch patterns and garment details. This part of the process happens on the blocking mats as you flatten and shape your sweater. As you draw the neckline, the sleeves, and the body outward on your mat, you are coaxing the garment into the shape and size it's meant to be. This process also involves pinning in some places to expand lacework or other details. As the garment dries, it will dry into shape.

Since our stitches don't always look perfect right off the needles (especially when working with plant-based yarn), the wet blocking process can make stitches and rows look more even than before. For me, a sweater doesn't feel finished until I've blocked it—I often rush right to the blocking water the minute I finish, even before I weave my ends (not because that's how it should be done, but because I'm impatient and know I can always weave them in later). I'm in a hurry to block my project, because **that's** the real finish line in my book, and I am always eager to see how it looks after it's off the mats. Many projects that disappointed me at the bind off transformed before my eyes on the blocking mats; this seemingly simple process can turn zeroes into heroes overnight. The bottom line, my friend, is that blocking isn't optional—it's an absolute must if you want to knit incredible sweaters and tops that look and feel great and fit the way they're intended.

Wet Blocking Basics

1. Start with a clean basin, like a bathroom sink or a large bowl. Fill it with lukewarm* water and a splash of softening fiber wash and submerge your garment. Let it sit for 20 to 30 minutes to give the fabric a chance to absorb water completely. (Five minutes won't usually do, but if the yarn label says to soak it for a particular amount of time, refer to those instructions for best results. However, I soak absolutely everything for at least 20 minutes, and I've never regretted it.)

2. When your garment has fully absorbed the water, drain the basin, press out as much excess water as you can (gently), and roll your garment in a flat, clean towel. (Be careful about your towel choice; if the yarn releases a bit of color while it's wet, you won't want to stain a nice towel.)

*Why lukewarm? While this may seem counter to the advice we've so often been given about soaking our knits, most surfactants (in this case, cleansers) work better—and more quickly—in warm (or hot) water, but for our purposes, lukewarm water will do the trick. Think of what it's like to shampoo your hair when you're camping, using ice cold water from the camp shower, versus washing your hair at home in hot water; there's a difference in the way the cleanser behaves at different temperatures. (And as a former soapmaker, I've spent years personally observing the behavior of natural cleansing agents on handknits, and I can attest that slight warmth in the water does help, and the more natural the product, the more the water temperature will matter.) I've tested this on a range of vibrant hand-dyed yarns, and the amount of color transfer was similar, regardless of whether the water was cold or lukewarm. Some cleansers (laundry detergent, for example) may be specially formulated to work just as well in cold water, but when in doubt, lukewarm wins the day.

3. Let your sweater roll-up sit for another 10 to 20 minutes to allow the towel to absorb a little more water, then unroll the towel and lay your garment on the blocking mats. (Time isn't super important here; I've been known to let mine sit in the towel all day, simply because I got busy and forgot.)

4. Use your hands to smooth out the sides and edges of your top. Smooth along the neckline, straighten the shoulders, and make sure any curves or details are laying nice and even. (If it's wonky on your blocking mats, it'll dry wonky!) Most designs benefit from the use of at least a few strategic pins to keep them in place as they dry, but blocking pins don't play nicely with some plant fibers. When in doubt, use fewer pins than you might use if you were blocking a wool sweater, but do pin strategic spots that might need a little training to dry where you want them.

This includes the curve of a neckline, lower edge details, lace panels, etc. The blocking advice for each pattern in this book will tell you if pinning isn't recommended with the particular yarn used in the pattern, but yarn substitutions will make a difference. I love to use comb-style blocking pins whenever I can, but even just taking the time to smooth out your sweater with your hands and make sure all the edges are smooth, flat, and even can make a difference.

5. After about 24 hours (depending on the temperature and humidity in your home), the top surface should feel relatively dry. At this point, gently flip the garment over and smooth it back into place on the mats to give the back a chance to dry, too. (If you pin it on the first day of drying, it shouldn't be necessary to pin it again when you flip it over. Just make sure it's flat and even on your mat.) When it's dry, it's ready to wear!

storing your knits

If you're anything like me, you probably have more than a few handknit garments in your closet (unless you're a newer knitter, in which case, it won't be long). Rotating different pieces for the weather (or for your mood), can be a fun way to keep your wardrobe interesting, and it can make old pieces feel new again, especially if you haven't seen them for a season (or two). But storing your handknits takes a little extra planning to keep them fresh and safe for their next day out.

In a perfect world, we would give our handknits a fresh new soak with fiber wash and lay them out flat again to dry before we packed them away for the season. It would be the ideal way to go, and I wish I had the time, energy, and general willpower to do that. But since I don't have the nerve to preach something that I don't do myself, I'll share the second-best method, which is *almost* as good, and much more practical. (If you do have the time to soak and lightly re-block all of your knits before you pack them away each season, you have my full admiration and respect.)

But anyway, *for the rest of us...*

First, check your garments to ensure that they look and smell clean (or at least don't look or smell unclean, if that makes sense). If you do see anything suspect, it's best to spot-clean the area and let it dry completely before you store it away. This is a good idea for any areas that have stains or might absorb excess skin oils or odors (such as the underarms). Rinse just that area of the garment under lukewarm water, then dab a little fiber wash over the area with a clean cloth. Let it sit for ten minutes and rinse the spot again under the water. By spot-cleaning just that area, you can avoid the extra work of soaking the whole garment and waiting days for it to dry, since small areas usually dry more quickly. But beware: Do not—under any circumstances—put your garment away damp. *Not even a little bit damp!* Plant fibers like cotton and linen are prone to mildew if they don't get a chance to dry completely. Spot cleaning is not only a great way to preserve your handknit garment for many years of wear, but it can also help deter pests like moths, which are drawn to soiled areas and sweat stains—even on plant fiber. The longer something sits in storage, the more time the stains and body oils will have to break down and discolor the fiber, so putting them away clean is best.

> **Note:** If your top is quite noticeably stained or smelly, then a full soak with fiber wash is the really the best and most appropriate option. Keep in mind that these patterns are for warm weather wear, which means they may get a little sweatier than your usual woolly knits. But if you only have a spot or two that need attention, the spot-cleaning method will do fine.

Second, store your knits flat or folded; don't store your plant-based knits on a hanger. To be honest, I don't store any of my handknit pieces on hangers, but especially not those made with plant fiber; they will stretch in ways you won't appreciate, and those hanger marks will be hard to get rid of. Instead, keep them folded, and stacked neatly in a cedar or plastic container (with a lid), and keep a few lavender or cedar sachets tucked in with them. Lavender and cedar have moth-deterrent qualities, and they impart a lovely scent on your garments (or at least I think they both smell lovely). I use sachets filled with dried lavender, and I give them a boost periodically with a few drops of lavender essential oil. (You'll want the real stuff, not imitation, but a little goes a long way, and even the good stuff isn't terribly expensive.)

When I bring my knits out for a new season, I'll check them over for any signs of damage, and ensure that there are no stains or other issues I missed when I put them away, then I'll use a hand-held clothing steamer to remove any creases or folds. By storing your tops with cedar or lavender—and assuming you put them away clean—they should already smell forest fresh, and you can always give them a quick spritz with fabric spray to refresh them.

Wrapping Up

If you'd told me in my early knitting days that I would one day develop a passion for cotton, linen, and other plant-based yarns, I wouldn't have believed you. Wool was (and still is) my first love. But I have also learned to love these strong, practical plant fibers for their ability to extend my handmade wardrobe well beyond fall and winter. I love them for the way they move and breathe, and even their unique textures have become a welcome part of my knitting routine. I've learned to savor the feel of different kinds of fiber as they run through my hands; each one has a little something different to offer. Your love affair with plant-based yarn may not happen overnight, but by the time you've knit a few of the pieces in this book, I hope they'll win you over.

If this is unfamiliar territory, start with an approachable blend, something that feels familiar, then expand from there as you get comfortable working with new fibers. If diving straight into a project knit with 100% linen feels like a stretch, try a blend with linen, silk, and wool—something that feels more like home on your needles, but will give you the opportunity to explore the benefits of plant fiber. Visit your favorite local yarn store and see what they have on their shelves (and if you don't have one in your town, there are some incredible online stores that will take excellent care of you).

To support you in your *Knitting Light* adventure, you'll find pattern support, errata notes, and technique tutorials at www.oliveknits.com and—for any additional questions—you can reach me at admin@oliveknits.com. I hope you'll come to love these strong, versatile, and incredibly wearable fibers as much as I do.

acknowledgments

This book would not have been possible without the help of so many people, especially Erika Close (who saved my bacon right up to the eleventh hour), Heidi Hennessy, Heather Connan, Bristol Ivy, and Shelly Dinh. They went above and beyond the calling as friends, employees, and contractors, working early mornings and late nights to help me slide into the finish line on time. This book was no small feat, and it wouldn't have been possible without these wonderful humans at my side.

I would also like to thank the sample knitters: Leslie Caponey, Erika Close, Heather Connan, Shelly Dinh, Gilda Escobar, Ashley Grillo, Heidi Hennessy, Janet Kallstrom, Kim Pellissier, Rachael Reichmann, Nancy Taylor, and Ciel-Nicole Williams who helped me bring my ideas to life when there weren't enough hours in the day for me to knit them all myself.

I'm grateful for the testers, who navigated the earliest versions of these patterns, speedbumps and all, and they did so with kindness and patience. Bless their sweet hearts, they deserve medals: Cindy Arndt, Marie Arnett, Kim Arellano, Debra Austin, Tami Beall, Becky Clowers, Ruth Darelius, Lea Donahue, Erica Erignac, Elizabeth Etherton, JoAnn Fox, Meg Gallagher, Joanne Guennewig, Nydia Haberlie, Lynette Hansen, Paula Johnson, Rhonda Kehrberg, Linn Kotnour, Kathy Kyburz, Sharon Lake, Laura Lawless, Jenn Lewis, Connie Lowe, Paule Marcotte, Colleen McDermond, Sue Meehan, Candy Mulholland, Patti Neuman, Caroline Normandeau, Sharon Nye, Trudy O'Nan, Kari Oswald, Jamie Peterson, Nikki Peterson, Mara Powell, Shelly Randel, Myriah Riedel, Peggy Riedinger, Kassi Robinson, Cheri Rondeau, Jennifer Ross, Rhonda Russell, Deirdre Schlunegger, Naomi Schober, Audrey Seifman, Annice Sevett, Patty Shaw, Kay Simmons, Michele Soleski, Rose Tobelmann, Marcy Traeger, Ellen VanderWey, Amy Walker, and Patricia Waterfield.

I'm thankful, too, for my editors Emily Archbold and Sarah Monroe, who've helped me bring this book to life.

I would also like to thank Laurel Vischer, Carla Brauer, Arienne Dinh, and Jackie Martin for being willing to navigate the exciting new territory of modeling knitwear on hot summer days, proving that lightweight knits really DO hold up in real life. They wore everything so well, and the results speak for themselves on the pages of this book. I am incredibly grateful to have had the opportunity to work with photographer Annie Loaiza, once again. She makes everything—and everyone—look incredible.

I'm grateful for my husband, Scott, who dropped everything to help manage things at home so I could finish this book. He is my favorite person in all the world, and I'm lucky he's on this ride with me.

It takes a village, and I have the very best. Thank you all.

about the author

Marie Greene is an independent knitwear designer, best-selling author, and knitting educator whose innovative approach to seamless knitting has gained notice around the world. Marie is the founder of Olive Knits™ and Knit Camp®, and the author of *Seamless Knit Sweaters in 2 Weeks* and *The Joy of Yarn*, among others. You can find her seamless patterns, renegade knitting tutorials, and cheerful tales of her fiber life at www.oliveknits.com. Marie lives in the Pacific Northwest with her husband, two persnickety cats, and one absolutely ridiculous puppy. *Knitting Light* is her fifth book.

resources

To find resources and supplies featured in this book, please visit the following vendors. Many of the yarns I used are available through your favorite yarn stores and dyers.

- Bath Fiber Wash – www.oliveknits.com
- Berroco – www.berroco.com
- Coastal Effects Elemental – www.jorstadcreek.com
- Erika Night – www.erikaknight.co.uk
- HiKoo Yarn – www.skacelknitting.com
- JaMPDX – www.jampdx.com
- Juniper Moon Farm – www.junipermoonfarmyarn.com
- Knit Picks – www.knitpicks.com

- Knitter's Pride Blocking Pins – www.knitterspride.com
- Madelinetosh – www.madelinetosh.com
- Miss Babs – www.missbabs.com
- Purl Soho – www.purlsoho.com
- Rowan – www.knitrowan.com
- Scheepjes – www.scheepjes.com
- Schoppelwolle – www.skacelknitting.com and www.schoppel-wolle.de/en/
- Treasure Goddess Yarn – www.treasuregoddess.com

index